A Day of Digital Rest

An Interpretative Phenomenological Analysis

Natalie Scheiner

Grosvenor House
Publishing Limited

This book is published by
Grosvenor House Publishing Ltd
Link House
140 The Broadway, Tolworth, Surrey, KT6 7HT.
www.grosvenorhousepublishing.co.uk

A CIP record for this book
is available from the British Library

ISBN 978-1-80381-983-9

Authorship and Ethical Clearance

I, Natalie Scheiner, am the sole author of this dissertation. I obtained ethical clearance on the 22nd of July 2022 from the New School of Psychotherapy and Counselling and the Psychology Department of Middlesex University. This dissertation is being submitted as a partial fulfilment of the requirements for the DCPsych Counselling and Psychotherapy degree from both institutions. I declare that I have no conflict of interest and take full responsibility for the content and writing of this dissertation.

Dr Natalie Scheiner is an accomplished psychologist based in London, UK. With a deep passion for understanding the human mind and behaviour, she has dedicated her career to exploring various aspects of psychology, particularly focusing on relationships and parenting.

As a dedicated professional, Natalie possesses a wide range of therapeutic skills and approaches (after she's had her first coffee of the day!). Her expertise includes Existential Psychotherapy, Gestalt Therapy, Psychodynamic Therapy, CBT Therapy, Integrative Therapy, and Humanistic Therapy. Through her extensive training and practical experience, she has helped numerous individuals navigate through life's challenges and achieve personal growth and healing.

Beyond her professional achievements, Natalie is a devoted wife and mother. She finds joy and fulfilment in spending quality time with her husband and children (just not too much time!). In her spare time, Natalie enjoys taking long walks (well, longish!), immersing herself in captivating books, engaging in word games, and exploring new destinations through travel (so long as the journey doesn't exceed 5 hours!).

Natalie's book, *A Day of Digital Rest*, offers a unique perspective on the modern challenges of constant connectivity and the importance and ups and downs of taking a break from technology. In this thought-provoking academic work, Natalie explores the concept of a digital detox through the lens of Jewish Orthodox Gen Zedders.

Acknowledgements

I would like to express my gratitude to my research supervisors, Dr. Andreas Vossler and Dr. Miriam Tasgal, for their unwavering support throughout the completion of my thesis. Their continuous assistance, valuable feedback, extensive knowledge, guidance, and recommendations have played a pivotal role in reaching this stage of accomplishment. In the words of Sir Isaac Newton (1675), "If I have seen further, it is by standing on the shoulders of Giants." I would also like to extend my gratitude to my fellow peers who have accompanied me on this journey, sharing valuable knowledge and providing support throughout the process and I am thankful for the guidance and support received from each of my tutors at the NSPC.

I would like to convey my heartfelt appreciation to the eight participants who generously contributed their time and willingly shared their experiences, without whom this research would not have been feasible. Thank you for your openness, honesty, and valuable insights throughout the study. Your participation has been instrumental in advancing our understanding of this field.

My deepest gratitude goes to my husband and children. My husband has been my unwavering supporter, believing in my ability to complete this doctorate even when I couldn't envision it myself. He has provided support in countless ways, enabling me to successfully reach this milestone. To my children, I want to apologise for the times when my immersion in writing caused me to neglect to respond to you. My focus on my work mentally separated me from my loved ones, but I want to thank you for not giving up on our relationship. Perhaps what kept you going was the reassurance that we were never more than six days away from a time when I could be fully present for you without technological interference.

Lastly, I want to express my heartfelt gratitude to Shabbat for its unwavering presence each week. As I commit to observing the Shabbat, I also commit to my family, assuring them that no matter the work or academic commitments, deadlines, or tempting opportunities that may arise, they will never compete with the profound beauty and significance that Shabbat holds for me.

Contents

Abstract

Online media saves time, increases leisure opportunities and offers users flexibility and control (Wajcman, 2016). However, experiencing excessive technology use is common among young people, and concerns about its impact are shared by individuals and institutions (Syvertsen, 2020). The growing popularity of digital detox as a remedy for excessive digital use is evident. Strategies to address this issue include the adoption of usage-tracking apps and self-control tools (Global Mobile OS Market Share 2023 | Statista, 2023), as well as engaging in digital retreats (Stäheli & Stoltenberg, 2022). This study aimed to explore the experience of combining technology use with a weekly digital detox for 25 hours every Shabbat, using Interpretative Phenomenological Analysis (IPA). The analysis revealed five Group Experiential Themes and eighteen sub-themes that are presented as the main findings. The analysis explores the effects of digital detox on relationships, the manifestation of anxiety during this period, and, conversely, the improvement of well-being. The themes also highlight how time is experienced during the digital detox on Shabbat and how feelings of authenticity emerge on Shabbat in contrast to weekdays where technology is present. Addictive behaviours towards technology are examined, as well as themes related to activities and routines during Shabbat. It was also found that only half the participants were able to maintain their digital detox while growing up, signifying a maturation process taking place across time and parental influence is discussed with this in mind. The implications of these findings are explored in relation to clinical practice and for society, and further areas of study in this area are identified.

Chapter 1

1.0 Introduction

'No one can foresee the radical changes to come. But technological advances will move faster and faster and can never be stopped. In all areas of his existence, man will be encircled ever more tightly by the forces of technology. These forces, which everywhere and every minute claim, enchain, drag along, press and impose upon man under the form of some technical contrivance or other— these forces, since man has not made them, have moved long since beyond his will and have outgrown his capacity for decision.' (Heidegger. M, p.51, 1969)

Data shows that technology usage is rising year on year and that human behaviour is affected and shaped by it (Aiken, 2016). Technological devices extend to all areas of our lives and are with us from the moment we wake up until we fall asleep and the rate at which we trade information with individuals is incomparable to a mere generation ago (Wendland et al., 2019). According to Ofcom (2022), young adults spend the most time online, with 18-24 year olds spending 5 hours and 6 minutes online daily on average. As of 2021, in the UK, it was found that 88% of all adults had a smartphone, whereas only 17% of adults had a smartphone in 2008 (Hiley, 2022).

Significant technological advancements arose in the course of the 2010 decade and became expeditiously inbuilt as part of our daily lives (Palandrani, 2022). These technologies are used widely by observant Jews aside from the 25-hour period of unplugging beginning at dusk on Friday. Generation Zers, born between 1997 and 2012, amongst observant Jews, are for a day a week, required to disengage from technology. How young people from Generation Z experience this period of digital abstinence, given that they have grown up with and are surrounded by digital media in their everyday life, is the subject of this study.

For millennia, it has been the practice of observant Jews to abstain once a week from many 'weekday' activities between dusk on Friday and Saturday nightfall. This is in fulfilment of the Biblical instruction 'The seventh day is a Sabbath of the Lord our God; you shall not do any work…' (Deut. 5:14-15). Overtly prescribed in a number of places in the Old Testament with innumerable binding explications in the Talmud, the Sabbath or 'Shabbat' and 'Shabbos', as it is known colloquially, has been the bedrock of Jewish life for time immemorial. Whilst details of what Shabbat should look like aside from the command to *rest* are missing from the text of the Bible itself, this is left to the Talmud. There is one exception; Exodus 35:2 states, 'You shall not kindle fire in any of your dwelling places on the Sabbath day'. This has been the basis on which the turning off and on of all and any electrical devices has been prohibited on

Shabbat, other than through the use of an automatic timer. As an aside, for all matters pertaining to health and safety, these laws are always suspended.

There is a lack of research on the impact of a regular digital detox on young adults. We know little about the attitude that young people have towards weekly unplugging from technology and for many people it is not a realistic option. Some sources allege that up to fifty per cent of Jewish Orthodox teenagers in the USA are unable to desist from texting on Shabbat (Lipman, 2011). This statistic suggests that there may be a generational gap in adhering to traditional practices. It also highlights the potential challenges that arise when trying to balance religious practices with the use of technology, especially for younger generations who have grown up as digital residents.

1.1 Definitions

Digital Technology (DT) in this study will refer to technology that is electronic, internet or computer-based. These will include computers, televisions, audio and visual devices, tablets, phones and smartphones. Using digital technology also includes the usage of apps such as those on social media, online forums, websites, email, Skype, YouTube, Facebook, WhatsApp, Instagram, Twitter and Snapchat.

The Orthodox Jewish population globally comprises sub-groups with distinctive histories, customs and a variety of authority structures of their own, notwithstanding an adherence to a single body of principle laws and close familial ties. The participants that take part in this study are all *Shomer Shabbat*, a term used to describe a person who observes and adheres to the Shabbat laws. The Hebrew word 'Shomer' means to guard, protect or keep (Glickman, 2019). Many Ashkenazi Jews of European settled heritage will refer to Shabbat as Shabbos but for the purpose of this study, the word 'Shabbat' used by Sefaradi Jews of North Africa and Middle Eastern settled heritage has been used as it is the pronunciation used in Modern Hebrew. The word 'Shabbat' is related to the Hebrew verb to 'cease' or to 'rest'. It is the seventh day of the Jewish week and is the day of rest and abstention from work (Elias et al., 2020). For those that observe laws pertaining to Shabbat, this abstention extends to any active engagement with all digital technology for a 25-hour period from sunset on Friday until sundown on Saturday every week of the year.

Millennials as a term refers to anyone born between 1981 and 1996 and are aged 25-40 years old. Those born from 1997 onwards, aged 24 or younger, are part of a distinct generation known as Generation Z, also known as Gen Z or the Zoomers (Dimock, 2019).

1.2 Personal Interest

My personal experience of observing a weekly digital detox during Shabbat is mostly positive. Primarily, it relieves me of commitments or problems that are not immediately in front of me, thus shrinking my world to the immediacy of my surroundings. It facilitates increased connection with my family in a way that seems unattainable during the rest of the week.

The digital detox affords me the opportunity to sit down to eat with my family, play games and relax with them free from device disturbance and interruption so we can enjoy quality time together. The benefits of this to myself and my family extend throughout the week, both as a shared memorable experience and as a common anticipation to the upcoming Shabbat, where there will be a new opportunity to digitally detox and connect with family members in a different way. Connections with extended family and friends are also enjoyed on Shabbat in a way that isn't achievable on weekdays. I also enjoy reading books and newspapers, which I don't do when my smartphone is on. Before the start of our digital detox, each family member switches off their device and consigns it to a designated place. For myself, there is a sense of freedom and relief in switching off however, there is preparation that is required. For example, it is a final chance to address any messages and emails and general technology-related tasks that require attention.

During the summertime, some of my family members often face the common challenge of boredom, especially on the long Shabbat days. This arises from their unfamiliarity with not having a device to engage with, even for brief moments, as they are accustomed to doing on weekdays. Personally, I find it difficult when I can't search for information or realise that I have an online task to complete, which now requires patience as it cannot be addressed until the end of Shabbat. The pressure of ensuring that all digital tasks are completed before the start of Shabbat can also create a sense of tension. I have never broken my detox, but if it were not a family-wide experience or a religious commandment, I doubt that I would have the resolve to stick to it. Moreover, I believe that the widespread nature of constant connectivity among younger individuals presents new challenges in observing Shabbat, making it more difficult than ever before. I am curious to explore the experience of disconnecting from the lifeline that technology provides them.

Returning to my device following the 25-hour unplugged period infuses me with mixed feelings. Partly it is curiosity about what I may have missed, but it is also worries about what I may have to address. There is trepidation about work and commitments that my device represents that have now re-entered my world. The children disappear once they are reunited with their devices and the home is filled with external distractions that sometimes feel intrusive following a sheltered period without them. My husband and my Gen Z children have some shared and some opposing attitudes towards their own digital detox. This relates much to their personalities, their age and maturity and what their devices represent to them.

I do not seek to use this study to promote or market Shabbat observance in any way. Indeed, the Jewish tradition actively discourages potential converts as there is an established belief and understanding that all of humanity has their own spiritual relationship and journey and they do not require a Jewish lifestyle and Jewish adherence to achieve their own fulfilment. What I am interested in is whether the benefits of being completely switched off from all of one's technology for a day each week has any impact on the lives of young Jewish adults and what that impact may be. I wonder whether the specific act of digital disconnection has anything of value that is transferable to the wider population, for both Jewish and non-Jewish people alike, and whether it can be observed without Shabbat, and if so, how this occurs is the subject of this study.

1.3 Social Interest

Misra et al. (2014) discreetly observed participants from a distance during a ten-minute conversation to learn how a silent mobile device placed on the table or held in a participant's hand affected conversations. Hierarchical Linear Modelling methods found that when mobile communication devices were not present, conversations were reported to have higher levels of empathic concern and were found to be more friendly. This raises the question of the implications of the nature of social life within the pervasive atmosphere of computing devices.

In two experiments, Przbyliski and Weinstein (2014) found that conversations are superficial even when silent phones are present during face-to-face conversations, as the very presence of mobile phones presents an obstacle to meaningful conversation. Mehrabian (1981) found that human conversations express only 7% of communications in words, 38% by the tone of their voice and 55% by body language. Empathic communication is restricted by online mediums of communication (Konrath et al., 2011). As a reaction to studies such as these, some companies have initiated policies to transform the way that employees are expected to use electronic communication. Media giants such as Apple have taken an interest in the potential problems caused by excessive DT usage and have implemented an operating system, iOS 12, with a beta version that includes a Screen Time feature designed to encourage awareness and control of how users manage technology (Fairyington, 2018).

Previous research has predominantly focused on the negative consequences of excessive technology use rather than exploring the potential benefits of moderating its usage. The proposed research in this study is likely to attract the attention of social scientists, parents, teachers, psychologists, and high-tech companies who share an interest in promoting responsible digital technology usage while emphasising the importance of maintaining in-person connections, and legislators interested in the right to disconnect. Additionally, individuals interested in understanding the impact of the Shabbat experience on young people, particularly in terms of unplugging from technology, as well as those curious about the lived experience of a weekly day without technological devices on Shabbat, may find this research relevant.

The study investigating digital detox presents the opportunity to explore several potential outcomes. It may reveal the necessity of achieving a healthy balance in the digital age. The preparation, effort, and willpower required for regular detox might be perceived as challenging. This research could offer valuable insights into facilitating the adoption of detox periods for individuals struggling with excessive use of digital media.

1.4 Research Question, Objective and Aim

This study will examine the ways in which eight participants experience the absence of technology for 25 hours weekly whereby they are otherwise fully engaged with it. The way in which a 25-hour digital detox is experienced by young adults is relevant to knowledge about well-being when unplugged from all forms of DT, and the impact on face-to-face relationships in the absence of DT. There is a demographic of observant, orthodox Jewish people who practise a weekly period of digital detox whose experience I am interested in studying. They abstain from active engagement with all technology for a day a week every week of the year. Given that this community practises weekly abstinence from technology, the participant pool is already available. The reason for choosing Gen Zers within this group is that they have come of age with the increased potential facilitated by DT and they have different characteristics, needs, attributes and work styles as a result (Singh & Dangmei, 2016). The research question is, 'How do young Jewish adults experience the digital detox over Shabbat?' The objectives are 'to gain insight into the experience of a digital detox over Shabbat for eight Gen Z participants' and 'to provide insight for others interested in the experience of how Gen Z's experience a digital detox every Shabbat'. The aim is 'to explore the experience of a digital detox over Shabbat for Gen Z's.'

Chapter 2: Literature Review

2.0 Introduction

The literature review will begin with an introduction to a narrative literature review followed by an overview of how the literature search was conducted. It will then specify the target population of the study, which is Gen Z, and explain the rationale behind selecting this age group. The philosophies of several notable thinkers regarding technology are explored. Martin Heidegger emphasises the importance of acknowledging technology's presence in our lives, as it plays a fundamental role in shaping our worldview. Martin Buber examines the nuances of different relationships, such as the "I-Thou" and "I-You", and considers how technology influences our understanding of these relationships. Viktor Frankl focuses on the search for meaning in life and suggests that technology can provide insights into the significance it holds for the younger generation, particularly Gen Z, and the ways they find meaning in the absence of their devices. The discussion also delves into the perspectives of proponents of technological determinism, including Bernard Steigler and Leo Marx, as well as those who advocate for cultural and social determinism like Raymond Williams.

Given the pervasive presence of the Internet in our lives and its significant impact on various aspects, such as work, social interactions, and leisure activities, the literature review will highlight the positive and supportive role that technology plays in users' lives. It will then present studies that have identified challenges associated with the prevailing culture of constant connectivity. Since there is limited knowledge regarding people's attitudes towards unplugging from technology, the review will also consider studies that have explored digital detoxes, analysing their strengths and limitations. Furthermore, the significance of Shabbat is explored, shedding light on its importance for observing Jews. The laws regarding the abstinence from all technology during Shabbat are outlined, and the philosophies of Rabbi Sacks, Rabbi Eliyahu Dessler, and Rabbi Joseph Soloveitchik are included to provide insights into Jewish philosophical perspectives on rest during this sacred day. The review will delve into the concept of Shabbat as a day of abstaining from technology. It will explore studies that focus on various aspects of observing Shabbat, examining the implications and experiences associated with disconnecting from technology during this time. Finally, the review will introduce the concept of a half-Shabbos as a response to the challenges faced in maintaining a digital-free day for Jewish teenagers who struggle to cope with the restrictions of Shabbat.

2.1 A Narrative Literature Review

When considering the appropriate type of literature review to undertake, the two primary options available were a narrative review and a systematic review, which are recognised as standard approaches in the field. A systematic review applies rigorous methodology, which aims to address a specific research question while minimising bias and enhancing the reliability of the findings. The narrative review offers a comprehensive overview and summary of existing literature, allowing for a broader exploration of the topic without strictly adhering to a structured methodology (Ferrari, 2015). Despite the availability of both narrative and systematic review approaches, the decision was made to conduct a narrative review for this study.

The objective of conducting a narrative literature review is to present an unbiased and thorough summary of existing knowledge on a particular topic, drawing upon previously published research (Holroyd-Leduc, 2002). By synthesising relevant studies, a narrative literature review offers readers a comprehensive understanding of the subject matter and aids in contextualising the gathered information (Sofaer, 1999). The review of existing research serves to validate the research topic by highlighting its significance and relevance (Hart, 1998). It collects and presents relevant research so that the reader is supplied with a summary of existing knowledge in the various fields connected to the research topic. The role of the literature review is to account, via progressive narrowing, for how current research has contributed to the topic at hand.

2.2 Literature Search

I conducted a comprehensive literature search across various platforms to gather relevant information for my research. I utilised databases such as Psychinfo, JStor, APA Psycarticles, Wiley Online Library, EbscoHost, Elsevier, academia.edu, Researchgate, Sage Journals, Medline, CINAHL, and Google Scholar, primarily accessed through the Middlesex digital library. Specific resources, such as books, chapters, and journals, required purchasing. Considering the dynamic nature of digital technologies and their widespread use, I focused on studies published from 2007 onwards, coinciding with the introduction of the iPhone, which significantly impacted people's relationships with their phones. I excluded papers in languages other than English. To ensure relevance, I employed key search terms including 'technology', 'mobile phones', 'digital detox', 'technology abstinence', 'digital abstinence', 'Shabbat', 'digital Shabbat', digital Sabbath', 'digital sabbatical', 'technology fast', 'digital cleanse', 'tech-free', 'digital break', 'digital free', 'digital detox interventions', 'timeout', 'intentional abstinence', 'disconnecting', 'disconnectivity', 'technostress', 'intrusive technology', 'unplugging', 'digital distraction', 'Gen Z', 'Generation Z', 'Zoomers', 'centennials', 'digital residents' and 'digital natives'. The search was done in a cycle whereby keywords were shifted and combined differently. A snow-ball technique was also helpful, using key publications to find further references.

2.3 A Philosophical Approach to Technology

It would be reasonable to expect, given the prevalent usage of technology, that scholars, experts, and professionals would widely discuss the philosophy of technology. However, this is not the case: 'technology has never joined epistemology, metaphysics, aesthetics, law, science, and politics as a fully respectable topic for philosophical inquiry' (Winner, 1997, p.55). The closest philosophy on technology pertains to the critical examination and significance of artificial aids to human behaviour. Although it is not only that technology aids human behaviour, it is that it also acts as a dynamic and transformational force to human activity and has altered what gives us meaning. Technology does not merely facilitate an increase in production but has profoundly altered the production process and reinvented the meaning of the constitution of 'work'. The universal developments resulting from the widespread use of technology are what distinguish and characterise modern times from earlier periods in history, the impact of which can be found not only in the realms of communication, transportation, manufacturing, and agriculture but also in our social and moral lives (Winner, 1997).

2.4 Martin Heidegger and the Essence of Technology

> '...the essence of technology is by no means anything technological.' (Heidegger, 1969, p.4)

Martin Heidegger (1889-1976), one of the most influential German philosophers of the 20th Century, best known for his contributions to phenomenology, hermeneutics, and existentialism, writes about technology (Heidegger, 1969). In ancient Aristotelian philosophy, *Techne* represented the essence of technology, signifying the process of bringing something forth. However, in

Heidegger's perspective, the essence of technology in modern times can be understood as *Ge-stell*, which encompasses the framing, construction, and exposition of the world (Huttunen & Kakkor, 2021).

> *'Everywhere we remain unfree and chained to technology, whether we passionately affirm or deny it. But we are delivered over to it in the worst possible way when we regard it as something neutral; for this conception of it, to which today we particularly like to do homage, makes us utterly blind to the essence of technology.' (Heidegger, 1977, p.39)*

In this quote from Martin Heidegger, he expresses his perspective on the relationship between human beings and technology. Heidegger argues that regardless of whether we embrace or reject technology, we are still bound to it and influenced by its presence in our lives. He suggests that our attachment to technology is often unconscious and involuntary. Heidegger warns against perceiving technology as something neutral or impartial. He believes that this common viewpoint blinds us to the true nature and impact of technology. By considering technology as neutral, we fail to recognise its essence and the ways in which it shapes our existence. A lack of awareness of the effects of technology will lead to a loss of freedom and a diminished sense of authenticity. Hence, it is crucial to examine our relationship with technology and how we perceive its implications on our lives (Dreyfus, 1995).

Heidegger posits that we see nature and, increasingly, humans as fodder for technical operations. We can escape this enslavement not by spurning technology but by recognising its associated risks. When a worker is rated only in terms of their production abilities and the value of their human capabilities are shrunk to measures of their utility, all humans become diminished into dispensable resources that lose their independence and uniqueness as they shape themselves to fit into a mould dictated by society. Human abilities become a means for technical procedure only. Heidegger thinks about the essence of technology where technology is understood beyond machines and technical procedures but in the way in which we encounter all structures and entities. We believe that as humans we control technical activity and that technology is there to facilitate our endeavours but, in effect, we are controlled and directed by means of technology, thereby reinforcing our dependence. Heidegger seeks to free our thinking from this phenomenon, to save us from what he believes we have been shackled. Heidegger is horrified not so much by the harmful effects of technology but by how it has reordered society by its essence. That is to say, it has transposed human beings and inhibits our ability to truly experience others (Blitz, 2014).

Heidegger argues that calculative thinking is primarily concerned with computation, while meditative thinking engages in contemplation of the overarching meaning that encompasses all existence.

> 'Calculative thinking computes. It computes ever new, ever more promising and at the same time more economical possibilities. Calculative thinking races from one prospect to the next. Calculative thinking

never stops, never collects itself. Calculative thinking is not meditative thinking, not thinking which contemplates the meaning which reigns in everything that is. There are, then, two kinds of thinking, each justified and needed in its own way: calculative thinking and meditative thinking.' (Heidegger, 1969, p.46)

Both forms of thinking require significant effort, time, and practice. However, calculative-technological thinking has become predominant, leading to a perception of the world as quantifiable and calculable. To challenge the dominance of technological thinking, Heidegger suggests a simultaneous affirmation and negation of technology (Huttunen & Kakkor, 2021). The aim of this study is to investigate a nuanced approach to technology, where a simultaneous pattern of affirmation and negation is employed. This approach entails utilising technology for six days a week while abstaining from it on the seventh day.

2.5 Martin Buber on Technology and Interpersonal Relationships

'We cannot throw it off, and our difficult task and responsibility remains to carry the human and humane values into technology itself.' (Buber, 1967, p.184)

Martin Buber, (1878-1965) was an Austrian and later Israeli Jewish existential philosopher. His work draws on the significance of communication and openness in relationships (Huston, 2007). He is known for his book 'I and Thou' (1923), which was translated into English from its original in German in 1937. Buber proposes that humans convey existence in two ways. 'I' towards 'It' and 'I' towards 'Thou'. The 'It' of 'I-It' refers to the world as we experience it. The 'Thou' implies our relationship towards God, the eternal Thou. It describes the world of relations (Buber, 2012). The relation itself can be a form of contemplation wherein relating deeply to another in an 'I-You' experience encompasses a present-moment encounter with another, free from theoretical knowledge and ideas but directly aware of the presence of the other human being. The 'I-You' experience affirms the relationship by the experience of the other individual in their uniqueness, authenticity, compassion and reciprocity. When one enters into contemplation in an 'I-You' mode, one enters into a direct relationship with the object of the contemplation (Garcia. A F, 2015).

On the other hand, the 'I-It' emphasises relationships with impersonal objects, such as those that can be manipulated, dissected or put to work for a purpose. This includes people when they are characterised as objects. The word 'it' signifies distance between oneself and the object. It is natural and unavoidable as we all categorise, conceptualise and plan in our lives. We cannot exist without it; however, it is in the 'I-You' state where we are directly aware of another human being and where deep relationships can be maintained (Garcia. A F, 2015).

Despite Buber's considerable work and extensive writings about the importance and uniqueness of interpersonal moments, concerning technology, Buber took a surprisingly practical approach. He presents himself as a 'realist' asserting that one must not discard the progress that has been made in technical engineering and that what is needed is the 'humanisation of technology' rather than the 'demonisation' of it. It is precisely within technology 'that true interhuman relations would occur' (Buber & Schapira, 1985, p.310). Buber rejected the criticisms of technology and asserted that we are destined to carry technology with us and cannot shirk it. Our duty towards it is to carry humane values into technology itself (Biemann, 2016). By consciously shifting our perspective from an instrumental 'I-It' mode to a more relational 'I-Thou' mode, we can strive for more authentic and meaningful interactions. This study will explore how these are maintained offline while living in a digital world.

2.6 Victor Frankl and Meaning in Life in a Digital Age

> '*Man's main concern is not to gain pleasure or to avoid pain but rather to see a meaning in his life. That is why man is even ready to suffer, on the condition, to be sure, that his suffering has a meaning.*' (Frankl, 1963, p.136)

Victor Frankl (1905-1997) was the founder and distinguished professor of Logotherapy. He was born in Vienna in 1905, gained his doctorate in medicine and philosophy and then during the Second World War, he was an inmate for three years in Auschwitz, Dachau and other concentration camps. His work before and after the War focuses on meaning in life and also meaning in suffering, which to Frankl, is an inevitable component of human life (Frankl, 2006, 2019).

According to Frankl, the noölogical dimension refers to the uniquely human experience of going beyond our surroundings and entering a realm of deep thoughts and insights (Frankl, 1988). Frankl suggests that individuals should strive to create this tension within themselves in order to rediscover their life's meaning. This ongoing tension provides a person with a sense of motivation and purpose (Frankl, 2006, 2014). Frankl believed that pursuing emotional balance is mentally beneficial, but it is the tension created by striving towards meaningful goals that truly gives purpose to one's life. Therefore, Frankl argued that being in a state of noö-dynamics, where this tension exists, is healthy and desirable, even though emotional stability can be comforting (Frankl, 2005).

Various studies have consistently found that close relationships are a significant source of meaning in people's lives. For instance, when individuals were asked to express what gives their lives meaning, the most commonly mentioned aspect was their meaningful connections with others (Nelson et al., 2019). Extensive research has highlighted the importance of meaning in life as a fundamental human need, which has a profound impact on both psychological and physical well-being (Vail & Routledge, 2020). People who perceive their lives as meaningful tend to experience greater longevity, improved health, and higher levels of happiness compared to those who perceive their lives as less meaningful.

In as much as the participants of this study find meaning in their interpersonal relationships, especially with family and friends, we need to consider whether those relationships and, therefore, the meaning of those relationships of a different essence when technology is absent. Furthermore, in their time alone, insofar as they experience meaning by themselves, or through social events, is that time enhanced or of a different essence with the absence of technology? Are participants in this study experiencing a noölogical dimension of existence in their time away from their phones? This study aims to address these questions.

2.7 Technological and Social Determinism

'What sort of entity is technology? But the truth seems to be that it is not an entity at all.' (Marx, 1997, p.983)

The philosophy of technology presents two opposing ontological and epistemological positions that offer different perspectives on the relationship between technology and society. Technological Determinism suggests that technology is the driving force in shaping human life and society. Social or Cultural Determinism, on the other hand, argues that humans drive technological changes, as society and culture influence how technologies develop (Thomas, 2019).

Bernard Stiegler, a French philosopher and cultural theorist, opposes Technological Determinism, claiming that there is no clear distinction between humans and technology because they are inseparable. He argues that being technical is an inherent part of being human, not just something humans possess or do. He pointed out that the uncontrolled flow of information through technology has led to various struggles in education and society. Stiegler is concerned that a wrong understanding of technology can hinder its effective use, impede its adoption, and limit its transformative potential (Stiegler, 2011). According to Stiegler, human life truly takes place when individuals socially interact through technology. He believes there are three interconnected aspects: the individual, the technical, and the social and that human evolution occurs in three ways: psychologically, technically, and socially. To illustrate this, he uses the example of ants, where understanding a social ant requires considering its physical environment and interactions with other ants (2011). Stiegler also highlights that what began anthropogenically (originating from humans) continues technogenically (influenced by technology). He terms this ongoing relationship between humans and technology as "epiphylogenesis" (Lemmens, 2011), emphasising how they mutually shape each other throughout human evolution.

Leo Marx, an American cultural historian, criticises technological determinism and defends human agency in relation to technology (Sacasas, 2014). He introduced the concept of reification, which means reducing technology to mere objects, ignoring their connection to humanity. This view sees technology as specific things like cars, power plants, or computers without considering the broader context of their use. It becomes problematic when technology is given human-like qualities and exerts influence over our actions.

By attributing causal power to "technology", they divert our attention from human factors (Marx, 1997).

Raymond Williams, a Welsh cultural critic, novelist and social theorist, questioned the concept of technological determinism by highlighting the intricate interplay of historical and social factors in shaping information and communication technologies (Williams, 2003). His contributions to cultural studies provide valuable insights that extend beyond his time and can even be applied to contemporary phenomena like digital convergence despite his lack of personal experience with it. 'Determination is a genuine social process, but it should never be seen as an all-encompassing and completely predictable set of causes.' (Willams, 2003, p.139). Social phenomena are not predetermined; instead, they emerge within a range of possibilities influenced by various social forces and pressures. In the context of television, these factors encompass 'the distribution of power or wealth, social and environmental legacies, and the dynamics of different social groups' (Willams, 2003, p.139). Williams highlighted the significance of various factors, such as power distribution, social and physical inheritance, and the relationships between different social groups in shaping phenomena like television. His ideas encourage a distinct understanding of technology's development and its interaction with society.

In summary, the philosophy of technology presents contrasting views. Stiegler cautions against a flawed understanding of technology, emphasising the interconnectedness of the individual, the technical, and the social. Marx's concept of reification reduces technology to mere objects. Raymond Williams challenged the concept of technological determinism by emphasising the complex interplay of historical and social factors in shaping information and communication technologies. This study on the weekly digital detox experience during Shabbat is linked to the concept of technological determinism, recognising that technology influences human life and society. It is also connected to social determinism, as the choices humans make in their interactions with technology shape the course of humanity.

2.8 Who are Gen Z?

Generation Z, also identified as Generation I, Gen Tech, Digital Residents, Digital Natives, or Gen Wii, is distinguished from its predecessors through its profound connection with technology (Singh & Dangmei, 2016). Each generation has been formed by the technological advancements of its time. For instance, Baby Boomers matured with television's growth, Generation X experienced the computer revolution, while Millennials came of age amidst the internet surge. However, for Generation Z, born after 1997 and nurtured during the 2000s, these technologies have been an integral part of their upbringing. When the iPhone was introduced in 2007, the eldest Gen Zers were just 10 years old. This generation has grown up as digital residents with scant memories of a pre-smartphone world. Their formative experiences have been largely shaped by on-demand entertainment, constant connectivity, and social media (Dimock, 2019). The central role of technology in their identity has resulted in significant changes in youthful behaviours, attitudes, and lifestyles (Singh & Dangmei, 2016). It is important to study this generation as they transition into adulthood (Dimock, 2019).

The digital era's growth has brought about questions concerning the potential impacts of smartphone usage on individuals, relationships, and communities (Lanette, 2018). Gen Zers' upbringing in the age of digital connectivity distinguishes them from prior generations, and the role of digital technology (DT) in their lives is critical to their identity formation, social interaction, and engagement. Generation Z might share a few traits with Millennials, but their development in a significantly different world has led to distinct attitudes, habits, and perspectives. A defining feature of Generation Z is their exposure to racial diversity. They are more likely to have grown up in diverse family structures, making them more accepting of differences in race, sexual orientation, or religion.

Another key characteristic of Generation Z is their inherent ease with technology. While Millennials experienced the rise of technology and social media, making them "digital pioneers" and "digital residents", Gen Z was born into an era of unprecedented technological innovation where information was readily available and social media was pervasive. These technological advancements have had mixed effects on Gen Z. It has provided them with an ocean of information, making learning more accessible and proactive. However, an abundance of screen time has been linked to detrimental effects on physical and psychological health, disruptions in sleep patterns (Nakshine et al., 2022) and adverse social and neurological consequences (Lissak, 2018).

Economic pressures, such as the stress of the rental market, have also shaped Gen Z, leading them to value stability, conservative spending, stable jobs, and smart investments. A common feature of Generation Z is the mental health challenges they face, often referred to as the "loneliest generation" due to the extensive hours spent online that may result in feelings of isolation and depression (Bakhtiari, 2023b; Future Care Capital, 2022; Growing Up Lonely: Generation Z, n.d.; Psychology Today, 2022). This generation's mental health is also impacted by the world's turbulent state. Increased political activism among Gen Z in the United States has led to heightened stress levels around issues like gun control, police brutality, and climate change. Yet, their technological prowess and use of social media platforms allow them to make informed purchasing decisions. They are inclined towards sustainable products and brands, even willing to pay a higher price. They value personalised products and are attracted to brands that echo their political views. They are considerably progressive, with a high probability of viewing LGBTQ rights advancement positively (The Annie E. Casey Foundation, 2023). According to Mintel (2023), there are approximately ten million Gen Z's in the UK today, which accounts for around 15% of the population. Despite Generation Z often being depicted as a highly socially and environmentally conscious generation, Mintel's data reveals that while they do care about these issues, living a more sustainable lifestyle is not their foremost priority. Enhancing their appearance, travelling abroad, and pursuing hobbies are ranked higher in priority for Generation Z.

2.9 The Supportive Role of Technological Devices

Technological advancements have converted the public into a global society with influences in many realms. Smartphones have experienced unparalleled adoption rates, surpassing the adoption rates of any other technology in human history (Pew Research Center, 2018). The adoption rate of smartphones in the United Kingdom has consistently grown yearly, reaching a rate of 94 per cent in 2023 (Statista, n.d.). These handheld devices have become deeply ingrained in daily life to the extent that many individuals express an inability to envision life without them (Smith A, 2015). Given the widespread acceptance of smartphones worldwide, it is reasonable to assume that these devices contribute to human well-being. They provide constant access to valuable information, entertainment, and connections with distant friends and family members. For brevity, this discussion will focus on three specific studies that demonstrate the numerous benefits of smartphones and other digital devices in the realms of education and relationships.

Educational process and learning environments are one area that has been transformed by an increasing trend to use social media and smart technology for teaching and learning, which provide platforms for knowledge sharing and learning in synergy due to improved communication (Latif et al., 2019). Various perspectives on learning with regard to social networks have been highlighted in literature, including the motivational aspect of social connections, collaborative teaching approaches, and the enhancement of learning through immediate feedback and active engagement (Alabdulkareem, 2015). The "social constructivism theory" (Piaget, 1953) emphasises the role of interaction and socialisation in facilitating students' learning and the construction of their knowledge and personal learning processes. This theory supports using social media for educational purposes, as it enables participative learning and serves as a set of constructivist tools for teaching and learning (Kalasi, 2014). Teaching in the 21st century is considered to be an exciting endeavour due to the abundant resources, opportunities, and possibilities for collaboration. Social media, as a cost-effective and highly accessible tool, enables global collaborations (Kalasi, 2014). It has been reported that approximately 80% of young individuals have accounts on social networking sites (Mintel, 2023), making it an integral part of their lives. Social media platforms have provided a platform for young people to showcase their talents and access relevant opportunities with just a single click. Students can share their problems and issues and receive multiple recommendations from their online peers and teachers.

In a review of articles searched from online data, the use of smartphones and social media in the context of medical education was examined (Latif et al., 2019). The review searched articles identifying the significance of smartphones and their application in medical education. Facebook, WhatsApp, and Edmodo were investigated as learning tools, along with an analysis of the latest trends, benefits, and challenges associated with utilising social media applications for educational purposes. The method they used was searching for relevant articles sourced from online databases, such as PubMed, ERIC, and Google Scholar. Various keywords, subject terms, and descriptors were employed to identify the appropriate sources, including terms such as social media, learning, Facebook, WhatsApp, Edmodo, students, and medical education. Advanced search options and filters were utilised to ensure the retrieval of the most relevant articles. Boolean operators were also utilised to expand or refine the search as needed.

Based on their systematic review, the authors concluded that social media is not only a powerful tool for social interactions but is also an important instrument used for teaching and learning. Resources can be shared, which permits flexible and collaborative communication via the Internet. Engagement and feedback are both remote and immediate, thus facilitating the speedy dissemination of knowledge. This allows teaching to be an exciting activity due to the resources and opportunities available on a single click. However, many studies ignore the technostress experienced by teachers who have to teach using multiple dimensions. Previous studies (Markowitz et al., 2018; Qi, 2019; Wang & Li, 2019) have revealed that university administrators experience technostress when it comes to implementing educational enhancements through information and communication technologies, such as mobile learning, blended learning, and virtual reality-based learning. The study also found disadvantages, such as addiction to media applications and time wastage, and they debate these distractions against the supportive framework that current technology provides. The study fails to mention the number of studies that were reviewed, and it does not address the user experience of the students;

however, it is important in highlighting some of the strengths that have been brought about via digital technology.

In a study (Atske, 2020) across eleven developing countries, researchers from the Pew Research Centre conducted a series of focus groups consisting of groups of 10 adults for an hour and a half to better understand how they think about their mobile phones and the impact of their mobile phones on society. All the focus groups across the countries required participants to have at least some interest in politics and were recruited to ensure diversity with regard to levels of education, employment status, rural and urban location and the duration that they have owned their phones. The results were largely positive, with a majority of people saying that their mobile phones impact themselves personally and the economy positively. They also broadly agreed that their phones allowed them to stay in touch with friends and family far away, where they could exchange news and information. In all countries, participants said that their mobile devices freed them rather than tied them down, although they were more divided about whether their phones helped them save time rather than made them waste time. While this study was extensive and recent, it was conducted within developing countries in Asia, Africa, and South America and did not represent users of DT in the UK. It also does not include information about different gendered uses of the internet or examine the effects of DT on mental well-being.

While critics argue that the internet has had a negative impact on society due to it weakening our social interactions (Putnam, 2000), analysis has also confirmed that the internet enhances the lives of its users (Hamburger & Hayat, 2011). Hamburger and Hayat (2011) examined results from participants from 13 countries that took part in the World Internet Project (Putnam, 2000). This project analysed the answers to a questionnaire to study the influence of different media channels on facets of people's lives. The participants that answered the questionnaire to the 2009 report numbered 22,002, aged between 12 and 84. Their responses were examined, and it was revealed that the impact of the internet differs depending on the reasons for its use. The study separated distinctive purposes for internet usage amongst participants, such as social interactions with family members, friends, colleagues, and people who share hobbies, recreational activities, political interests, and religion. It was found that variables of age, income, and education impacted the amount of internet usage that participants' social lives depended on, and all but one of the study's hypotheses were supported by a positive correlation between internet usage and increased social interactions. This study is useful in demonstrating that there are ways in which social relationships can be enhanced by the internet rather than diminished. However, when comparing the breadth of the internet from 2011 to 2023, the terrain is vastly different. Instagram was in its infancy stage, conceived in 2010, whilst Snapchat was conceived in 2011, not known about at the time of this study, as was TikTok, which started in 2016 and WhatsApp was still in its infancy, born only in 2009 (Ortiz-Ospina, 2019). Considering how vast and widespread the internet's expansion has become since 2011, there is room for further examination as to its effects on individuals and, more so, how young people manage a detox from the continual influx of information that has become increasingly prevalent over the decade and more since this report was published.

2.10 The Complexities of Continuous Connectivity

Numerous studies have documented the problems associated with technology use and overuse, highlighting their impact on physical, mental, and emotional health. While several studies address the issue of technology-related stress, two specific studies will be mentioned here to highlight the research gap that exists regarding the potential benefits of using technology while also incorporating regular breaks. These studies demonstrate the need for further investigation into the effects of technology use on health and well-being and specifically explore the possibility of taking weekly breaks from technology to mitigate the negative consequences.

In contemporary research, technostress is defined as the stress triggered by the usage of information and communication technologies (Ayyagari et al., 2011; Li et al., 2020; Ragu-Nathan TS et al., 2008). Previous studies have examined the impact of technostress, particularly in the context of mobile device usage. The consequences of technostress can manifest in physical, psychological, and behavioural aspects. Negative physical reactions include restlessness, headache, and fatigue (Arnetz BB et al., 1997), while psychological effects may involve burnout, reduced satisfaction with technology, and job dissatisfaction (Ayyagari et al., 2011; Scott et al., 2009). Decreased productivity, performance, and declining innovation are other common behavioural effects (Ragu-Nathan TS et al., 2008; Saylor Academy, 2012). However, limited studies have specifically focused on the influence of technostress resulting from smartphone use.

Identifying a research gap, Yao and Wang (2022) aimed to investigate the antecedents and outcomes of technostress related to smartphone use among university students, who represent a distinct population with widespread smartphone usage. The study aimed to shed light on students' smartphone usage patterns and potential intervention strategies. Students often experience *compulsive smartphone use, life invasion, and information overload* due to constant Internet connectivity and various smartphone applications. *Life invasion* pertains to individuals' subjective perception of their daily lives being encroached upon due to the excessive dominance of various ICT tools, including social networking sites (Cao & Sun, 2018; Scott et al., 2009). The widely used social software, WeChat, serves as an example where students are online 24/7, often prioritising smartphone usage over important activities such as learning, attending meetings, sports, and face-to-face conversations. Life invasion has been positively associated with technostress in previous literature (Ragu-Nathan TS et al., 2008; Tarafdar et al., 2007). Therefore, the study hypothesised a positive association between life invasion due to smartphone use and technostress among university students. In this study, researchers measured students' academic self-perception, which refers to their confidence in their academic abilities and self-evaluation of academic performance. They further hypothesised a positive association between technostress and poor academic self-perception among students.

Data was collected from a public university in southern China over a two-week period using an online questionnaire administered via WeChat to approximately 600 potential respondents across various majors. The final analysis included 540 responses using SPSS 20.0 and AMOS 24.0. The results indicated that compulsive smartphone use and information overload were positively associated with technostress, and a positive association was found between technostress and poor sleep quality among university students. Furthermore, technostress was found to potentially contribute to students' poor academic self-perception. The predictive effects of compulsive smartphone use and information overload on technostress suggest that controlling these stressors may help alleviate technostress among students.

This study, being recent, may closely reflect the attitudes of university students toward their smartphone use. However, further research is needed to understand how UK students perceive their smartphone relationships and their experiences of technostress, considering potential cultural differences. Researchers conclude that exploring prevention mechanisms to address students' compulsive smartphone use is crucial. Further research is needed to investigate whether a weekly digital detox, for example, can mitigate technostress resulting from digital overload and compulsive smartphone use.

In a study conducted by Thomée et al. (2011), excessive mobile phone use was found to be associated with sleep disorders and musculoskeletal issues. The researchers suggest that these factors contribute to feelings of depression, anxiety, and stress as individuals feel the pressure to be constantly available. They set up to investigate this using a prospective cohort of young adults aged 20-24 years. To gather data, a random selection was made from the general population in Sweden, including 10,000 men and 10,000 women born between 1983 and 1987. Participants completed a questionnaire at both baseline and a one-year follow-up. In 2007, a questionnaire covering health, work and leisure-related exposure factors, background information, and psychosocial factors was distributed to the selected population via post, with the option to respond online. Incentives were provided as rewards for participation (Ekman et al., 2008). One year later, individuals who indicated their willingness to participate in further studies were invited to complete an identical questionnaire. The non-participation and dropout rate was 79%, resulting in a remaining sample of 4,156 participants who completed both questionnaires.

All analyses were conducted using SAS software, version 9.2. The findings indicated positive associations between high mobile phone use and current stress, sleep disturbances, and symptoms of depression in both men and women after adjusting for relationship status, educational level, and present occupation. Availability demands were linked to current stress and symptoms of depression in men and with all mental health outcomes in women. Being awakened at night by the mobile phone was associated with current stress, sleep disturbances, and symptoms of depression and overuse of the mobile phone was associated with current stress, sleep disturbances, and symptoms of depression in men and with all mental health outcomes in women. The strongest associations were observed for accessibility stress in relation to mental health outcomes, with accessibility stress being associated with current stress and symptoms of depression in men and with all mental health outcomes in women.

Most young adults indicated that they were required to be accessible and reachable via their mobile phones throughout the entire day or at all times. A significant number of participants reported subjective overuse, which may suggest a potential addiction to the mobile phone or its various functions. The use of mobile phones places significant demands on an individual's ability to set limits on usage and accessibility. Norms regarding mobile phone usage are shaped through interactions with others. If a young person perceives that "everyone else" is always available, they may experience stress when they themselves are not accessible. In this study, perceiving the accessibility provided by mobile phones as stressful was identified as a clear risk factor for reporting symptoms of mental health issues. Therefore, perceiving something as a "problem" could indicate a broader issue and serve as a warning sign to take measures to avoid constant accessibility and overuse. It is important to note that this study was conducted solely in Sweden and was based on data from 2007, which means that the technological landscape has significantly evolved since then. The researchers acknowledge a healthy participant selection bias and potential bias towards lower mobile phone exposure. The participants in this study found feelings of anxiety associated with being inaccessible. This highlights a research gap in exploring whether undergoing a digital detox with the support of family and friends could serve as a protective factor against the stress of disconnection. This is particularly relevant for young people who may feel that "everyone else" is always available and connected to technology.

2.11 Beneficial Outcomes of Brief Technology Breaks

Researchers documented how smartphones have the ability to subtly diminish the emotional benefits of face-to-face social interactions. They suggest that this happens through two main pathways. Firstly, by constantly providing access to information and entertainment, smartphones can divert our attention away from giving full focus to our friends and family in our immediate social environment. Secondly, smartphones may replace casual social interactions. By enabling tasks like ordering food or finding directions without the need to interact with others, smartphones eliminate the necessity of engaging with people in various daily activities (Kushlev et al., 2019).

The researchers began with the assumption that smartphones are intentionally designed to capture attention, indicating that they can be highly distracting in daily life. They discovered that students exhibited more symptoms of inattentiveness during a week when they were instructed to keep their phones within reach with alerts turned on, compared to when they were instructed to keep their phones out of reach with alerts turned off (Kushlev et al., 2016). To investigate whether such distractions interfere with the benefits of face-to-face social interactions, the researchers conducted a field experiment at a science museum in Vancouver (Kushlev & Dunn, 2019).

They recruited 200 parents visiting the museum with their children and randomly assigned them to use their phones as much as possible or as little as possible during their visit. Before leaving the museum, the parents completed a questionnaire about their experience, including their level of distraction, perceived social connectedness, and the extent to which they felt a sense of purpose and meaning in life. The results showed that parents who maximised their smartphone use felt less socially connected, had lower feelings of meaning, and experienced more distractions compared to parents who minimised their smartphone use. The effects on social connectedness and meaning were partially mediated by the increased sense of distraction. Thus, smartphones interfered with the well-established benefits of spending time with children by providing a source of distraction in a potentially rewarding social context (Nelson et al., 2014). One limitation of this study was that parents were informed in advance about the possibility of minimising or maximising their smartphone use, which may have influenced their responses to the questionnaire based on their own theories about smartphones or assumptions about the researchers' hypotheses. I also have concerns about the ethical implications of requesting parents to maximise their smartphone use in front of their children.

To minimise potential biases and expand the research to another significant social activity, researchers conducted a field experiment at a local café (Dwyer et al., 2018). They invited 304 participants to dine with friends or family members at the café without disclosing the study's connection to smartphones. Smartphone use was manipulated by instructing half of the groups that they would receive a one-item survey via text message after placing their food order and keeping their phones on the table with alerts on. The other groups were told they would complete the survey on paper and were asked to place their phones in a basket on the table. After the meal, all participants completed a questionnaire about their experience. Participants with access to their phones reported enjoying the experience less than those without access. They also reported feeling more distracted when they had access to their phones, and distraction partially mediated the negative impact of phones on enjoyment. While no significant effects were observed on other variables, such as pleasant affect, social connection, and boredom, combining all the outcome variables indicated that participants' overall subjective experience was consistently diminished when they had access to their phones. Therefore, in this rewarding social environment, smartphones generated feelings of distraction and undermined the well-being benefits of sharing a meal with friends or family. This study demonstrates that face-to-face interactions are improved when spending limited time with friends without the presence of phones. However, it does not explore the experience of being without phones for an extended period of 25 hours in various situations, where individuals are unlikely to spend a substantial portion of that time with friends.

2.12 Applying a Detox to Digital Technology

Research shows that about 61% of people admit they are addicted to the internet and their digital screens, and approximately 25% of 18 to 44-year-olds cannot recall the last time their phone was not within reach (Sreenivas, 2021). Constant connectivity can harm one's quality of life, leading to sensory overload and overwhelming experiences. Taking a break from social media apps and spending time away from screens can benefit mental and physical well-being (Sreenivas, 2021). Both the time span and the range of digital devices for a digital detox period can vary from spending an hour or two without a mobile phone to a detox period lasting a few weeks. The devices abstained from may be the mobile phone only or may include all computers, televisions, and online media and games (Syversten & Enli, 2019).

According to the Oxford Learner's Dictionary, a digital detox is 'a period of time when a person does not use digital devices, such as smartphones or computers, especially in order to reduce stress and relax'. Digital Detox as a temporary break has been seen as an opportunity for professionals to heighten consciousness and a time to practice self-regulation with the purpose of reducing stress and allowing one to feel more present. It taps into the phenomenon for those who seek authenticity, a counter experience to that experienced online, which can be associated with artificial communication (Syversten & Enli, 2019).

In a study (Roberts & Koliska, 2014), 891 students from 10 different countries and 12 different universities were asked to blog about their experiences following a period of unplugging from 'ambient media' for a period of 24 hours. 'Ambient media' describes the information-rich environment commonly available to adult populations in the developed world and increasingly in the developing world. It is comprised of networks, websites, and apps that allow users to share information and also the mobile devices that allow for the transmission of this information. It refers to the world of information that serves as awareness systems with which users cannot maintain knowledge and activities that seamlessly integrate into everyday life. This study was interested in how these awareness systems, made possible via ambient media, affect its users.

Only half the sample was able to abstain for the full period. The most recurrent theme was dependence or addiction to media technology, followed by sentiments of distress and anxiety. This surfaced because of feeling like a failure at not being able to meet expectations that come with being constantly connected and withdrawal from being separated from the devices that represent emotional connectedness. Some students compensated for the loss of their devices by making deeper connections to those in their proximity. However, they still felt its absence, and some participants were at first not able to find replacements for the void left by the absence of their digital devices. The third theme revealed feelings of relief from the necessity to be preoccupied with media technology.

The results of this study indicate the extent to which students are becoming increasingly dependent on media technology, and leaving this technology for a brief period is akin to leaving the real world. Feelings of frustration and anxiety surfaced when participants felt they were unable to track the movements of their friends and family or be able to provide information to others due to their lack of connectedness. Lievrouw (2001) argues that fundamental social behaviours have been altered due to new technologies. Themes of confusion and isolation were also frequently found where students affirmed their feelings of missing out and of not knowing what was happening to friends and family as well as the wider world. They emphasised missing connecting with parents, friends, and significant others during their 24-hour digital detox. The lowest overall frequency was feelings of content or calm, as many found that the media devices that they were abstaining from represented their daily routines, such as alarm clocks, maps, navigators, music, and entertainment needed for exercise, relaxation, and for commutes. Some students were not able to ask strangers for directions or able to walk without music and declared that they were unable to cope. This study validated the findings from various studies that ambient information is linked to awareness systems that our lives have become a part of. The students of this study were not practiced at having a digital detox, they kept their detox in isolation from their families and communities, and it does not say whether they were advised about how to use their time instead.

(Thomas et al., 2016) conducted a comprehensive study to examine the costs and benefits associated with constant digital connectivity across different age groups. The research involved surveying 446 participants ranging in age from 14 to 79. The study focused on participants' feelings and attitudes toward unplugging from computer-mediated communication (CMC), which encompassed activities such as email, instant messaging, social media usage, and video chats. The researchers aimed to understand how different age groups perceived the act of unplugging, identify the perceived costs and benefits of being unplugged, and explore alternative activities individuals would engage in during a 24-hour unplugged period. The study sought to deepen the understanding of the role of CMC in people's lives and address concerns about the potential negative impact of heavy CMC reliance on the development of young digital residents.

The participants were diverse in terms of gender and race, and they were categorised into four age groups: adolescents, emerging adults, middle adults, and older adults. The participants completed a 20-minute online survey comprised of closed and open-ended questions, as well as a psychometric questionnaire measuring loneliness. Recruitment was conducted through Facebook, colleges, and high schools, with participants accessing the survey through a provided web link. Data analysis utilised a mixed method design, with quantitative analysis used to address age-related questions and test the correlation between CMC usage and loneliness, and qualitative analysis employed to identify themes in the narrative responses to open-ended questions about unplugging attitudes.

The findings revealed that participants had mixed emotions when considering the prospect of unplugging, with adolescents displaying less anxiety compared to emerging adults and middle-aged adults. The study identified feeling addicted to digital communication technology as a common reason for wanting to unplug. However, there were significant obstacles to unplugging, such as being the sole person disconnected from devices among friends and family who were habitually engaged with their devices. Additionally, the pressure to constantly be available to colleagues at work made the idea of disconnecting from digital technology seem impractical.

Participants anticipated that unplugging would allow them to spend quality time with loved ones and engage in face-to-face interactions, which they perceived as gains from the unplugging experience. However, they also acknowledged that unplugging would result in a loss of connection with others, creating a dilemma as digital devices offered both opportunities for connection and barriers to real-time interaction with important people in their lives. This finding supports the notion that CMC usage competes with real-time sociability and intimacy (Turkle, 2017).

Adolescents were significantly less likely than other age groups to believe they would gain any benefits from unplugging while emerging adults recognised more benefits compared to adolescents. Adolescents reported anticipating more negative emotions associated with unplugging, such as boredom and loneliness. By contrast, emerging adults considered unplugging an opportunity for personal reflection, solitude, and engaging in enjoyable activities alone, highlighting their awareness of the need for 'me time' that is inhibited by their constant engagement with CMC. Notably, the study did not find a high frequency of adolescents reporting the anticipated benefit of alone time.

Reading for pleasure emerged as the most preferred activity overall, although it sharply declined among adolescents, whose top activity was engaging in physical exercise. This may indicate that excessive device usage hinders physical exercise. The study also found that feelings of addiction to digital devices and spending excessive time on devices were not necessarily linked to feelings of loneliness. The anticipated anxiety levels related to unplugging did not differ significantly based on whether the experience was rated positively or negatively.

The findings suggested that individuals with prior experience of voluntarily abstaining from CMC felt less anxious about unplugging in the future, particularly among adolescents. This indicates that becoming accustomed to unplugging may require practice, and more voluntary experiences can reduce anxiety surrounding digital detox. The researchers concluded that completely refraining from CMC usage is not feasible or advisable for most individuals, given its increasing ubiquity. However, periodic experiences of temporary unplugging may become a mainstream practice due to the identified reasons, such as having more time for meaningful connections with friends and family, reducing distraction and cognitive overload, and escaping the pressure of constant availability to work colleagues.

While this study provided valuable insights into participants' attitudes and feelings toward a hypothetical unplugging experience within a diverse sample, it should be noted that the findings were based on opinions rather than actual data. The researchers recommended further investigation of individuals' actual experiences with unplugging, whether for 24 hours or longer durations. They suggested collaborating with organisations like Digital Detox or Sabbath Manifesto for future research endeavours.

In a study, Conroy et al. (2022) examined the experiences of fourteen individuals aged 18-30 regarding their ownership and usage of smartphones. The focus of the research was on understanding the participants' engagement with and disconnection from their smartphones. By employing an Interpretative Phenomenological Analysis (IPA) methodology, the researchers aimed to gain deeper insights into the context in which individuals detach themselves from their devices and the wider implications this has on their lives. All participants in the study were located in the United Kingdom. The researchers formulated two primary research questions to guide their investigation. The first question explored how young adults between the ages of 18 and 30 discuss their experiences of excessive reliance on smartphones. The second question investigated the experiences of these adults in their attempts to overcome overreliance on smartphones.

All participants were students who use smartphones regularly. The recruitment method was via six weekly email invitations sent on consecutive weeks to psychology students at the researcher's institution. There were twenty-eight initial responders, and finally, 14 took part in the interviews; these were students who responded to the follow-up emails. The superordinate theme of phones being like an addiction arose with four subthemes: 'convenience/productivity and overreliance', 'subjugated needs', 'lost leisure time and pastimes', and 'thwarted agency'. A second superordinate theme was 'it's difficult to maintain abstinence' with four subthemes of 'scope for self-deception', 'intertwining of devices with life', 'possible social repercussions', and 'transference to other devices'.

The study revealed a strong desire among participants to decrease their smartphone usage, and their accounts reflected frustration associated with the challenges of reducing the amount of time spent on their smartphones. The researchers reached a conclusion that participants in the study recognised both the practical benefits and enjoyment associated with using smartphones while also acknowledging the importance of modifying their usage habits. Notably, the findings indicated that reducing smartphone engagement or completely abstaining from it could pose challenges, including negative social consequences. These challenges underscored the intricate and demanding nature of attempting to change smartphone usage patterns. The researchers expressed their hope for future studies to explore further individuals' dependence on smartphones and their experiences in trying to alter their device usage habits, building upon the evidence presented in this research.

The focus of this study was not on a comprehensive digital detox but rather on exploring the attempts made by participants to abstain from technology.

When participants considered detoxing from their phones, they still had access to other devices like laptops, meaning that a complete digital detox was not achieved. Various strategies for digital detox were employed, such as having phone-free days and using 'lockout apps'. The success of these strategies varied within and between participant accounts, making it challenging to pinpoint specific strategies' effectiveness based on the findings. The study's limited representativeness is a result of its participant pool consisting solely of psychology students from the same university. This characteristic of the sample restricts the study's generalisability, as it does not adequately represent a broader and more diverse population.

Digital Free Tourism (DFT) refers to a specific form of tourism where access to the internet and mobile signals is intentionally absent or restricted (Li et al., 2020). There is a growing trend among vacationers seeking 'digital downtime' and a desire to disconnect from technology, as reported by the Scottish tourism sector (National Trust for Scotland, 2023). This has led to the rise in popularity of resorts and travel packages that provide opportunities for tourists to unplug from the internet, such as the emergence of 'black hole' resorts in the UK and North America, which now cater to luxury holiday experiences (Digital Detox Holidays & Luxury Getaways – Carrier, n.d.). Many island destinations also promote similar digital detox holidays as selling points for their tourism (Li et al., 2020). Moreover, retreat programs that temporarily deprive participants of digital devices have gained popularity, offering a way to address internet addictions, manage stress, and enhance overall resilience in work and life (Smith & Puczkó, 2015).

Researchers (Egger & Wassler, 2020) were interested in understanding the motivations behind tourists willingly choosing to engage in DFT, rather than perceiving it as a travel inconvenience. They specifically targeted participants born after 1980, whom they considered digital residents and the group most susceptible to dependency on digital technology. Participants were recruited using experience-based sampling, and the inclusion criterion was a self-confirmed voluntary engagement in a DFT holiday within the past two years, with digital detox as one of their main motivations for travel. Participants were initially recruited using social media platforms and later, a snowball effect took over. Data was collected through semi-structured interviews, with a total of 17 interviews conducted either face-to-face or via telephone, each lasting 25-35 minutes. The interview data were analysed using research software Nvivo, and several main motivations for DFT emerged, including Escape, Personal Growth, Health and Well-being, and Relationships, with underlying subthemes identified for each category. While these motivations align with traditional tourist motives, participants highlighted the negative influence of technology on these factors, leading them to opt for DFT as a means of mitigating these issues. Participants generally agreed that their travel experiences were more enriching when disconnected from technology, although they also recognised the usefulness of technology to some extent. Using a snowball effect as a recruitment method for participants who have shared a holiday poses a problem due to the inherent bias created by their shared experience. This shared experience might have involved discussions about their holiday, potentially excluding individuals who had different perspectives or experiences regarding their digital-free time. As a result, those who felt differently about their digital detox may have been inadvertently excluded from the sample.

Notwithstanding, the practical implications of this study are relevant to tour operators and other stakeholders in the tourism industry, providing insights into the motivations behind DFT. Mental health and wellness practitioners can also recognise the growing demand for disconnection and the need to address this aspect of travellers' well-being. It is worth noting that younger generations may resist completely cutting off technology use, but DFT appeals to prospective tourists as a way to limit or reduce technology dependency while still enjoying the benefits of immediate surroundings.

The investigation into the digital detox experience of Generation Z on Shabbat provides a comparable encounter to Digital Free Tourism (DFT), wherein individuals willingly partake in a weekly digital-free break, sharing the objective to improve their connection and appreciation of the immediate environment.

2.13 The Significance of Shabbat

'Six days you shall labour and do all your work, but the seventh day is a Sabbath of the Lord, your God. You shall not do any work.' (Exodus, 20:9–10)

Shabbat has been singled out as more important than all the other Jewish festivals. The Hebrew writer Achad Ha'am famously wrote, 'More than the Jews have kept Shabbat, Shabbat has kept the Jews' (1856-1927). Remembering the Shabbat day to keep it holy is included in the Ten Commandments and Rabbis dwell on the blessings of keeping the Shabbat for all Jews. Traditionally, Jews have held Shabbat in high regard based on deep religious convictions as the Shabbat is a sign and perpetual witness for the covenant between God and the Jews. As a religious institution, Shabbat has many restrictions where many physical exertions are prohibited and spiritual and intellectual occupations are both prescribed and encouraged (Millgram, 1947).

The rabbinic understanding of 'work' is not based on the amount of physical effort involved. For example, lighting a torch from an existing flame was prohibited despite requiring minimal actual labour. The biblical prohibition against kindling a fire does not directly pertain to the concept of work. While heavier burdens are permitted to be carried within the home, light ones may not be carried into the public domain. The advent of inventions such as the electric light, phones and computers, which were non-existent in ancient times, has become deeply ingrained in the lives of modern individuals. According to a strict interpretation of rabbinical law, these devices should not be used on Shabbat (Eisenstein, 1961).

The prohibitions of Shabbat come from the construction of the Mishkan (Tabernacle), a portable sanctuary that held the tablets of the Ten Commandments, among other sacred items (Exodus and Leviticus). This Mishkan accompanied the ancient Jews throughout their journey, symbolising God's presence among them. The Mishkan served as a dwelling place for God's presence in the world, emphasising the act of creation. Similarly, on Shabbat, the aim is to invite God's presence into our lives by refraining from creative work and acknowledging that we are not the ultimate masters of our existence. To determine what constitutes 'creative work', the principles established during the original construction of the Mishkan apply. Tradition identifies thirty-nine categories of creative activities. Numerous books delve into these concepts and provide detailed guidelines for observing Shabbat, addressing various situations that may arise and offering guidance on how to handle them appropriately (Palatnik, Aish.com).

'The Sabbath is a focused one-day-a-week antidote to the market mindset. It is dedicated to the things that have a value but not a price. It is the supremely non-market day. We can't sell or buy. We can't work or pay others to work for us. It's a day when we celebrate relationships.' (Sacks, 2021, p.116)

The Western world in modern times has experienced significant transformations that have impacted traditional religious practices. The Enlightenment has influenced people's thought processes, while technology has revolutionised their way of life. The focus has shifted from a God-centred theological approach to a more human-centred and autonomous perspective. Metaphysics has been constrained by rationalism and positivism, and there has been a shift from respecting authority and hierarchies to emphasising individuality and egalitarianism (Angel, 1997).

In modern times, the observance of Shabbat among non-Orthodox Jews has significantly declined. This shift can be attributed to a change in mindset. While it is true that many Jews have the ability to refrain from work on the Sabbat, they have lost the tradition of dedicating this day to prayer, study, and relaxation. The introduction of the five-day workweek has transformed Saturdays into a day for various secular activities, such as shopping, watching movies, and doing sports. These activities clearly deviate from the essence of Shabbat (Eisenstein, 2022).

Even for those Jews who actively strive to maintain Shabbat observance, they often encounter conflicts due to the evolving nature of our lifestyle. For instance, a Jewish family that desires to attend synagogue services on Shabbat may face the challenge of living too far away to walk there. In order to participate in the services, they would need to violate the Sabbat by using transportation. It is evident that the changing circumstances of our contemporary existence have posed obstacles to the traditional observance of Shabbat, leading to a significant decrease in its practice among non-Orthodox Jews (Eisenstein, 2022).

In ancient times, the observance of the Sabbath held a powerful message as a form of protest against slavery. Today, it continues to serve as an antidote to the pervasive stress of our lives, offering one of the most effective means of finding respite. Rest plays a vital role in putting everything into perspective. In the midst of a constant stream of pressures and obligations, we often lose touch with the natural rhythms of work and rest, the balance between exertion and relaxation, striving and savouring the fruits of our labour. Our hurried pace prevents us from truly appreciating the beauty around us. Our frequent travels can lead to a loss of direction. It is essential, at regular intervals, to pause, take a breath, and simply be present. This intentional break from constantly striving and becoming allows us to experience a profound difference in our well-being (Sacks, 2019). Shabbat observance serves to ground and centre us to notice what is really important in life (Dein & Loewenthal, 2013).

According to Rabbi Dessler, the Shabbat day's creation marked the ultimate fulfilment of the entire creation process. The Shabbat is not just a day of rest but a world of restfulness called "menuchah", which should not be confused with laziness, a destructive and deadly trait. Menuchah represents a break from the material and physical world, allowing for spiritual repose and peace. This state of being is a prerequisite for experiencing the divine revelation in the world and represents the ultimate fulfilment of creation (Dessler, 1985).

Rabbi Soloveitchik (1903-1993) asserts that dignity cannot exist without responsibility, and one can only take on responsibility when one is capable of fulfilling one's commitments. Only when individuals reach a level of freedom and creativity in their actions and thoughts can they truly carry out the noble duty of responsible behaviour bestowed upon them by God. The expression of human dignity, manifested through the awareness of responsibility and the ability to fulfil that responsibility, can only be realised when individuals have gained control over their surroundings (Singer & Sokol, 1982). The expression of human dignity, which includes a sense of responsibility and the capability to fulfil that responsibility, can indeed extend to having control over digital devices. In today's digital age, when technology plays a significant role in our lives, the responsible and mindful use of digital devices has become crucial.

Jewish people comprise 0.2% of the global population. Within that percentage, according to the Pew Research Centre (2020), 39% of them in the USA often or sometimes mark Shabbat in some way that is meaningful to them. In that context, it may be just by lighting Shabbat candles on Friday nights, but it does not include observing all of Shabbat laws, including laws pertaining to abstaining from technology. We can deduce from this data that the number of Shabbat observant people is tiny. In that context, this population is uniquely exposed to the contrast of engaging from technology fully and, by contrast, complete abstinence.

Marks et al. (2018) conducted a study where they looked at sacred family practices in the Jewish context of Shabbat, believing that several insights of value can be gained from exploring Shabbat as a family practice. Leading family therapists and researchers have written extensively about how family rituals and practices serve to strengthen family life (Fiese et al., 2002; Marks, 2004; Walsh, 2010). Family professionals seek strategies to help families to create a feeling of 'we-ness' and closeness where families contain meaning and unity (Walsh, 2010). The research was interested in how the Shabbat can bring this and how members of the family interact on the Shabbat to facilitate this closeness.

Thirty families, including mothers, fathers, and children, were interviewed in a semi-structured interview between 90-120 minutes long. Families were from across the USA, and their level of religious observation was varied. Thus, experiences would be very broad. Reflexivity by three researchers who were not Jewish but Mormon and the breadth of Shabbat observance of participants encompassing 30 families would have been challenging. They sought to represent insider perspectives from the point of view of outsiders. Strauss and Corbin's grounded theory was used as the method. Shabbat-related rituals were identified as bringing increased harmony to family life on this day. However, the absence of technology as a factor in Shabbat observance was omitted from the interviews, which points to a research gap.

Michaels (2016) found that whilst non-scholarly sources encourage a practice of regularly unplugging from technology, few studies examine the potential benefits of decreased use of electronic/digital media. In a phenomenological inquiry about the benefits of unplugging weekly, Michaels's study was conducted on six adult Jewish women from around the USA who unplug as part of their weekly Shabbat observance. Semi-structured interviews were conducted using three arts-informed creative methods of data collection: storytelling, photography, and collage, hence combining verbal and symbolic exercises to help participants discover their perceptions of many dimensions of holistic health at a deeper level. Data was analysed within the realms of the mental, physical, spiritual, social, and environmental.

The findings indicated that weekly unplugging yielded comprehensive health advantages across various dimensions, including mental, physical, spiritual, social, and environmental realms. Five of the interviews were conducted via a chat platform, and one was conducted face-to-face. Michael's status as a Jewish woman was viewed as a strength because, as an insider to the culture, she was able to understand things intuitively that may have been lost by an outsider. It was also a limitation because she may have been blindsided by pertinent data that would have been picked up on by an outsider. Michaels found that most enthusiasm from the participants was gleaned from the verbal interview over the symbolic methods. However, the author observed that by interviewing via a chatroom, non-verbal cues were missed, such as smiling and laughing, which often occurred in the face-to-face interview, as was eye contact. There was also a high dropout number. From the original fifteen women who volunteered to take part, only six continued to participate until the end due to time constraints. This research focuses on the holistic health benefits for female participants who unplug weekly, thus leaving a gap to explore the experience of Generation Zers in the UK who unplug and, if there are benefits, what they might be.

Emerging themes from a study (Dein & Loewenthal, 2013) that aimed to examine the perceived costs and benefits of Shabbat observance among practising

Jews were: Shabbat as a special day, giving time to contemplate profound issues, withdrawal and rest from mundane concerns and deepening relationships. Whilst mental well-being was found to improve, some were prone to worry more due to a lack of distractions. The study focused on the mental health implications of rituals in Judaism as prescribed in the fourth commandment.

Thirteen orthodox Jews took part in a qualitative analysis; nine were from London, UK, and four were from the USA, seven males and six females; they were a mixture of married, single, and widowed. The inclusion criteria specified that they would all be over 18 years old and self-defined as orthodox and Shabbat observant. Semi-structured interviews of one hour were offered either face to face, written, or by telephone, and the age range of participants was 20-81 years.

Interviews were analysed thematically by the researchers, and a preliminary identification of themes was made. Illustrative quotes established thematic reliability. Participants reported a sense of rest and relaxation and also freedom, enhanced spirituality, and the opportunity to reflect on ultimate values. Many had an improved mood from weekdays on Shabbat from Shabbat observance, but preparation for it filled the week. There were also paradoxical aspects of worse worry as the freedom from work and weekday concerns created, for some, a vacuum where worries filled the space. This was accompanied by a feeling of helplessness to act. Depression could set in due to an inability to stop thinking about things that can't be solved due to the inactivity associated with Shabbat restrictions. Technological unplugging led to a lack of distraction and more time to think bad and depressing thoughts that were exacerbated on the Shabbat.

This study explores various aspects of Shabbat observance and covers a wide range of experiences, including an examination of the impact of digital abstinence on individuals on Shabbat. The researchers recommend further phenomenological research as to mental health associations with religious attendance, belief, and coping. Moreover, as the median age of participants was 44.2, and the study was conducted in 2013, many responders may not have the same values attached to DT as Generation Zers in 2023.

Speedling (2019) conducted a study to explore how individuals who were not part of communities that commonly practised Shabbat-keeping could benefit from celebrating a weekly Shabbat or day of rest. The research aimed to fill the gap in existing literature, which lacked studies on individuals incorporating a Shabbat where it was not the norm. It also lacked empirical research on the transformative effects of Shabbat-keeping. The study sought to understand how celebrating a weekly Shabbat promotes transformation in various dimensions of well-being, including psychological, social, physical, spiritual, cultural, and environmental aspects.

For the study, Speedling interviewed ten women who had been practising Shabbat-keeping for at least six months. Participants were recruited through flyers posted in libraries, food co-ops, and local coffee shops, as well as through social media and personal contacts. Semi-structured, in-depth interviews were conducted, and participants were provided with journals to reflect on their Shabbat practices and experiences. The participants in the study were women between the ages of 20 and 63 with diverse backgrounds, including African-American, Caucasian, Filipina American, Hispanic, Italian, and Scandinavian. They all had a college education and were raised in Christian households, although two had converted to Judaism and one identified as an eclectic pagan. None of the participants were part of communities where regular Shabbat-keeping was the norm.

The study identified six common themes among the participants: Shabbat-keeping enhanced self-awareness, improved self-care, enriched relationships, developed spirituality, positively influenced the rest of the week, and involved evolving Shabbat-keeping practices and philosophies over time. The author concluded that Shabbat-keeping, seen as a sacred gift from Judaism, can serve as a remedy for modern-day stresses and contribute to the well-being of individuals, communities, and the planet.

2.14 The Challenges of a Digital Detox on Shabbat

Some say that half of Modern Orthodox teens text on Shabbat (Lipman, 2011). In August 2014, a new development called the Shabbos App was introduced to the Jewish community. The purpose of this app was to enable texting on Shabbat while adhering to the guidelines of Halacha (Jewish religious law) (Phillips, 2019).

The Shabbos App was developed to cater to Jewish teenagers who observed most aspects of Shabbat but not all, a practice commonly referred to as 'half Shabbos' (Blum, 2017; Lipman, 2011; Telushkin, 2014). In the Jewish English Lexicon (2023), 'Half Shabbos' is defined as a form of observance typically practised by teenagers who adhere to all aspects of Shabbat except for one: they use digital communication such as texting, SMS, or tweeting during Shabbat, and sometimes also use other electronic devices like tablets.

The practice of keeping 'half Shabbos' has become a new phraseology because it is so widespread. These individuals would participate in family observances and engage in Shabbat-related celebrations, refrain from activities like watching television or using electronic entertainment, and even avoid driving or riding in motor vehicles. However, one aspect they couldn't or chose not to abstain from was using their smartphones to text each other. The Shabbos App emerged as a solution, offering a means to text while technically complying with the rules of Shabbat. While the Shabbos App never made it to the production stage, it is still worth examining the promotional video released to introduce the app. This video sheds light on the developers' intention to appeal to the ambivalent nature of Modern Orthodoxy within the Jewish community. The reaction to the app was divided, with some members expressing enthusiastic support while others felt disgusted by the concept. This polarisation indicates that the topic of texting on Shabbat was a contentious issue. The ambivalence is significant as it demonstrates that people still hold strong opinions on the matter. If Modern Orthodox individuals were not concerned about upholding tradition while navigating the modern world, there would be no controversy surrounding such apps. Moreover, Modern Orthodox parents and other concerned adults seek to guide their children on an observant Jewish path, leading to the development of apps like the Shabbos App, even if they were never brought to market (Phillips, 2019).

'Addicted' and 'bored' are the two most frequent justifications that teenagers identified for breaking their Shabbat observance (Rosenblum, 2012). Rosenblum identifies that this data demonstrates that Jewish teens are not immune to trends in general society. Thus, Shabbat in of itself cannot be a protective factor against youth using their digital technology in the face of addiction and boredom. The author cites these as problematic because an addiction implies a lack of belief in one's free will, and boredom expresses a shallow sense of self where a sense of self-identity needs to be constantly affirmed by one's friends. A positive experience of Shabbat, which is underpinned by the parents' preparation to enhance the Shabbat experience in the home, is suggested as a possible antidote to this growing problem.

2.15 Conclusion

There is an evident research gap in the literature about what a digital detox conducted weekly for 25 hours over Shabbat is like for Gen Z. It is encouraging to note that there are studies exploring the experience of having a digital detox and different ways of having it. Considering the literature demonstrating the adverse effects of excessive technology on health and well-being, this is good news.

The justification for the current study is that whilst there are multiple ways of conducting a digital detox, there is no literature that examines the experience of unplugging weekly from all devices on Gen Z – the generation that grew up into adulthood with mobile phones – and abstaining from them over Shabbat with all its implications. Conducting this literature review has served to highlight the limitations of current academic research into the practical reality of what Gen Z experiences when being off all their devices in a consistent and predictable manner, together with their families and communities in the context of Shabbat.

The existing literature pertaining to the experience of a digital detox is mixed, and the contexts are varied. Shabbat provides a context that has not yet been explored. It may be limited in its generalisability however, the research topic is one where lived experience is relevant and pertinent. The concept of a digital detox is increasingly recognised in today's prolific technology culture and exploring it in the context of Shabbat is one way of understanding its meaning and value to its participants.

Numerous countries have recognised the pressures stemming from constant connectivity and have implemented legislation to address the right to disconnect. For instance, France enacted a law in January 2017 that required employers to negotiate agreements with unions for the right to disconnect from technology outside of working hours. Similarly, Italy granted the right to disconnect to remote workers, while Spain introduced a new set of digital rights that encompassed the right to disconnect for maintaining work-life balance. In Belgium, employers with more than 50 employees were mandated by law in 2018 to discuss disconnection and digital tool usage with workplace health and safety committees. In April 2021, the Irish government introduced a code of practice that officially granted all employees the right to disconnect from work during non-working hours. In December 2021, the Portuguese parliament implemented new legislation, including the right to privacy, which prohibited employers from contacting employees during their designated rest periods (Sinead, 2022). The UK has witnessed a significant increase in remote and hybrid working, particularly accelerated by the COVID-19 pandemic, leading to a re-evaluation of the necessity of in-office work. While this digitally connected world has provided greater flexibility, it has also compromised the work-life balance for some individuals (Jones & Bano, 2021).

Although legislation has been enacted to address the right to disconnect in some European countries, there is a lack of research exploring workers' reflections on these rights and whether improvements have been observed as a result of these legislations. Jewish individuals, through the practice of Shabbat, not only have the right to disconnect but are mandated to do so. This study focuses on examining the experiences of young adults during this designated period of disconnection, considering its potential impact on various aspects of their lives.

The existing research on digital technology has primarily focused on the negative consequences of overuse rather than exploring the potential benefits of limiting its usage. This literature review examined studies identifying that digital technology can be supportive and studies acknowledging the harm it can cause, especially when used excessively. Some studies have examined the advantages of limiting technology use, including the effectiveness of digital detoxes. However, there is a lack of research specifically investigating the experiences of planned periods of abstaining from technology-related activities, as well as a scarcity of literature on the emerging secular unplugging movement.

Researchers have explored the observant Jewish population in general, but there is a gap in the literature when it comes to examining the specific benefits of unplugging on Shabbat for individuals from Generation Z. Therefore, further research is needed to investigate the potential advantages of unplugging from technology during designated times, particularly focusing on the experiences and outcomes for the younger generation.

Chapter 3: Methodology

3.0 Introduction

This chapter commences by stating the rationale for using qualitative research. It then explores the philosophical underpinnings of phenomenology, beginning with Husserl, the progenitor of phenomenology, followed by Heidegger's assertion that knowledge is intricately tied to our existence in the world, Merleau-Ponty's perspectives on the embodied nature of relationships and their relevance to research are discussed, as well as Sartre's ideas on the ongoing process of self-discovery. It then delves into an examination of qualitative research, followed by providing an overview of the ontological and epistemological positions that inform the research. The chapter proceeds to emphasise the utilisation of a constructivist approach achieved through the researcher's interaction with the participants. The application of Interpretative Phenomenological Analysis (IPA) is explained, along with a justification for its selection and an exploration of how hermeneutics are applicable to the analysis. Limitations of IPA are then discussed, and alternative methodological approaches that were considered are then examined. The credibility of the study is acknowledged, followed by a reflexive account of the methodological process (Hoepfl, 1997).

3.1 The Rationale for Qualitative Research

Qualitative research employs a naturalistic approach, aiming to comprehend phenomena within specific contextual settings. It involves studying real-world situations where researchers refrain from manipulating the phenomenon of interest (Patton, 2002). Qualitative research encompasses a wide range of methodologies that generate findings through approaches other than statistical procedures or quantification (Strauss & Corbin, 1990). It is characterised by an emphasis on exploring phenomena in real-world settings, where the phenomenon of interest unfolds naturally (Patton, 2002). Unlike quantitative research, which aims for causal determination, prediction, and generalisation of findings, qualitative research focuses on illuminating understanding and extrapolating insights to similar contexts (Hoepfl, 1997).

Over the last few decades, qualitative research has attained prominence in the social sciences and helping professions (Merriam. S. B, 2002). This study was conducted using a qualitative research method as I'm interested in the nature and quality of the experience of unplugging from all forms of DT for a day a week. Qualitative methods enhance understanding of experiences within a context by providing rich descriptions of phenomena. Qualitative methods can also help to locate distinct patterns within experiences, moving from description to substantial explanations (Sofaer, 1999). Qualitative methods are employed to address inquiries concerning individual experiences, interpretations, and perspectives, predominantly from the participant's point of view. Such data typically resist quantification or measurement due to their inherently subjective nature (Hammarberg et al., 2016b). Given these considerations, a qualitative methodology was selected for this study.

3.2 Husserl

Edmund Husserl (1859-1938), the founding figure of phenomenology, emphasised the importance of returning to the direct experience of consciousness and suspending our preconceived notions. Husserl encouraged us to approach phenomena with fresh curiosity by setting aside our assumptions through a process known as "bracketing" or "eidetic reduction". This involves examining each aspect of experience in its own right and exploring different possibilities through free imaginative variation. Husserl's concept of "transcendental reduction" goes even further by focusing on the content of conscious experience and describing it through its elemental features. Husserl's philosophy has influenced the reflective process undertaken by IPA researchers, as it aligns with his exploration of the conscious contents of lived experience (Smith et al., 2022). Husserl's call for phenomenological reduction, aiming to focus on the essential features of experiences, resonates with this study's aim to identify and analyse the core themes and structures that emerge from participants' accounts. IPA researchers engage in a process of reduction to identify and understand the essential aspects of participants' lived experiences, uncovering the underlying meanings.

3.3 Heidegger

Martin Heidegger (1889-1976), a German philosopher and student of Husserl, diverged from Husserl's approach to phenomenology. He shifted his focus away from transcendence and towards the hermeneutic and existential essence in phenomenological inquiry, questioning the possibility of knowledge outside of interpretation (Smith et al., 2022). Heidegger argued that all knowledge is situated within a particular stance, whether it be language, people, or relationships. We cannot separate the thing itself from our understanding of "dasein", our being in the world. Heidegger emphasised that dasein, our existence, has been neglected in Western philosophy, either because it is inaccessible or taken for granted (Heidegger, 2008).

According to Heidegger, we not only exist in the world, but we also engage with the world through objects, projects, language, relationships, knowledge of death, and culture. These aspects are inseparable from our understanding of our experiences in the world (Finlay, 2011). Dasein requires a reflexive awareness that extends to acknowledging the existence of others (Heidegger, 2008). IPA researchers learn from this perspective that relationships, language, and our being in the world are always in relation to something, making meaning and interpretation central to phenomenological inquiry (Smith et al., 2022). Heidegger's philosophical ideas and concepts can provide a theoretical foundation and inspiration for conducting Interpretative Phenomenological Analysis (IPA) research. Heidegger's phenomenology emphasises the subjective experience and understanding of individuals within their lived world. This aligns with the core principles of IPA in this study, which aims to explore the lived experiences of individuals and their unique interpretations of the phenomena of a digital detox on Shabbat.

3.4 Merleau-Ponty

Maurice Merleau-Ponty (1908-1961), the French philosopher, was influenced by both Husserl and Heidegger's work and commitment to understanding being-in-the-world but he developed it in the direction of noticing the embodied nature of our relationship to that world and how our individual stance influences our perspective. Our sense of self is holistic and looks at the world rather than being encompassed by it (Smith et al., 2022). Merleau-Ponty observed that we live in the world in a bodily way and consciousness is perceptual and embodied. It is grounded in the world that is construed and constituted by the individual who perceives it. Merleau-Ponty draws on Gestalt psychology, insisting on an intermingling of sensory possibilities, a way of bodily experiencing objects in our everyday lives (Finlay, 2011).

In IPA research, Maurice Merleau-Ponty's perspective on the embodied nature of our knowing and experience in the world holds great significance. According to Merleau-Ponty, each person's experience is deeply personal and tied to their embodied position in the world. While we can observe and empathise with others, we can never fully share their experiences, as they are shaped by their unique embodied perspective. For qualitative researchers, including IPA researchers, Merleau-Ponty's emphasis on the role of the body in shaping our understanding of the world is crucial. Practical activities and relationships, rooted in the physical and perceptual affordances of the body-in-the-world, hold greater significance than abstract or logical considerations (Anderson, 2003). The pivotal role of embodiment aligns closely with the importance of emotional experience. As Ratcliffe (2019) suggests, our emotional experiences are mediated through our feeling bodies, similar to how we perceive entities through tactile sensations. In IPA research, this perspective encourages researchers to explore how participants' bodily experiences and interactions with their surroundings contribute to their lived experiences and interpretations of phenomena. Furthermore, Merleau-Ponty emphasises the significance of perception and the situatedness of perception within a specific context. This research aims to capture the nuances of participants' experiences of their digital detox on Shabbat and their subjective interpretations. Merleau-Ponty's ideas can guide researchers in recognising the intricate interplay between perception, context, and the meanings ascribed by participants (Murray et al., 2014).

3.5 Sartre

Jean-Paul Sartre (1905-1980), a French existentialist philosopher and writer, provides insights into the phenomenological experience by examining objects, experiences, and concepts in human consciousness (Finlay, 2011). Sartre's concept of "existence before essence" emphasises the ongoing process of self-discovery rather than pre-existing essence. According to Sartre, human nature is characterised by freedom of choice and responsibility for one's actions. He further develops Heidegger's philosophy by exploring personal and social relationships, highlighting the significance of the presence or absence of "the other" in our perception of the world. Sartre's analysis of individuals engaged in projects in the world captures the embodied, interpersonal, affective, and moral dimensions of these encounters, offering a clear glimpse into the phenomenological analysis of the human condition (Smith et al., 2022). In IPA, "existence precedes essence" aligns with the focus on understanding the participants' subjective interpretations of their digital detox and how they construct meaning of it in their lived experiences.

3.6 Ontology and Epistemology in Scientific Research

Ontology and epistemology are two of the relevant positions that are significant in relation to the application of science. Ontology is the assumptions we make about the kind and nature of reality and what exists (Richards, 2003). Ontological assumptions respond to the questions of what is there to be known or what is the nature of reality. It is defined as the study of being (Crotty, 2003). Ontology, as a branch of philosophy, is the science of what is, of the kinds and structures of objects, properties, events, processes and relations in every area of reality (Nuccetelli-Hurtado/Nudler, n.d.).

Understanding our assumptions surrounding what constitutes 'real' knowledge is crucial as it significantly influences how we choose to investigate knowledge. It is, therefore, not surprising that ontological discussions are considered vital in research (Bracken, 2010). In general, there are two prominent ontological positions: objectivism and subjectivism. A fundamental distinction can be made between both positions. An objective ontological stance suggests a belief that there is an external reality whose existence is independent of knowledge of it. On the other hand, a subjectivist ontological position believes one cannot know an external objective reality apart from one's subjective experience (Saunders et al., 2009).

Epistemology can be defined as how we can generate dependable knowledge (Tomlinson, 2023). Epistemology not only captures an individual's personal relationship with their study but also includes the nature, scope and limitations of knowledge, thereby helping to ground personal reflections (Berger, 2015). Epistemology refers to the study of knowledge and how we acquire it, which significantly impacts the design and implementation of research. These methods of acquiring knowledge may include conducting interviews to grasp public opinion on a particular topic, observing individuals in their natural settings, utilising surveys sent by mail for independent completion, or analysing people's viewpoints expressed in newspaper editorials. Each data collection method carries its own set of epistemological assumptions regarding how knowledge is obtained (Saylor Academy Open Textbooks & Saylor Academy, 2022). Two primary viewpoints within this field are positivism/post-positivism and constructivism/interpretivism (Ponterotto, 2005). Researchers adopting a positivist perspective approach individuals under study in a manner similar to objects, considering that the truth behind their experiences, including interpersonal and social interactions, can be objectively examined. Constructivism/interpretivism asserts that humans actively construct knowledge as they interpret their experiences within the world (Constantino, 2008; Pascale, 2011).

This research delves into the subjective experiences and interpretations of participants regarding their experience of refraining from using technology during Shabbat and the resulting effects. The study acknowledges the absence of objectivity, as participants perceive technology and its impact through their personal perspectives. Consequently, this study adopts a subjectivist ontology and embraces a constructivist epistemological perspective.

3.7 A Constructivist Approach

The process of meaning-making is crucial in qualitative research, and qualitative researchers often focus on understanding how individuals construct meaning in their lives. IPA is a linguistically-based approach, as language is used to express meaning and experience (Oxley, 2016). What the participant says to the researcher is connected to the reality of the experience, and what they say is their reality. This approach aligns with constructivism, which acknowledges that different people perceive and interpret the world in unique ways (Willig, 2016; Oxley, 2016). Individual experiences influence perceptions and understanding of events and behaviours.

While we cannot directly enter someone else's mind to explore their reality, we can indirectly access these phenomena through various research methods, such as interviews, questionnaires, and observations. Qualitative research recognises that individuals have diverse interpretations of reality due to their unique life experiences. Researchers adopt a constructivist perspective to understand how individuals construct meaning in their lives (Denicolo et al., 2016).

3.8 An Idiographic Approach

The idiographic approach stands in stark contrast to the nomothetic approach traditionally employed in psychology. Idiography emphasises the significance of individual particulars and specific details. In this regard, IPA serves as an exemplary research methodology that aligns well with the idiographic approach, as it focuses on small samples of participants selected from 'expert groups', without attempting to generalise findings more broadly (Oxley, 2016). In a typical IPA study, each case is examined independently, recognising its individuality and significance, and subsequently, a comparative analysis is conducted to identify commonalities and distinctions among the cases within the "expert group" (Hefferon & Gil-Rodriguez, 2011). As a researcher, I fall in between an emic approach, which focuses on understanding phenomena from within the cultural group under study and an epic perspective, where I'm an outsider or observer carrying out the investigation (Markee, 2012).

3.9 Rationale for Choosing Interpretative Phenomenological Analysis (IPA)

In this research, Interpretative Phenomenological Analysis (IPA) was chosen as the preferred method due to its alignment with phenomenological inquiry (Sullivan & Forrester, 2019). As a psychotherapist practising phenomenological approaches, I found a resonance between my therapeutic work and the interview process used in this study.

IPA is a methodological approach that emerged in psychology but has since been applied across various disciplines, particularly in health sciences (Pringle et al., 2011). Developed by Jonathan Smith, IPA aims to rigorously explore individual subjective experiences and social cognitions (Smith et al., 1995). The primary focus of IPA is to investigate how individuals make sense of their life experiences and navigate significant events (Smith et al., 2009). This aligns with the qualitative research paradigm, as IPA emphasises subjective experiences that cannot be easily quantified without losing their richness.

While IPA is experientially focused, it acknowledges that the researcher can only gain an understanding of the participant's experience through what they express, as direct sharing of the experience is not possible (Oxley, 2016). IPA emphasises the active role of the researcher in the dynamic research process. The researcher's own conceptions and interpretations play a crucial role in making sense of other personal worlds, leading to a process of interpretative activity known as the double hermeneutic (Smith, 2003). Choosing IPA for this research was influenced by my own experience of weekly unplugging and the reflexive insights it provided regarding how Generation Z individuals experience a weekly digital detox. Through IPA, I aim to gain comprehensive and rich analysis by integrating interpretation into the research process (Pietkiewicz & Smith, 2014).

Phenomenology, as formulated by Husserl, focuses on how individuals understand and perceive their world by exploring consciously experienced phenomena (Willig, 2021b). Interpretative phenomenology aims to grasp the essence and quality of perceived phenomena. IPA, consistent with its phenomenological roots, seeks to understand the participants' perspective, taking their side and asking critical questions about their experiences (Willig, 2021b).

Given the research question focused on the experiences of Gen Z individuals practising a weekly digital detox, IPA was chosen as a highly suitable methodology for this study. IPA aligns well with the qualitative research paradigm, emphasising a detailed exploration of individual experiences and subjective meanings. The idiographic approach of IPA is particularly valuable in understanding how each participant makes sense of the phenomenon of digital abstinence for 25 hours each week. This methodology allows for a comprehensive analysis of the unique perspectives within the participant pool, consisting of individuals who regularly engage with technology for six days and abstain on the seventh. By employing IPA, the study aims to uncover the rich and nuanced understandings of this specific group, shedding light on their experiences and perceptions of digital detoxification.

3.10 Hermeneutic Phenomenology in Interpretative Phenomenological Analysis

Hermeneutics, originally developed as a method for interpreting Biblical texts, has evolved into a broader theory of interpretation (Sullivan & Forrester, 2019).

In the context of phenomenological inquiry, hermeneutic phenomenology focuses on understanding the quality and meaning of experience. It recognises that the researcher's own values and perspectives shape the interpretation process, highlighting the importance of reflexivity (Willig, 2008; Billin, 2011). Unlike mere description, hermeneutics emphasises the interpretative aspect of phenomena, emphasising contextual meanings (Oxley, 2016).

In the case of IPA, it draws from phenomenology to explore how participants make sense of their experiences while incorporating hermeneutic principles to delve into the interpretative activity involved in analysis. IPA research operates at the level of individual experiences, offering specific insights into participants' unique perspectives (Sullivan & Forrester, 2019). The researcher's own pre-existing knowledge and assumptions play a crucial role, necessitating ongoing reflection on their influence (Oxley, 2016).

The process of interpretative phenomenological research involves a "double hermeneutic", where both the researcher and the participant engage in a mutual interpretative process. The researcher strives to understand the participant's experience while the participant is making sense of their own experience (Sullivan & Forrester, 2019). This interactive nature highlights the significance of interpretation in amplifying context and understanding. It encompasses a hermeneutic circle, where assumptions and beliefs are continually challenged, and evolving meanings are tested and refined (Willig & Billin, 2011).

It is the researcher's active involvement and interpretive role which are essential in making sense of the participants' personal worlds. This two-stage hermeneutic process involves the exploration of participants' experiences by the participants themselves, followed by the researcher's efforts to interpret and understand those experiences (Smith, 2003).

3.11 Limitations of IPA

IPA has become a widely used methodological approach for many students across various academic levels (Hefferon & Gil-Rodriguez, 2011). However, there have been concerns expressed by scholars regarding misconceptions surrounding the nature of phenomenological research, specifically in relation to IPA. Max Van Manen (2017) is troubled by the perception of IPA as primarily a therapy-oriented research methodology rather than a true phenomenological approach. This misinterpretation often results in IPA being seen as a straightforward form of thematic analysis with less emphasis on interpretation, leading to it being perceived as an easier option (Braun & Clarke, 2006).

Students frequently face pressure to include a large number of participants in their IPA studies, which goes against the core principle of idiographic exploration in IPA (Reid et al., 2005). Another aspect that has been highlighted is the limited recognition given to the crucial role of language in IPA as well as other phenomenological studies (Willig C, 2008). The question arises as to whether both participants and researchers possess the necessary communication skills to effectively convey the nuanced aspects of their experiences.

Furthermore, while IPA focuses on perceptions in line with other phenomenological inquiries, this narrow focus can be problematic and restrict our understanding. Phenomenological research seeks to comprehend lived experiences, but it does not necessarily explain the underlying reasons behind these experiences. Moreover, the assertion that IPA is primarily concerned with cognition exposes it to criticism, as certain aspects of phenomenology are not compatible with cognition, and the role of cognition in phenomenology is not fully understood (Willig C, 2008).

I have tried to compensate for these limitations by emphasising the phenomenological nature of IPA. IPA focuses on the lived experiences of participants, and it is distinct from therapy-oriented methodologies which involve interventions to facilitate client growth or healing. IPA research prioritises quality over quantity. Rather than aiming for a large number of participants, I focused on in-depth analysis of a smaller number of cases, allowing for a richer understanding of individual experiences. I tried to expand my understanding of participants' expressions and cognition beyond language. Phenomenological research aims to comprehend lived experiences holistically. Attention was paid to emotions, embodied experiences and social contexts which shape life stories and contribute to a comprehensive understanding of the phenomenon.

3.12 Alternative Methodologies

Qualitative psychology has experienced a remarkable surge of interest, representing a notable shift from the traditionally quantitative-focused approach (Smith, 2003). Before deciding to use Interpretative Phenomenological Analysis (IPA) as a methodological choice, it was crucial to become familiarised with various qualitative approaches, considering their theoretical foundations and practical procedures. In this study, two alternative approaches considered were Grounded Theory (Charmaz, 2014) and Narrative Analysis. However, these alternatives were ultimately rejected, and I will provide the rationale behind these decisions.

3.13 Grounded Theory, Charmaz

Grounded Theory (Charmaz, 2014) was one of the alternative methodologies considered for this study. Like IPA, it embraces a constructivist approach and involves the collaborative reconstruction of the research process. Grounded Theory adopts an inductive approach, moving from specific observations to broader generalisations (Sullivan & Forrester, 2019). Notably, theories developed within Grounded Theoretical frameworks are firmly grounded in the data, necessitating the researcher to set aside preconceived theoretical assumptions and instead construct theories based on the emergent patterns and insights derived directly from the data (Urquhart, 2013). The researcher maintains a flexible position, analysing emerging stories and prioritising significant issues. Grounded Theory extends beyond a mere technique, offering a framework for theory development (Sullivan & Forrester, 2019).

After careful consideration, IPA was deemed a more suitable methodology for this study. It was selected because it enables a deeper exploration of the essence and quality of experiences, placing emphasis on understanding rather than theory generation. This aligns with the objective of comprehending the nuanced aspects of the phenomena under investigation.

3.14 Narrative Analysis

Narratives offer a means to bring order to the apparent chaos in our world and hold ontological significance as they shape our understanding of reality. In narrative research, interviews are conducted to allow participants to provide detailed accounts of their experiences, with the researcher emphasising this intention (Smith, 2003). Building rapport and collecting background information about the participants and interviewer are important steps. The researcher engages in interpretation to convince the audience of the narrative's character rather than merely describing it, considering personal, interpersonal, group, and social contexts. This methodology is akin to television talk-shows where individuals share their stories, rather than documentaries where expert voices prevail (Murray, 2003). The structure of narrative accounts depends on factors such as the narrator, audience, and broader social and cultural contexts.

Narrative studies adopt a constructivist approach, assuming that individuals actively construct their world and assign meaning to it through narrative structures. Theme Analysis is a systematic method used in the narrative approach to identify core and subordinate themes in interviews and assess their development over time, weaving them together to provide consistency and meaning to clients' life stories.

Despite its relevance to some extent, Narrative Analysis (NA) was not deemed suitable due to its limited focus and inability to capture the desired lived experience of participants sought in this study (Smith et al., 2009). The field of narrative research would also benefit from a clearer definition of "narrative" and "narrative research" (Gottlieb & Lasser, 2001) before I would be comfortable using it.

3.15 Credibility

Whilst the tests and measures of validity and reliability that are used to ground quantitative methods cannot be applied to qualitative methods, these terms may assume applicability to enhance the credibility of qualitative research. To avoid criticism for non-scientific findings, methods need to be made transparent in the analytical procedure, and rigour needs to be demonstrated (Noble & Smith, 2015). Validity refers to the precision with which findings accurately reflect the data whilst using integrity in the application of the methods. Reliability refers to the consistency applied during said procedures (Noble & Smith, 2015).

To ensure that the credibility of the study is maintained, there are a number of factors that need to be accounted for. For example, consideration of any personal biases the researcher may have and to acknowledge those biases whilst being critically reflective. Any biases can be addressed with other researchers with the aim of reducing them. To keep records that demonstrate a clear trail of the process whilst ensuring interpretations of data are consistent and transparent. To seek out similarities and differences across participants to ensure that all perspectives are paid attention to. To clearly demonstrate how interpretative conclusions were reached via interpretations within the analysis. To invite participants to validate their data by allowing them to comment on the interview transcript and final themes (Noble & Smith, 2015). Some of these considerations make up my reflexivity section below.

3.16 Reflexivity

Reflection is a central theme of IPA studies, and to support the researcher to engage with this, it is helpful for the researcher to keep a reflective diary (Oxley, 2016). A researcher's beliefs and ideological stance are parts of their positioning and are useful areas to explore as part of a reflexivity statement (Berger, 2015). Whilst conducting this research, I continually reflected on my own experience of my weekly digital detox on Shabbat in light of my interview questions. I explored this with family members, my therapist and friends and noticed some varied experiences as well as shared ones. Having three Gen Z children afforded me a unique window into how a digital detox over Shabbat, for individuals who are fully engaged with their technology on the other six days a week, is experienced and how individual temperaments and needs affect and influence their experience and the meaning they attach to it. The variety of their experiences allowed me to keep an open mind as to the range of experiences and meaning-making that I may encounter among my participants. I found it most helpful to keep this diary in my phone as thoughts could pop up anywhere at any time and, aside from Shabbat, my phone is always with me.

Chapter 4: Method

4.0 Introduction

Between October 2022 and April 2023, a total of eight semi-structured interviews were conducted. This section will highlight the significance of sampling in the context of Interpretative Phenomenological Analysis (IPA) methodology, describe the applicability of the sample in this study, outline the inclusion and exclusion criteria, discuss the recruitment process, and address the ethical considerations associated with conducting the research. The chapter will then provide an overview of the research interview itself, followed by a brief description of the transcription process. Additionally, it will include a discussion on the pilot study that was conducted. Subsequently, the seven steps of analysis employed in this study will be explained, detailing how they were applied. Finally, a reflexive account of the methodological processes will be provided.

4.1 Sample

When conducting interview research with an idiographic aim, it is common to select a small sample size to ensure that each individual case can be given significant attention and thoroughly analysed. This approach allows for a more in-depth exploration of the unique perspectives and experiences of each participant. For studies utilising Interpretative Phenomenological Analysis (IPA), researchers are typically advised to include a range of three to sixteen participants (Smith et al., 2009). This guideline enables researchers to maintain a balance between capturing diverse perspectives and conducting a comprehensive analysis of each participant's case. Phenomenological analysis is a method of research that is taxing and prolonged. Consequently, researchers tend to work with small sample groups in any one study (Willig & Billin, 2011). IPA aims to focus on the details of the experiences and perceptions of the participant group. A sample of eight young adults were interviewed: five females and three males. Participants were recruited on the basis that they could provide accounts of their experience in terms of detail and depth, as the quality of the data depends largely on the richness of the data (Willig & Billin, 2011).

4.2 Inclusion and Exclusion Criteria

To delineate a sample universe, a set of inclusion criteria or exclusion criteria, or a combination of both, must be specified for the study (Luborsky & Rubinstein, 1995). Inclusion criteria should specify an attribute that cases must possess to qualify for the study, while exclusion criteria must stipulate attributes that disqualify a case from the study (Robinson, 2013).

The inclusion criteria for the study were males or females aged between 18-24 years old, and they were single and living at home. Single means that they are not in a relationship with a partner whilst living at home. This is because, during the digital detox period, there may be a difference in the experience of single participants who are in a romantic relationship compared to those who are not. The justification for the criteria is to keep the sample group as homogenous as possible (Smith, 2003). Sample universe homogeneity can be achieved along a variety of parameters, such as demographic homogeneity, graphical homogeneity, physical homogeneity, psychological homogeneity or life history homogeneity (Robinson, 2013). Interpretative Phenomenological Analysis is explicit that homogenous samples work best in conjunction with their philosophical foundations and analytical processes (Smith et al., 2009). By maintaining a measure of sample homogeneity, IPA studies remain contextualised within a defined setting, and any generalisation from the study is made cautiously to that localised sample universe.

The exclusion criteria were anyone outside of the inclusion criteria, participants or families who do not adhere to digital detox during Shabbat and anyone that I know. The more specific these criteria are, the more homogenous the sample becomes.

4.3 Recruitment

The recruitment of participants for interviews relies on the researcher's creativity in effectively reaching out to the target population. One approach to achieve this is through advertising, which can be done using various methods such as print, face-to-face, and, increasingly, online platforms (Robinson, 2013). In my study, I utilised an app to design a recruitment poster, which I shared with friends and family via WhatsApp, requesting them to help spread the word as widely as possible. Additionally, I invested in advertising the poster on a popular Jewish website called EverywhereK, which reaches 18,000 email subscribers who observe Shabbat, making it more likely to attract suitable respondents. The poster was visually appealing, designed in the shape of a mobile phone to capture attention, and clearly outlined the inclusion criteria. It was distributed approximately two weeks before the first interview to allow potential participants sufficient time to respond, undergo vetting based on the inclusion and exclusion criteria, and review the participant information sheet and consent form before signing and returning them.

Once a potential participant met the criteria and expressed interest, I promptly scheduled the interview at a mutually convenient time and as soon as possible to maintain their engagement. A participant initially reached out via WhatsApp after seeing the advertisement on a WhatsApp group. To ensure the integrity of the study, no financial incentives were offered for participation, as this can potentially influence participants to provide fabricated information in order to receive monetary rewards (Robinson, 2013). Instead, I relied on participants' genuine interest in the subject matter and their willingness to reflect on their experiences. This approach was supported by the pilot study participant, who mentioned that her motivation for volunteering was her personal interest in the topic.

To expand the participant pool, I employed a snowball method, where current participants were asked to recommend acquaintances who might also qualify for participation, creating referral chains (Robinson, 2013). This allowed for the recruitment of additional participants through trusted connections, ensuring a potentially suitable and engaged sample. By employing various recruitment strategies and maintaining ethical considerations, such as clarity in the study purpose, informed consent, and participant vetting, I aimed to gather a diverse and engaged group of participants for the interviews.

4.4 Ethical Considerations

Researchers encounter ethical challenges throughout the various stages of their study, encompassing aspects such as anonymity, confidentiality, informed consent, and the potential impact of both the researchers and the participants on each other (Sanjari et al., 2014). Protecting participants from any potentially harmful consequences arising from their involvement is also a crucial responsibility of researchers. Informed consent is widely recognised as an essential component of research ethics across different fields. For qualitative researchers, it is paramount to clearly define in advance the data to be collected and its intended use. The principle of informed consent emphasises the researcher's obligation to fully inform participants about various aspects of the research using understandable language. These clarifications should include details such as the nature of the study, the potential role of the participants, the identity of the researcher and funding source, the research objectives, and how the results will be disseminated and utilised (Hoeyer et al., 2005; Orb et al., 2001).

Many individuals consider it important to participate in research that may benefit their peers, community, or society as a whole. Therefore, qualitative health researchers should clarify that their research contributes to scientific knowledge and has the potential to make a meaningful impact (Holloway & Wheeler, 2010). Before embarking on the research, I completed an ethics module where I had to submit a risk assessment, participant information form, debrief form, and participant consent form to the ethics board in order to proceed with the pilot study. These forms guided me in effectively communicating the objectives of the interviews to potential participants and ensured that data collection and storage would be carried out anonymously to protect the participants. All interviews were securely stored with password protection to ensure confidentiality. Participant identification documents, such as consent forms, were also kept under password protection. I extensively discussed and deliberated upon these considerations with the course leader, peers, and supervisors. Adjustments were made based on advice from the ethics board to ensure compliance with the BPS Code of Ethics and Conduct (*Code of Ethics and Conduct | BPS*, n.d.).

Furthermore, I completed the Research Part 1 module and the Social, Cultural, and Ethical modules, which facilitated group work and discussions with tutors focused on ethical considerations in our own research. Throughout these modules, I consulted both my primary and secondary supervisors to ensure that ethical commitments to the participants would be upheld. These experiences and engagements helped me prepare for participant recruitment, the interview process, and the secure storage of data in a sensitive, ethical, and responsible manner. To protect the identities of all participants, their names are not included in the recordings and are instead identified by pseudonyms.

Given that the interviews were conducted via Zoom, it was essential to ensure that both the participants and I were situated in a private environment where interruptions were unlikely, and their privacy would not be compromised. Following the interviews, participants received a debriefing to identify and address any unforeseen harm or discomfort. Due to the small size of the Jewish community, there were instances where I had to decline participation from individuals I personally knew. Additionally, careful consideration was given to potential interactions with participants in my local area after the interviews.

4.5 The Research Interview

The semi-structured interviews followed a well-planned approach. During the semi-structured interviews, which each lasted approximately 50-60 minutes, I engaged with the participants using open-ended and non-directive questions to delve into their experience and insights regarding the subject under investigation (Willig, 2021b). Participants were asked for permission to audio-record the interview, and none of them objected. Recordings were stored according to the requirements of data protection legislation (Smith et al., 2009).

The research questions were grounded in an epistemological perspective that focused on understanding the participants' orientation in the world and their sense-making processes. Prior to the interview, an interview schedule was developed to guide the conversation and ensure comprehensive coverage of the desired topics (Smith, 2003). The schedule was shared with friends, family, and my supervisor for feedback and valuable suggestions. By anticipating various paths the interview could take, I approached the actual interview feeling more relaxed and able to listen attentively to the respondent. The pre-planned schedule prompted explicit consideration of the intended scope and content of the interview, emphasising neutral and non-leading questions (Smith, 2003). The aim was to explore participants' perspectives rather than provide explanations (Smith et al., 2022). I made a conscious effort to minimise my influence and allow participants to express their thoughts freely, using minimal prompts to avoid leading their responses (Smith, 2003).

The questions were sequenced logically and thoughtfully, addressing different areas of inquiry. Sensitive questions were strategically positioned later in the interview after participants had established a level of comfort. Creating a relaxed environment was important, and conducting the interviews over Zoom allowed participants to choose familiar and comfortable settings. Participants were encouraged to minimise distractions during the interview. A research contract outlining the measures taken to protect participants' safety and confidentiality was established to build trust and ensure ethical conduct. In my role as the interviewer, I assumed the responsibility of facilitating and guiding the conversation, placing emphasis on the participants' responses. Throughout the interview, I made a conscious effort to set aside any preconceived notions or existing knowledge, aiming to approach the participant's experience with a state of 'deliberate naivety' (Oxley, 2016). This approach enabled me to remain open and receptive to the participant's account of their reality without allowing any preconceived assumptions to unduly influence the interview process. When appropriate, I provided cues to further explore certain topics. The interview schedule served as a helpful reference, allowing me to maintain a relaxed demeanour and concentrate on the participant's input. While the conversation did not always strictly adhere to the predetermined order of questions, it flowed naturally, ensuring the discussion remained within the intended scope (Smith, 2003).

4.6 Transcription

In IPA, it is necessary to maintain a verbatim record of the data. The primary focus of IPA lies in understanding the meaning and content of participants' accounts. Therefore, detailed transcription of non-verbal aspects like long pauses is not required in the transcripts. Instead, any noteworthy information that stands out and is relevant to the interpretative process, such as laughter or facial expressions, was included as additional notes for analysis (Smith et al., 2022).

4.7 Pilot Study

In accordance with Research Project 1 (RP1) guidelines, a pilot study was conducted as a preliminary step in this research. Abigail, a 19-year-old student, was recruited through an advertisement posted on a WhatsApp group. After Abigail expressed interest, we arranged a suitable time for the interview after she had provided her signed consent to participate. The pilot study interview proved to be successful, as both the participant and I, as the researcher, felt at ease during the interview, and I felt that it met my targets. As a result, it was decided that I should include it as part of the overall research.

4.8 Phases of Analysis

There is no single 'method' for working with the data. Instead, there is a set of standard processes and principles which can be applied flexibly according to the analytic task. A heuristic framework for analysis was used for this study, which followed a suggested set of seven steps (Smith et al., 2022).

4.9 Step One – Reading the texts

The researcher is tasked with immersing themselves fully in the data. In the initial stage of analysis, the focus is on uncovering meaning which may not be immediately apparent. Therefore, a process of engaging with the text and interpreting it becomes necessary. Each text is read and reread to ensure that a quick summary is avoided, and instead, the participant remains the central focus of the analysis. Through repeated readings, a model of the overall interview structure starts to take shape, allowing for an understanding of how certain sections of the interview might be grouped together (Smith et al., 2022).

During this stage of analysis, some instances of paradoxes emerged. For example, participants expressed the belief that a digital detox is best maintained when it is their own decision while also acknowledging the importance of their parents' role in supporting their digital detox.

4.10 Step Two – Exploratory Notes

This step was intertwined with the first step, as I took notes with an open mind while reviewing the transcript. My aim was to identify specific ways in which the participant expressed and comprehended their experience of a weekly digital detox. There were no strict rules dictating what to comment on; the objective was to generate a comprehensive and detailed set of notes based on the data. Certain parts of the interview may have warranted more comments than others. These notes, referred to as "exploratory notes", were recorded in the right margin of the transcript (Smith et al., 2022). Initially, these exploratory notes were descriptive and closely linked to the data itself. As I explored the transcript line by line and word by word, I gained a deeper familiarity with its contents and started to discern the participant's unique ways of discussing and understanding their experience. The exploratory notes allowed me to capture and summarise the most significant elements of the passage based on my interpretation.

4.11 Step Three – Experiential Statements

In the third and deepest level of analysis, the focus shifted to a more interpretative and conceptual examination of the data, exploring the underlying meanings. This level of analysis involved the use of psychological terminology and abstract concepts, going beyond the previous two levels (Smith et al., 2009). On the left-hand side of the analysis, I recorded experiential statements, which were previously referred to as "emergent themes". The change in terminology was explained by Smith et al. (2022) as a way to provide a clearer characterisation of how themes are described at this stage of analysis. The goal of these statements was to capture the essential points derived from the exploratory notes, reflecting a process of both description and interpretation (Smith et al., 2022).

4.12 Step Four – Searching for Connections

After conducting exploratory coding, I began to observe the emergence of themes from the data. This stage necessitated a shift in analysis, transitioning from directly working with the transcript to working with the analysis generated through exploratory coding (Hefferon & Gil-Rodriguez, 2011). It was important to proceed cautiously to avoid excessive fragmentation of the participant's experience. Initially, there were 14 emergent themes, which were subsequently clustered together based on their relevance and interconnectedness and were reduced to four themes. However, certain themes emerged that appeared to deviate from the emerging pattern. These instances of dissonance, referred to as disconfirmatory 'cases', involved narratives or themes that significantly differed from those of the majority of other participants (Smith et al., 1995). In response to such dissonance, I would revisit earlier transcripts to ensure that nothing vital had been overlooked or misunderstood. If it was determined to be an irregularity, a decision was made to exclude it from further analysis.

4.13 Step Five – Naming and Organising the Personal Experiential Themes (PETS)

Four overarching themes emerged from the analysis of the pilot, each consisting of 2-4 subthemes. This stage of analysis involved a creative approach, where I carefully considered how statements shed light on each other. To facilitate this process, I printed out the analyses and cut out individual experiential statements, with the participant's name and page number noted for easy reference. I laid out these statements on a dining table and moved them around as I searched for connections and similarities across statements, ultimately organising them into clusters.

Some experiential statements that couldn't be closely linked to the research question or other clusters were discarded, and in this way, the original 14 clusters were then reorganised into smaller groups until a final set of four themes was established. These groups of related experiential statements were referred to as Personal Experiential Themes (PETs), formerly known as superordinate themes (Smith et al., 2022). The process of forming and categorising PETs involved innovation and required moving back and forth between the original data and the experiential statements. It was crucial to ensure that the experiential statements contained an interpretive element and didn't remain too closely tied to the original data, as was the case with the exploratory notes. This iterative process created a hermeneutic circle within the analytic process (Smith et al., 2022). A table was then created, presenting the PETs as the highest level of organisation in bold uppercase, with subthemes listed in bold lowercase letters.

4.14 Step Six – Repeating the Process

This process was initially applied to the pilot study statements and then extended to all the cases. It was crucial to approach each case independently and honour its uniqueness. Care was taken to avoid replicating ideas already identified in the pilot study, allowing for the emergence of new analytic elements with each new case.

4.15 Step Seven – Developing Group Experiential Statements (GETS)

It was essential to avoid imposing a group norm and instead explore the points of divergence and convergence within each case. During this stage, some group names and the sequence of sub-themes were modified, and new sub-themes were added to accommodate new findings. The focus was on understanding the essence of each participant's experience, how they lived through their digital detox, and identifying connections across experiences. Key questions included identifying the most significant Personal Experiential Themes (PETs) across the data, examining how sub-themes resonated across different cases, identifying universal experiential features, and determining the level at which commonalities were shared. To facilitate the process, the material was physically moved around the dining table, and colours were used to visually distinguish different themes. Finally, the number of PETS was expanded to include a fifth and two to four sub-themes were contained in each.

4.16 Reflexivity

Qualitative IPA researchers must engage in self-reflection to consider how their presence and actions may influence the research process, both during data gathering and subsequent analysis. When gathering data, it is crucial to attentively listen to participants' language and experiences. As an IPA qualitative researcher, I was responsible for making sense of these experiences in a meaningful way while being mindful of my own contributions and position. Drawing on my experience as a therapist, I applied strategies to establish rapport and connection with participants during interviews. These included active listening, allowing participants to lead the conversation, using encouragers, being aware of nonverbal cues, and being comfortable with silence when participants needed time for reflection. I also learned to navigate when to delve deeper into a narrative or request clarification without interrupting the flow of thought. Unlike my role as a therapist, during the interviews, I had to carefully balance the depth of questioning to address participants' experiences while also considering the time constraints to ensure that the interview schedule could be completed within the allocated timeframe. I experienced a sense of responsibility, recognising that each interview was a unique opportunity to comprehend and interpret the participants' perspectives accurately while striving to avoid any misinterpretations. At the interview stage, concerns arose regarding participants' honesty in disclosing any instances of breaking their digital detox on Shabbat, as well as potential embarrassment in sharing such information. I was aware that the participants' level of honesty depended on the non-judgmental atmosphere I created and the comfort they felt in my presence. It was crucial to exercise caution in not posing challenging questions too early in the interview, as establishing trust was essential. Participants needed to feel confident that their confidentiality would be upheld throughout the process.

While I was working with the participants' statements to arrange them into Personal Experiential Themes and Sub-themes, I was conscious of keeping an open mind as to the themes I was finding, applying them to each participant individually. After all of the participants were transcribed, some new themes emerged that included common experiences felt by all or some participants. In addition to notetaking and records being kept, regular email exchanges and Zoom meetings were held between myself and both of my supervisors to discuss findings as they came about. This allowed me to be continually thinking about my work. Meetings intensified at the analysis stage of this work to ensure that it was understood and adopted correctly. Having a primary supervisor who was unfamiliar with the experience of digital detox over Shabbat helped me to maintain a phenomenological stance. Themes that had emerged from the pilot study were temporarily put aside and, when more participants were interviewed, these themes resurfaced for examination to see whether they reappeared across participants or whether they were an anomaly.

I was grateful for the structure provided by Smith et al. (2022), which guided my research process. Additionally,

I sought the assistance of my supervisors to gain additional perspectives on the development of Personal Experiential Themes (PETs) and General Experiential Themes (GETs), as their input was valuable in ensuring a well-rounded analysis.

Chapter 5: Findings

5.0 Introduction

A marker of IPA is the characteristic of the hermeneutic circle, which links part and whole. In this way, a narrative develops, adding a sense of coherence to the evolving investigation (Smith, 2007). This chapter aims to convey a 'story' through the narrative development of themes and to support findings with verbatim extracts from the interviews to demonstrate that efforts were made to validate interpretations by showing how conclusions were reached.

This happens within and across themes. Within each theme, selected participant quotations are cited. The quotations chosen were the ones that most closely reflected the theme in order to demonstrate to the reader how the theme was arrived at. Coherence is achieved by ensuring that each theme enhances the narrative. This also happens across themes where it is shown how the themes are interconnected (Nizza et al., 2021). To avoid excessive overlap, it is important to contrast themes in order to differentiate them (Braun & Clarke, 2006). During the process, there were instances where different statements overlapped with various themes as well as themes themselves overlapping. The creation of themes and the allocation of statements to those themes is a subjective task that depends on the perspective of the researcher.

The research identified five Group Experiential Themes (GETs) among the participants, which are presented in Table 1 using bold uppercase letters for clarity. Each GET is accompanied by sub-themes, represented in bold lowercase letters. To facilitate easy identification, each theme has been color-coded. These five themes and their respective sub-themes were derived through the interpretative phenomenological process. It is worth noting that some statements overlapped across multiple themes, and decisions were made regarding their allocation to specific groups.

The voices of the participants are used throughout and their quotations are taken directly from the transcripts. They are cited by their pseudonym and their age. The quotes are not left to speak for themselves, their significance is revealed in accordance with the hermeneutic cycle whereby the full meaning of the data is shown in the way that each participant makes sense of their experience through the researchers' engagement with the quotes and the picture as a whole (Smith, 2007).

Convergence and divergence are addressed by seeking a balance between commonality and individuality. The participants' unique idiosyncrasies are maintained whilst also seeking shared qualities across participants. Personal quotes are considered in the wider context of the data gathered across groups whilst the personal narrative is maintained thus adding texture to interpretations. This requires hermeneutic cycling between part and whole (Smith et al., 2009).

Table 1 Group Experiential Themes and Sub Themes

	Group Experiential Themes	Sub Themes
1	**DETOX AND RELATIONSHIPS**	• Real Presence • Positivity in relationships • Impact of community • Attitudes of others
2	**DETOX AND IMPACT ON SELF**	• Reading • Anxieties associated with digital technology • Wellbeing • Who might benefit?
3	**MEANING OF SHABBAT**	• Two different worlds • Active Engagement with Shabbat • Time on Shabbat • Feelings of authenticity
4	**MAINTAINING AND BREAKING A DIGITAL DETOX**	• Impact of parenting • Breaking the detox • Keeping the digital detox across time
5	**LIVING WITHOUT TECHNOLOGY**	• Routine during Shabbat • Experiencing the power of technology • Attitudes towards Shabbat

Table 2 Participants

Participant Name	Age	Male/Female	Occupation	Single	Living at Home	Shabbat Observant
Mendel	22	M	Student	✓	✓	✓
Shaul	22	M	Student	✓	✓	✓
Dov	22	M	Student	✓	✓	✓
Abigail	19	F	Student	✓	✓	✓
Sarah	24	F	Post-grad	✓	✓	✓
Leah	20	F	Student	✓	✓	✓
Orli	19	F	Student	✓	✓	✓
Adina	19	F	Student		✓	✓

5.2 Analysis

5.2.1 *Group Experiential Theme 1*

1. DETOX AND RELATIONSHIPS

This overarching Group Experiential Theme (GET) encompasses the participants' experiences in the context of social interactions, including their interactions with family, friends, and communities. The sub-theme of real presence emerged consistently in each interview, highlighting the importance of face-to-face communication and its unique qualities. The research revealed that the absence of technology had a significant impact on the way relationships were perceived and experienced compared to when technology was present. Additionally, it was observed that observing Shabbat within a community enhanced the spirit of Shabbat and contributed to the maintenance of a digital detox. The research also indicated that keeping a digital detox sometimes required explaining it to others or considering it in relation to individuals who do not observe or understand the practice.

Real Presence

This sub-theme sheds light on the distinction between the mere physical presence of family members and the genuine sense of presence within families. Despite the inclusion criteria ensuring that participants lived at home, the experience of true presentness was only identified during Shabbat. The participants attributed this disparity to the distractions caused by technology, which hinder people from fully experiencing and feeling the presence of others. On Shabbat, all participants felt a greater sense of being heard, which differed from their experiences on weekdays. This was partly because there was ample time available, but it was also due to the absence of technological distractions. In many ways, these two factors are interconnected, as the absence of technology creates spare time, which fosters genuine listening and communication among friends and family members.

Leah explains her experience of presence on Shabbat as being a time to really get to know one another without requests. She feels a sense of connection experienced by her parents who want to be close to her. Unlike weekdays when phones are present, their relationship isn't based on what one needs from another, such as money, favours or errands, but it's based on her essence as a person.

> '...during Shabbat everything's switched off so we have nothing to do other than spend time with each other and get to know each other properly, so I would say my interactions with my parents are a lot less ehm need based.' (Leah, 20, p.11)

Leah's experience reveals that during the week, her interactions with family members are primarily focused on utilitarianism and practical matters. In these interactions, there is little opportunity for genuine closeness or a deeper understanding of one another within the family.

Orly experiences Shabbat similarly to Leah. On Shabbat, communication has an intimate quality that is lacking on weekdays. Conversations on Shabbat connect the people around them.

> '...you get to know them on Shabbat, you get to, you know, speak and talk about your week...' (Orly, 19, p.4)

On Shabbat, Orly observes that spending time with her family without the distractions from technology allows for a deeper understanding of each other. During this time, they have the opportunity to catch up and learn more about one another. It becomes a mutual process of discovering and revealing aspects of themselves, leading to a deeper connection and a better understanding of each other's true nature.

Leah reflects that the ever-presence of technology acts as a barrier to deep connections. She experiences a sense of insignificance compared to the phone when interacting with others. Even if the phone is hidden, its influence is still felt, preventing others from fully focusing and listening to her. This lack of undivided attention leaves Leah feeling less important and hinders the depth of connection she desires.

> '...it's always in front, there's always this sense of oh we're talking but there's also something else on the side that's... that could be more important than you...' (Leah, 20, p.7)

Abigail is confident that on Shabbat there are no distractions that hinder her experience of her mother's presence. Incoming calls, emails, alerts and the pull of apps with games or social media interrupt conversations and compete for attention.

> 'I think there would probably be less… I think I would feel less that they were listening to me because I find that in the week that sometimes I'll be talking to my mum and she'll be on her phone, she won't be listening, but on Shabbat she doesn't have that so she does have to listen to me.' (Abigail, 20, p.29)

Abigail expresses her perception of feeling less listened to. Abigail says there would be less and then corrects herself to say that she would feel less. This experience gives her a sense of being diminished as if her presence becomes less significant when she is not truly heard. On Shabbat, her mother is compelled to listen to her, as if there is no choice but to be fully present and attentive. There is a clear longing to be noticed and heard, without the competition for attention posed by technological devices. It is implied that when these devices are present, Abigail's mother may not feel obligated to listen to her. Abigail states that during regular days without a digital detox, her mother's attention is diverted to her phone rather than actively listening to her.

Shaul feels that conversations occurring in the presence of phones are a battle against technology. He uses the word 'allows' which implies that there isn't permission to talk to parents when there is technology present or perhaps that there would be no point.

> 'Being away from that (technology) allows us to talk to them.' (Shaul, 22, p.2)

Shabbat provides a unique opportunity to experience the presence of family members in a way that is not achievable in the presence of technology. The constant demands of digital media will overshadow the presence of family members, as their need for attention often takes precedence.

> 'When someone's talking to me, I literally like take out one earphone and say like, I'm listening to music, literally like it just sort of shuts you off from people and you're in your own little bubble, I guess, and then on Shabbat everyone talks to each other.' (Adina, 19, p.9)

For Adina, whilst she is physically present with her family, she is also fully cognisant of being apart, residing in a zone all by herself where she is unreachable despite proximity. 'Shut off' seems like she is separated in a place of her own, distant and unconnected. She cannot feel connected to two things at once, if she's connected to technology, she is withdrawn from her family and the only time she can feel present with her family is when she is disconnected from technology, which happens on Shabbat.

In Orly's experience of family life, shared mealtimes are inconceivable;

> 'We can't have a family meal throughout the week because people will just call, there's all these like emails from work and all these things, and without the phone there isn't that distraction.' (Orly, 19, p.4)

Family mealtimes are only attainable in a family-wide digital detox as the distractions from technology make familial conversations impossible. Family may be present but the distractions caused by technology isolate Orly, leaving her feeling alone and unimportant as phone-related activities take precedence.

Leah highlights the contrast on Shabbat where she experiences a stream of conversation;

> '...the quality of conversation is it's less broken up, so it flows a lot better. It's a lot more natural and there's no underlying sense of ehm there's something else I need to do instead of you...' (Leah, 20, p.8)

In the company of technology, Leah is acutely aware of its existence, which diminishes her sense of importance. It creates a perception that others prioritise something else over being present with her, resulting in strained conversations and disrupted flow. Interactions feel forced and require more energy, lacking the natural ease and smoothness that would typically be present. Instead of being effortless, conversations become arduous and demanding, necessitating additional effort.

Sarah experiences an acute sense of presentness when having a digital detox as she finds that conversations focus on the here and now rather than external factors that are not directly related to her.

> 'It's very much focussed on like what's happening then as opposed to what's already happened, or yeah probably like what's already happened or been shared on social media.' (Sarah, 24, p.17)

On Shabbat, Sarah can feel really listened to and valued. Those around her want to hear Sarah's own thoughts and opinions, there is no interest in outside matters or news that has nothing to do with them. Interests not directly pertaining are not important, the only value is the present moment.

Dov goes as far as to say that talking like a human being is performed only in the absence of technology.

> '…you can have a meal where very little communication goes by cause you're on your phone, talking to people, and people call that talking, but eh on Shabbat day there's no phones, there's no reading, there's no you know WhatsApp group saying your second cousin has a second birthday and has a picture saying ooh how cute she is and you know very sweet it's like a baby. It's like let's talk like a normal human being.' (Dov, 22, p.9)

Dov's observation of his experience of being in the company of others with their devices is a feeling that he's no longer present to the extent that he believes that basic human qualities are lost. Dov does not consider phone communication to be normal human interaction even when sharing information about family. For Dov, interruptions on phones where information is shared have a non-human quality as it's not talking. He doesn't experience communication on phones as communication. He can only best describe this as feeling inhuman.

Later, Dov says how being in the presence of his Rabbi feels belittling because of technology.

'...he's (his Rabbi) always on his phone, like every three or four minutes, so having a very important conversation with him about the most important thing in the world, but he's always on his phone checking what came in. You do feel a bit not so important because they come before me, you know.' (Dov, 22, p.13)

Dov feels diminished, of no value, when the Rabbi is distracted by his phone in his presence. He knows he is close with his Rabbi, but the Rabbi is not there for him. He is not present to attend to him; no matter how important Dov's needs are, they are of no significance in the presence of the Rabbi's phone.

Dov's experience of technology is very negative. Whether it's at home with his family or when he's gone out to meet his Rabbi, he keeps getting the feeling that he doesn't matter. His cousin's birthday or an anonymous caller will take precedence over him, leaving him feeling at the bottom of the heap to the degree that he feels out of step with humanity. Dov is confused by this as he wonders how he can lose rank so speedily.

Dov also feels there is a difference between physical presence and pixels on a phone which represent reality but for him are not real.

'...the real world it's grounded, it's physical, I can't explain, like I can touch this table, I can touch this chair, I can touch this phone, I can touch myself, I can see it, I can relate to it. You know, that's what human beings are.' (Dov, 22, p.23)

Dov struggles with what the phone represents. He finds that he can relate to what he can physically see but he struggles with representations on screens, they make him feel ungrounded and unsafe and somehow inhuman. It feels that phones are a misdesign, a mistake of humanity, wrong in their existence and not real and he struggles to reconcile and accept presentness without presence.

Positivity in Relationships

This sub-theme became transparent because all the participants noticed positive aspects to their relationships, either with friends, family or both, on Shabbat. Bonds are tightened, families reconnect and relationships are built through face-to-face interactions without technology. This sub-theme builds on the previous one where participants felt listened to, in this sub-theme they are identifying bonds. Sarah observes a status of pausing to enjoy each other's company.

> '...you get to hear about everyone's week where people aren't rushing through the house and everyone's finally sitting down, has a chance to relax...' (Sarah, 24)

For Sarah, there is a sense of having waited a long time for this moment – it was anticipated. At the end of the week 'finally' each member sits and, in that sense, it evokes a feeling of presentness for the sake of taking interest in one another's week. She waits for this to 'finally' happen when the family inquire as to her activities. For her, relaxation happens when everyone is seated and she can talk about her week and hear about the week of her family members. Getting to relax in this way can't happen soon enough; it is important to Sarah who waits for it to 'finally' happen. The rush around the house that normally takes place on weekdays is counterproductive to Sarah's relaxation and she awaits a different state of sitting and catching up when she can finally relax.

Shaul observes positivity in his face-to-face relationships with his parents where he can have conversations with them that he might otherwise never have;

> 'I think it increases, like improves our relationship. It gives us a chance to talk about things that we might not otherwise talk during the week ehm so you know we talk more deeper like more personal concepts at a deeper level, which we don't do during the week, so I think it's very beneficial yeah.' (Shaul, 22, p.1)

He finds that deep conversations only occur on Shabbat as Shabbat affords him the time and space to explore himself in a deep way. Conversations on Shabbat move beyond the surface level and penetrate the depth of his soul because there's time and a lack of distraction by technology. This depth enhances his relationships as it 'gives them a chance' to talk. For Shaul, the presence of technology removes all chance of deep, meaningful conversation happening, but during a digital detox, he knows there is a chance it will happen.

Shaul reflects further saying;

> 'Ehm you know we have heart-to-hearts. We discuss very personal topics and ehm and really discuss

emotions and discuss feelings which we really don't during the week.' (Shaul, 22, p.2)

When Shaul says 'heart-to-hearts' it evokes a feeling of true connection, a connecting of souls that feels intimate and personal and there is space for his feelings. He is certain this does not happen on weekdays; it is only possible on Shabbat. It seems that the presence of technology removes the discussion of feelings and there is no room for him to address his emotions or his needs.

Leah discovers that her phone submerges her into a world where people appear more distant and consequently more desirable, and she contrasts this with her family that she reconnects with on Shabbat;

'Really just spending time with people, you know, you take for granted, you know, my siblings.' (Leah, 19, p.9)

Celebrities encountered via technology embody glamour, mystery, and inaccessibility, as they are individuals Leah is unlikely to meet in person. On the other hand, the people she lives with are easily accessible at any time, making them seem less intriguing. She becomes aware of their flaws and imperfections, which can make them appear ordinary and uninteresting. However, during her digital detox on Shabbat, Leah experiences a newfound appreciation for her immediate family, an appreciation that would be unattainable in the presence of technology. With the absence of her phone, Leah's siblings have the opportunity to reveal their own unique qualities, allowing her to see them as fascinating individuals worth getting to know.

Orly finds positivity in her relationships in a different way. She finds that Shabbat compels her to be discerning with her choice of friends;

> '...it (Shabbat) kind of you feel you manage to realise which friends you can have a conversation with. There's some friends that you genuinely can't have a conversation with you if you don't have your phone...' (Orly, 19, p.9)

With the presence of phones, Orly finds that it doesn't matter as much who she spends her time with; however, without phones, individual characteristics are exposed, and Orly feels more intolerant towards certain friends that she's more tolerant of during weekdays. Without phones, connections between individuals are strengthened, but for this to occur, the qualities of friends are evaluated. It seems that with the presence of phones, Orly regularly spends time with people she 'genuinely' cannot talk to; it is as if the phones either blind or shield her from reality.

Impact of Community

When considering the observance of a digital detox on Shabbat, one cannot ignore the impact of community in this endeavour. The digital detox on Shabbat leaves a void, a space that needs to be filled. There are many ways to fill the space and this section will explore how the vacuum is filled by community-related activities. This subsection was categorised within this PET because it examines the participants' relationships with their community and how these relationships interact with their digital detox practices during Shabbat. I considered the broader relationship between the participant and their community in analysing this aspect of their experiences.

Most frequently, the observance of Shabbat is not observed in isolation but in the presence of others who share the commonality of the experience. Only one interviewee lives outside of a Jewish neighbourhood, keeping Shabbat with her family but not within a like-minded Shabbat observant community. Two participants lived in Shabbat observant areas, but their friends lived in far away neighbourhoods and they weren't able to meet with their friends on Shabbat. All participants experienced Shabbat through the lens of community in different ways.

Living in a Jewish observant neighbourhood, Abigail found that on Shabbat, her parents were more flexible with their rules.

> '...like on a regular weekday, I'd never finish lunch and go to a friend's house, whereas on Shabbat I could walk alone. It wasn't such an issue, for whatever reason. I don't know...' (Abigail, 20, p.19)

On Shabbat, vehicles are not driven as part of the digital detox. Thus, in neighbourhoods populated with observant Jews, there will inevitably be many Jewish pedestrians. Being a small community, walking along the street will invariably mean that there will be many familiar people at any given time over the period of Shabbat. For Abigail, she picked up a message that Shabbat was a safer time to walk the streets, and she experienced her parents' loosening of rules despite her being unreachable by phone. She is confused by their ease of letting her walk alone when she can't be contacted by them, whilst when she does have her phone, they don't let her walk outdoors alone. This leaves her feeling that the community is safe on Shabbat, safer than being able to phone for help as there will be people around who will ensure her safety.

Abigail also takes advantage of social groups arranged by the community on Shabbat;

> 'We also had youth groups and things that were running on Shabbat that all my friends were going to so I would also go.' (Abigail, 20, p.19)

For Abigail, it's important that she lives in proximity to friends who are also keeping Shabbat and they have a common place to meet up. If her friends were going, she would also go as it's important for Abigail to spend her digital detox with friends and be where they are. She says 'all her friends'; she feels that by attending the youth groups she is surrounded by all her friends and, combined with being allowed to walk there alone, she feels a sense of security, safety and familiarity by her observance of Shabbat within a community also keeping it.

For Mendel, the experience of the community he experiences on Shabbat is one of giving back;

> 'I think there are big advantages to the community. The amount of volunteering, for example, that is being done on Shabbat is way more than during the

week. You know, people actually visit people in hospital and not to say that they don't do it during the week but, for example, I wouldn't have time during the week to look after my kid that I look after...' (Mendel, 22, p.13)

On Shabbat, Mendel experiences a void from the absence of his technical devices and he fills this by helping out. He acknowledges that volunteering takes place on Shabbat. If not for the digital detox, the void would not be there, and he would not be able to have time to volunteer, as the time for volunteering is made possible by the digital detox. He says they 'actually visit people in hospital'. He is noticing something that wouldn't normally happen but on Shabbat; he notices there's time for aspirations to become reality and actually happen. He calls his volunteering with a child 'his kid'. On Shabbat, he is undistracted and fully devoted to his task of looking after the child. By giving the child full attention, undistracted by technology, he can call the child 'his kid' as if the level of care he is able to give the kid is like he would give to his own child.

For Orly, Shabbat meals were a time for her parents to get to know community members, so growing up, guests were a part of her life;

> '...we made it so that only one of our meals on Shabbat we invite people over. We don't invite more than twelve people.' (Orly, 19, p.3)

Orly's family are devoted to the community and regularly invite a large number of guests. For Orly growing up in this way, community time and Shabbat are intertwined as this was a way of life for her on Shabbat. Shabbat for Orly is synonymous with community life and connections. This is specifically done on Shabbat when phones are away so that focusing on guests is possible. Like Mendel's volunteering, guests on Shabbat are entertained in lieu of time spent on technology. Whilst hosting visitors is also a positive commandment in the Torah, it is not on Shabbat specifically that this is commanded to be done. Shabbat is chosen as an appropriate time because it is the only time of the week that Orly's parents can devote themselves to this endeavour as they won't be distracted by technology. The digital detox affords them community time in this way. When Orly mentions that '*we* don't invite more than 12 people', it implies that she perceives herself as a co-host alongside her parents. This suggests a strong sense of togetherness and unity within the family, as they collectively host guests in a manner that fosters a feeling of solidarity.

Orly's parents are mindful that their own children need and deserve their parent's attention on Shabbat and that is why only one of the Shabbat meals is devoted to visitors whilst the other Shabbat meals are designated as family time. Therefore, their children know that only on Shabbat will they have their parent's full attention for a significant portion of time. There is a sense of predictability for Orly knowing that on Shabbat there will be one meal for guests but also one meal for her, and it seems like this was instituted at some point in the past ('we made it'). It was thought about and considered and decided that the perfect balance for family and community on Shabbat is one meal for each. This leaves

Orly feeling that she is a priority for her parents as, whilst they have diverted interests, they don't cease to acknowledge her needs too and their wish is to institute a meal devoted to their family that Orly can rely on.

Leah experiences the community behind her, helping her to feel the vibe of Shabbat;

> 'There's a massive community effort to make, to bring the atmosphere of Shabbat out, so there's loads of events, things for children to do ehm going to shul (synagogue) every week eh you really feel the community has become much more cohesive.' (Leah, 20, p.17)

Leah experiences a strong community effort to uphold the observance of Shabbat. The community organises events and activities to engage the youth and attends Synagogue regularly, which is essential for the survival of Shabbat. This collective backing makes Leah feel included and supported in her commitment to Shabbat. Being part of a larger community project gives her a sense of belonging and purpose. Rather than feeling isolated, she feels empowered and encouraged to disconnect from her phone and embrace the group's energy.

Attitudes of Others

Some participants, especially being students, had both Jewish and non-Jewish friends or both Shabbat observant as well as Jewish but non-Shabbat observant friends. All participants came from Jewish observant families. Some participants had to consider their digital detox through the eyes of the other.

Orly's parents invited guests who were not observing the digital detox on Shabbat and, whilst she knew they came with their phones, she experienced a respect for Shabbat where they wouldn't take their phone out on Shabbat;

> 'So, the likelihood is that they have their phones with them, but we haven't had anyone whip one out in the middle of the meal.' (Orly, 19, p.3)

Orly knows it's a likelihood that guests had their phones on them although she could not say for certain. What she knew for certain is that at no time did guests use their phones or indicate that their phones were on them thus imbuing in Orly a sense that Shabbat observance is respected by outsiders. This leaves her feeling that she is doing something important and worthwhile in her digital detox on Shabbat.

Leah has non-Jewish friends at university and has to manage their attitudes;

> 'I do know that they might forget and might message me, or they'll ask me about it and won't really understand it, and sometimes there's a little bit of ridicule, which I personally don't mind so much, but it doesn't make it easier.' (Leah, 20, p.18)

By contrast to Orly, Leah has to contend with explaining the inexplicable. She feels mocked by friends and is held in contempt as her friends continually forget her practice of detoxing; it is a foreign tradition in the modern world. She puts on a brave face, saying she doesn't mind so much but nevertheless, it hurts and she suffers the challenges of it. In addition to the scorn, Leah knows that she will miss out on messages sent to her which she expects to receive on Shabbat. This is another aspect of her digital detox that she needs to manage.

Sarah has Jewish but secular friends who know about her Shabbat observance and will nevertheless message her on Shabbat;

> 'I know that my friends, you know, will be on their phones and might message even though most of them know not to bother texting as they won't hear from me.' (Sarah, 24, p.4)

Sarah is confident in her observance – she doesn't care that her friends will have to wait until Shabbat is out to get a response. She is indifferent to them or their messages on Shabbat as they are irrelevant to her; they don't make up part of her day. Unlike Leah, her friends are Jewish so they know and understand her observance, yet they message her anyway. In both Leah and Sarah's experiences with friends, they cannot be left out of digital life (despite others knowing about their detox) and both Sarah and Leah show unwavering commitment to their digital detox despite being pulled in by others to engage.

Abigail is frank about missing out. She takes it for granted that her way of life is dissimilar to her peers and she takes a pragmatic view. There is no wavering of her commitment just a casual acceptance that there will be the challenge of missing out. There is a feeling of being left apart but it's dismissed in a matter-of-fact way. Shabbat is ingrained in Abigail and for her there is no conflict, just fact;

> 'Well, the majority of my friends, especially now post-high school, are not religious and don't keep Shabbat, so there are actually things going on or they're messaging me things and I'm missing out.' (Abigail, 20, p.26)

Adina experiences a range of responses to her digital detox and finds that she needs to have trust to feel understood in her observance;

> '...depends on the level of trust in that friendship. Like a lot of my friends like are really interested in it and they completely understand that and a lot of them are actually, quite a few of them, not a lot of them, quite a few of them are like really envious that wow you're so lucky that you have this family time and you are just not online and whatever. They're really envious, but a lot of people just don't understand it.' (Adina, 19, p.12)

She notices that for some friends her digital detox is foreign and is met with suspicion whilst for other friends her detox makes her an interesting person. For others, she is the object of envy for having more family time. It seems significant to her peers that a detox means time spent with family, perhaps she has explained it in this way to them or perhaps they deduced this as a natural consequence. Either way, the point of their envy is having time with family, it is something that adult children feel they miss. Adina feels lucky to have the time with her family and this allows her to have a cavalier attitude to other friends to whom she feels misunderstood.

5.2.2 Group Experiential Theme 2

2. DETOX AND IMPACT ON SELF

The selection of this second GET was based on the numerous mentions of how the digital detox on Shabbat influenced the individual participants in various ways. They commonly expressed that Shabbat provided an opportunity for reading and also highlighted the anxieties associated with digital technology. Additionally, they reported positive effects on their overall well-being. Participants were then asked whether they believed the benefits they experienced were unique to them or if they thought others could also benefit. The final sub-theme explores their responses based on their own personal experiences with technology.

Reading

Each participant in the study shared their unique experience of how Shabbat presented a precious opportunity for reading or learning. While some cherished the pure joy of immersing themselves in books, others found the absence of technology during Shabbat made reading more appealing. Interestingly, even those who expressed a deep appreciation and love for reading admitted to being constrained by distractions that limited their reading time to Shabbat. Some participants reflected on how reading was an activity they cherished during their younger years but gradually neglected as teenagers when smartphones entered their lives. Abigail's narrative perfectly aligns with this common pattern observed among the participants;

'When I was a kid I read a lot, I was a big reader, ehm, now with uni and things I typically only really read on Shabbat, but I can read about three books on Shabbat.' (Abigail, 20, p.9)

Abigail's love for reading is evident. During Shabbat, she can devour three books within just 25 hours, showcasing her passion for literature. However, as she entered her teenage years and obtained a phone, reading took a backseat to activities on technology. Without the structure of Shabbat, Abigail would struggle to find the motivation to read, except for what is required for her university studies. On Shabbat, free from the distractions of technology and with ample time at her disposal, she rediscovers the joy of reading. Once engrossed in a story, she becomes completely immersed, free from the nagging feeling that there are other tempting activities vying for her immediate attention.

Adina has no reservations that Shabbat is the only time she would read.

'I know that I'm a massive reader and the only reason I'm a reader is because ehm of shabbat, right? Otherwise, when would I read?' (Adina, 19, p.8)

Through her rhetorical questions, Adina acknowledges that, outside of Shabbat, there is no time for reading, despite being an avid reader. The rhetorical questions suggest a certainty that I, the researcher, would agree with her. It comes across as obvious to her that anyone who observes Shabbat would feel the same way as she does with regard to reading on Shabbat. It is interesting to notice how technology usage undeniably overpowers her love for books. It seems that only a complete digital detox can reignite her passion for reading. This highlights the significant influence technology has over long-held hobbies and interests.

> '...and the mental benefits of reading are like phenomenal. It reaches from being able to empathise with people who you wouldn't understand if you hadn't read to ehm to just literally improving your grammar, so like the mental benefits of being able to focus on other things...' (Adina, 19, p.8)

Despite being aware of the benefits of reading, such as its pleasure and constructive nature, Adina finds herself consistently choosing technology over books. While she acknowledges the value of reading, it seems that when faced with the choice between reading and technology, the latter always takes precedence.

Like Abigail and Adina, Leah also shares a similar experience of reading on Shabbat. While she has diverse interests, the distractions of weekdays prevent her from fully engaging in them.

> 'I have a lot of interests that I find I don't... that I can't do during the week because I find I'm so distracted by everything else. I love to read, I love to do extra stuff, but I find that it all naturally falls on

Shabbat because that's when I don't actually have any other distractions...' (Leah, 20, p.9)

Initially, Leah describes her situation as 'finding' herself unable to partake in her preferred activities throughout the week. However, upon deeper contemplation, she corrects herself and recognises that she 'can't' engage in them. Despite her strong desire to read, she feels powerless as if there is a greater force that restrains her. This is largely due to the abundance of distractions that surround her. In addition to her work and social obligations, the persistent presence of her phone serves as a continuous source of diversion, inhibiting her from indulging in her beloved pastime of reading.

Anxieties Associated with Digital Technology

It is evident that phones hold significant meaning for the individuals in this study belonging to Generation Z, as revealed by the unanimous sentiment expressed by the participants in the previous section. They all shared a common feeling of being unable to engage in reading or pursue their favourite activities during weekdays due to the distracting nature of their phones. This section will explore the anxieties associated with the presence of phones and apprehensions rooted in the very nature of these devices.

Adina raises concerns about the negative impact of phones, particularly social media and the news, on her well-being.

'...when we're on Instagram we're literally just sitting there comparing our bodies and comparing our faces to everyone else and that's not normal, and when we're on the news we're just hearing about death every second, and when we're on WhatsApp we're like, obviously, there's good sides to all social media but I think like being very honest with yourself and recognising how like deeply stressful like technology really is, is probably very helpful to make people want to refrain from it.' (Adina, 19, p.7)

She has noticed how these platforms can induce anxious feelings within her. Specifically, she finds that Instagram fosters insecurity as she compares herself to others whom she perceives as more attractive. Despite recognising this negative effect, she finds it challenging to break away from the scrolling habit, feeling trapped by the act itself. It conveys a sense of being held captive, unable to detach from the sedentary activity. Furthermore, Adina discusses how consuming news, particularly global tragedies involving unfamiliar individuals, adds to her overwhelm. While she believes that understanding the detrimental effects would motivate people to disengage, her own struggle to break free from the allure of technology presents a conflicting reality.

Adina also recognises that phones create a persistent pressure to present an idealised version of oneself, one that may not reflect reality;

> '...In my own family, like when we're all together as a family, there's always a few people on their phones and photos, that's a massive distraction. Everything has to look perfect and there's a very big like... pressure to make it all look good so we get a good photo...' (Adina, 19, p.8)

This pressure detracts from the ability to fully enjoy the present moment, transforming what could be a relaxed and authentic experience into a time fraught with the need to conform and appear a certain way. The presence of phones introduces an element of pressure, shifting the focus from genuine enjoyment to the constant need for validation and social acceptance. As a result, the natural ease and acceptance of oneself are compromised, giving way to a constant striving for external validation and a sense of belonging.

Abigail experiences something similar to Adina where the enjoyment of living in the moment is hampered by the presence of technology;

> '...if you do have your phones, someone could be taking a picture of you at that time and it could be an unflattering picture or a video, and in the background you can hear what you are saying and maybe it's not something that you want to get out, and there's no risk of that on Shabbat because there isn't a phone there to record or take a picture or send a text to your friends telling them what you've said or anything like that.' (Abigail, 19, p.23)

Whilst Abigail trusts her friends, she can't help but feel uneasy about the lack of privacy as the presence of phones creates a lingering doubt in her mind. Any moment can be captured, any words can be stored and potentially used against her in the future, leaving her with a sense of vulnerability and loss of control. This concern about the potential for embarrassment from the violation of shared experiences remains ever-present unless it's Shabbat when the absence of technology provides a sense of peace allowing her to relinquish these worries.

Dov finds that he feels miserable, messy and disgusting when he's on technology;

> 'Ehm often if I use screens I feel a bit depressed and a bit yucky.' (Dov, 22, p.23)

Dov has recognised that the time he spends on his technology does not bring him joy. Instead of informing and uplifting him, it leaves him feeling dejected and unhappy;

> 'I'm very bad at telling emotions over text, something bad over text. Some people are really good at it – I'm just, struggle with it.' (Dov, 22, p.11)

Dov explains the big difference between having face-to-face conversations versus communicating on his phone. He feels that without non-verbal cues, such as body language, facial expression, and hand gesticulations that often accompany speech, he is left lost and confused. This frequently leaves him wondering about the intentions of the sender and, by extension, how his replies will be received by the receiver. This creates an anxiety that he does not experience when talking face-to-face with people. He repeats the word 'bad' in the following sentence. He is 'bad' at relaying his true feelings, it comes across as 'bad' and perhaps if the news is 'bad' it's made worse via communicating it by phone. What makes it harder for him is his belief that others are good at it, implying that he is lacking in this skill. He is behind other people, he can't do something that others can do well, thus furthering his sense of uneasiness associated with his phone.

Whilst Dov struggles with explaining himself via text, Shaul finds that he cannot put his phone down;

> 'It gives me a chance to unwind to not always be so immersed in the business of ehm seeing what's going on and seeing what everyone else is doing.' (Shaul, 22, p.9)

Shaul finds that he can relax when he's not in 'the business'. 'Business' denotes a state of intense activity and being consumed by its demands. In drawing this parallel, Shaul equates his immersive engagement with his phone to being involved in a demanding business. When one is deeply engrossed, they can't see anything beyond the subject that they are submerged in and, in this way, Shaul is accurately describing his experience of being on his phone. He refers to it as his occupation, living in the world of social media, where he finds himself constantly observing and monitoring other people's activities.

Shaul observes that detoxing from being in a state of business is helpful in the grand scheme of things, however, in the short term it increases stress;

> 'I think I'm maybe more stressed on Shabbat, towards the end of Shabbat especially, 'cause I want to go on my phone as soon as possible. But I think

overall, the grand scheme of things, it helps to deal with the stresses of life.' (Shaul, 22, p.8)

Shaul is observing the difficulties of a digital detox. It is stressful for him to not have his technology, and this is a weekly challenge. He needs to have sight of the overall benefits in order to find the willpower to see it through. This is especially the case towards the end of Shabbat, by which time his stress levels are high, mimicking withdrawal symptoms as if it were a drug;

> 'More difficult eh yeah that, being away from my phone, is always difficult I think, especially on a Friday when I'm in the middle of trying to organise something, some something's happened and I have to deal with it and to put your phone away for Shabbat okay for the next 25 hours I can't think about this and you, for the whole Shabbat, you're curious to know what... how was that situation resolved. You're not going to know for the next 25 hours. Ehm yeah, that's definitely difficult.' (Shaul, 22, p.9)

Shaul emphasises the difficulty of setting aside his phone before Shabbat. Regardless of what he may be engaged in, such as personal commitments, following a news story, or staying informed about the well-being of distant friends or family members, or even if he's in the middle of watching a film, he acknowledges the challenge of disconnecting when the designated time arrives. 'Always difficult' implies that he hasn't got used to it. It's a weekly stress he has to contend with that hasn't got easier with practice.

Dov reflects that screens stop growth;

'You're stunted, almost emotionally, you're stunted by screens.' (Dov, 22, p.24)

They act as a blockade that inhibits emotional expression. Dov cannot grow, nor feel his feelings, he loses touch with reality as he is prevented from developing properly.

Leah reflects on the contrast between being switched off from technology to turning it back on following Shabbat;

'...as soon as you go back to technology that's when everything, because you're taking in so much information, there's no space to breathe, there's no space to think...' (Leah, 20, p.20)

Leah's experience of returning to her devices is akin to feeling choked as if her freedom and personal space are constricted. The weight of this overwhelming burden leaves her with a sense of suffocation, hindering her existence despite her initial willingness and excitement to re-enter this detrimental state. The benefits of her digital detox quickly dissipate in the face of these constraints.

Some participants faced emotional challenges associated with being unable to take action and feeling out of control without their phones. Abigail, for instance, experienced anxiety during her digital detox periods, primarily stemming from a sense of being out of control in various situations where she was faced with her own presence along with an inability to act.

'If like, for example, I've left something unresolved before Shabbat, then I'm thinking about it the whole

Shabbat, then that can be like, quite inconvenient.' (Abigail, 20, p.7)

In this example, Abigail contemplates the difficulty of being alone with her thoughts during a digital detox. With her phone, she had the ability to either distract herself from these uncomfortable emotions or reach out to her friend, using technology as a means to address and resolve misunderstandings. However, in the absence of this ability to take immediate action, she remains with no choice but to sit with her distressing feelings and her need to confront them directly. This uneasiness does not subside but remains the entirety of Shabbat. The discomfort cannot disappear until she is reunited with her phone. Abigail's phone represents an ability to address difficult feelings so she does not have to feel them in their rawness.

Shaul identifies a similar challenge to Abigail with regard to his digital detox. He refers to being in a state of discomfort during the span of Shabbat. This feeling will not go away on its own, it can only be resolved once he is back on his phone.

'...or the whole Shabbat you're curious to know what, how was that situation resolved, you're not going to know for the next 25 hours, ehm yeah that's definitely difficult.' (Shaul, 22, p.9)

Shaul struggles with a lack of access to information outside of his present environment. It is a challenge to sit with his immediate surroundings. He feels the need to know things, the curiosity is unfamiliar as with his phone he would have a way to access a solution. The inability to act on his thoughts and sit with uncertainty is distressing.

This sub-theme explored examples associated with digital technology. On one hand, phones bring about anxieties for their users, while on the other hand, being disconnected from their technology during Shabbat introduces a different set of anxieties. These two forms of anxiety are not mutually exclusive and many participants experienced both simultaneously. They found relief from the anxiety of being constantly connected to their phones, yet they also felt a desperate longing to be back on their phones.

<u>Wellbeing</u>

This sub-theme conveys the positive effects of a weekly digital detox on Shabbat. For some participants, the positive results are obvious and immediate whilst for other participants, it is hard work. Shaul articulates it with an analogy;

> '...it's almost like a therapy I guess where a therapy session can be very intense and very tough mentally but you know in the long run it's helping you.' (Saul, 22, p.8)

Shaul is fully aware of the hardships that come with his digital detox. He draws a parallel between this process and undergoing therapy. Just like therapy sessions that require deep self-reflection and often bring up painful emotions, Shaul sees his weekly detox as a similar endeavour. It's not an easy journey, and he describes it as mentally challenging. He knows that enduring this discomfort is necessary for personal growth and positive outcomes, even though the immediate benefits may not be apparent. Just like therapy can lead to healing and transformation, Shaul believes that his digital detox can bring positive changes if he has the strength to endure the struggles that come with it.

Whilst Shaul knows that the benefits to his digital detox are in the long term, he is also cognisant of immediate benefits despite the challenges;

> 'I would say that it gives me a more positive ehm mindset, or like mentally it helps me. I have that break to my week ehm so that if I didn't have that break maybe I would wanna, my mind would be more chaotic or I'd be more emotional so having that break helps me a lot.' (Shaul, 22, p.2)

Knowing that his years and months are punctuated by the cycle of weeks is positively beneficial for Shaul's sense of well-being. Shaul experiences mixed feelings on Shabbat but he is certain that his overall health would suffer if he was not observing his digital detox. The break from technology on Shabbat keeps his emotions in check; he feels he would have no control over his feelings without a weekly digital detox. He also refers to 'chaos' in his mind. He believes there would be a jumbled mess, unpredictable behaviour, randomness and confusion if not for having a weekly, predictable break.

The following phrase indicates how Shaul uses his detox in order to gain maximum benefit;

'On Shabbat I get the opportunity to actually think and eh explore my own thoughts.' (Shaul, 22, p.4)

Shabbat is the time when Shaul can order the chaos by thinking. Technology inhibits thinking as one busy activity is followed by the next, however on Shabbat, Shaul can take a break from these all-encompassing activities to make sense of his world in his own head so that his real self can emerge.

Adina similarly experiences discomfort associated with her digital detox and she offers the following reflections;

'I think it's uncomfortable sometimes. Sometimes uncomfortable, but I think the reason it's uncomfortable is because it's really good for us, ehm like no pain, no gain.' (Adina, 19, p.4)

Adina finds the experience of disconnecting from her technology to be challenging and even painful, but she sees a purpose behind the discomfort. She recognises that if she can endure the pain and discomfort, there will be long-term benefits for her well-being.

Adina demonstrates maturity in her understanding that valuable things often require effort in the following sentence;

'...there's a bit of tension or whatever and an argument's about to happen, right? People will honestly just repress it and go on their phones.' (Adina, 19, p.9)

Adina has recognised the importance of embracing challenging emotions as part of her personal development. Within her family, she has observed a pattern where stress and conflict are often avoided and replaced with phone usage as a means of distraction until the difficult emotions fade away. In this context, the phone serves as a refuge, offering temporary relief from life's hardships. However, Adina understands that this avoidance, in the long term, does not contribute to harmonious relationships at home or inner peace.

For Sarah, the break from technology is analogous with feeling unconstrained;

'Shabbat is freedom from technology.' (Sarah, 24, p.8)

Shabbat is a time to feel unencumbered by the demands of her phone. There is no pressure to be doing something else and a sense of immunity from life's pressures descends.

Later, Sarah expands on the concept of freedom;

'I think the absence of technology just allows people to think about what they need, how that week's gone and kind of digest everything.' (Sarah, 24, p.15)

She realises that Shabbat provides her with the opportunity to feel liberated and focus on herself, her well-being, and her personal growth. It's a time when she can create mental space to reflect on the events of the week, assess her successes, identify areas for improvement, and internalise meaningful messages. Sarah likens this process to digestion, where her mind assimilates information and experiences in a thoughtful and intentional manner.

Sarah has observed that Shabbat has a positive effect on her well-being by being able to think without distractions or without a nagging feeling that she might be doing something else.

For Abigail, Shabbat is a time to be free from bad news;

> '…so Shabbat was nice, like during Covid I stopped reading the news so much and Shabbat I was free of all news, there were no messages, no updates and that was definitely beneficial.' (Abigail, 19, p.25)

Abigail recognises the positive impact on her well-being during Shabbat as a direct consequence of not having access to negative news. Particularly during significant global events like the COVID pandemic, Abigail felt that the constant influx of news invaded her life and heightened her levels of stress. Beyond major world events, the daily barrage of information, arriving rapidly and often filled with pressures, takes a toll on her health and overall well-being.

Mendel recognises that Shabbat serves as a punctuation mark in his week, offering a valuable framework to reconcile and process the rapid pace of activities that occurred from Sunday to Friday. It provides him with an opportunity to absorb and reflect on everything that has transpired. During Shabbat, he can recharge and rejuvenate before the start of the upcoming week, knowing that once again, activities will unfold at a fast pace;

'...I think that especially nowadays when I know everyone says this that life moves so fast ehm and I think having a few hours to catch up and like sort of take it all in.' (Mendel, 22, p.8)

Mendel's reference regarding his life moving at a rapid pace, followed by his need to 'take it all in', implies that during the week, while engaged with his phone, he struggles to absorb and process his activities effectively. Furthermore, the endless possibilities for additional engagement facilitated by technology prevent him from reflecting on his experiences, as the phone perpetuates a constant stream of activities at an ever-increasing rate. It is during the pause on Shabbat that Mendel finds solace and the opportunity to manage the overwhelming onslaught of constant stimulation. Mendel has engaged in conversations with others and discovered that his experience is widely shared among his friends. They, too, acknowledge that life seems to progress rapidly for them, leaving little time for pause or reflection.

Leah emphasises the importance of disconnecting from technology in order to feel truly connected;

'...just being more connected in being able to think about things properly with a clear head, I think that's really important to me.' (Leah, 19, p.14)

The connection she is referring to is connecting with her own self. By disengaging from the digital world, she creates space in her mind to absorb and process information, allowing her thoughts to come together coherently. When constantly immersed in technology, her mind becomes scattered and restless, preventing her from finding inner peace. Leah recognises the significance of having this mental clarity and space for her overall well-being.

Dov discovers that Shabbat brings a sense of invigoration and renewal, as it provides him with a precious opportunity free from any competing demands on his time;

> '…ehm it's refreshing in a sense also as well cause you, you have nothing to text, no one to email or text you just completion in a sense, real shevisa (rest).' (Dov, 22, p.3)

During Shabbat, he experiences a complete respite, unlike any other time, where he can fully unwind and rejuvenate. This unique experience of uninterrupted tranquillity and peace nourishes him on a deep level, allowing him to recharge and replenish his energy.

Orly perceives Shabbat as a space that truly belongs to her, highlighting the contrast with the rest of her time when technology tends to dominate and dictate her activities;

> 'Time for myself is really, really good, like introspectively yeah, so it's really, really fun. I really, really enjoy thinking deeply so I get that opportunity, which I get very excited for throughout the week.' (Orly, 19, p.7)

When she is engaged with technology, her time is consumed by its demands and distractions. However, during Shabbat, when she intentionally disconnects from technology, she reclaims full control over her time. This sense of ownership and autonomy over her time is not limited to Shabbat alone but is something she eagerly anticipates throughout the week. It becomes a precious opportunity for her to reconnect with herself, engage in uninterrupted self-discovery, and nurture her personal growth. The frequent use of hyperboles in her expression emphasises the intensity of her emotions and the significance she attributes to this experience.

Orly summarised the feeling that all the participants felt and encapsulated it succinctly in the following way;

> 'Yeah, it's kind of like I get to kind of just it's like, a survival tool.' (Orly, 19, p.8)

Orly engages in deep reflection, struggling to find the right words to convey her profound visceral experience. However, she eventually arrives at the perfect word that encapsulates her feelings. In weeks dominated by the hyper-alertness induced by her phone, she realises that the sustenance of her life and existence hinges on the complete act of switching off.

The dependence of Gen Z on their technology creates a heightened state of energy that they experience for a significant portion of their time. However, when they deliberately disconnect from this constant engagement, a noticeable void emerges, which poses its own set of challenges. Despite these observed difficulties, the participants in this section have come to understand the importance of this contrast in their day and age. They have recognised that by embracing moments of disconnection, they can enhance their overall well-being. Therefore, this sub-theme focussed on the acknowledgement of challenges while highlighting the positive impact that intentional disengagement can have on their well-being.

Who Might Benefit

This subtheme, included within the broader theme of 'Detox and Impact on Self', is situated in this context because the answer to this question relied on the unique experiences, mindset, worldview, and subjective perceptions of each participant. As a researcher, my intention was to explore whether the experience of a digital detox on Shabbat felt like an individual experience, was specifically for Jewish people or if they believed it could benefit particular groups of people. I approached this inquiry without any preconceived expectations, and I discovered that all participants shared the belief that a digital detox could have positive effects on others. They acknowledged the significance of sharing the valuable experiences they gained from their own detox and recognised that various groups of people could particularly benefit from taking a break from technology. The responses gathered during the research contribute to this specific subtheme;

'I think just being able to take a step back and seeing that not everyone looks like all people on social media that you are looking at every single day and just actually look around would make a difference.' (Abigail, 19, p.22)

Abigail recognised the significance of a digital detox, especially for individuals, particularly teenagers, who struggle with addiction to technology and are influenced by the curated lives of social media influencers. Constant exposure to the idealised and flawless images presented by these influencers can lead to distorted perceptions and insecurities among young people. By disconnecting from this virtual world, individuals can shift their focus to the real world and the people in their everyday lives who represent more realistic notions of appearance, behaviour, and eating habits. Stepping away from the immersive online experience allows individuals to gain perspective and recognise the true reality that may be obscured while being constantly immersed in the digital realm.

Sarah also identified teens who spend a lot of time on social media as being a group that would most benefit from having a digital detox;

> '...it's not the honest portrayal of reality, you know. Someone might be doing well, you know, sharing everything on social media, you know, financially well, but mentally they're waiting for all those likes and everything, so if especially high school age were to take a certain amount of time away from their phone that would definitely be better for their mental health.' (Sarah, 24, p.18)

Sarah observes that social media, with its emphasis on accumulating 'likes', reflects a deep human desire for validation. However, this constant need for external approval can be detrimental to one's overall sense of well-being and happiness. It prevents individuals from recognising and appreciating their own inherent fulfilment, as they become overly reliant on seeking validation from others. The only way to break free from this unhealthy cycle of seeking external validation is by disconnecting from social media and switching off from its influence.

Adina recognises a stark contrast between the false representations of life found in technology and the different reality that exists outside of it;

> 'I think that social media is the root of so many eating disorders and so many teenagers, teenage girls but I guess also teenage boys and so many young adults, ehm and I'd say if there's a group that would benefit so much from it it's anybody anyone who is struggling with any type of body dysmorphia or disordered eating or even anxiety, depression anything. Literally anyone who struggles with that. I think having a place to reground themselves and not be looking at models all day online... and also time away from having a place where everyone's focussing on how they look and everything's so imaged focussed ehm would be so beneficial. I think it would be so beneficial.' (Adina, 19, p.21)

Adina observes that social media often presents a superficial world, where individuals are primarily judged based on their external appearance. This shallow focus on physical attributes leads to a limited understanding of people's true personalities, qualities, and inner selves. Adina finds this phenomenon to be hazardous, as it can contribute to negative effects on mental and emotional well-being. She believes that individuals should be valued for their intelligence, opinions, values, and all the multifaceted aspects that make up their identities. Adina refers to the phone as being a 'place'. This denotes that in that place these significant aspects of a person's being are often concealed behind the camera lens, emphasising the importance of looking beyond superficial appearances to truly appreciate others.

Shaul identifies teens and Gen Z as being a group that would benefit from a digital detox;

> 'I think people my age especially or even people younger than me teenagers, ehm where with social media being so prevalent and being so ingrained in life, it would be so healthy to have to take time out.' (Shaul, 22, p.7)

Shaul recognises the distinction between the online world and the offline world. He uses the term 'ingrained' to highlight how deeply integrated technology is in the lives of teenagers and Gen Z. It becomes an inherent part of their existence, explaining why separating from their phones can be a challenging and even painful experience. Just like with any form of dependency, removing oneself from it can have significant side effects. However, Shaul emphasises that, in order to experience the benefits of a digital detox, temporarily disconnecting from the harmful influence of technology is necessary.

Orly feels that disconnecting from technology creates an opportunity to practice connecting with family;

> 'I think, if the family as a whole is finding communication difficult, I think just having that detox might be really, really beneficial.' (Orly, 19, p.16)

Being constantly connected to a phone can create a sense of being connected to everyone yet disconnected from meaningful interactions. Orly believes that families who choose to forgo technology at certain times would be compelled to engage with each other, fostering deeper conversations and a greater understanding of one another. Although it might initially feel unfamiliar and challenging, with time and practice, such interactions would benefit all family members.

Overall, participants expressed a strong sense of advocacy for the benefits of a digital detox and a desire to share these benefits with others, highlighting specific groups that could find it particularly helpful in navigating the challenges of modern technology.

5.2.3 Group Experiential Theme 3

3. MEANING OF SHABBAT

This GET delves into four sub-themes that emerged, all shedding light on how participants derived meaning from their digital detox on Shabbat. The participants frequently described Shabbat as a distinct world separate from their secular lives, which became a notable sub-theme. Additionally, participants demonstrated a sense of maturity when reflecting on their Shabbat experiences, discussing how they engaged with Shabbat and how they interpreted their digital detox. The theme of time emerged as participants discovered a new significance in the passage of time on Shabbat, while feelings of authenticity were also prevalent as participants observed a reality that often went unnoticed during the weekdays.

Two Different Worlds

Abigail observes that Shabbat exists in a distinct realm, separate from the weekdays;

> '...It's like it's nice to be a bit turned off from the world, kind of.' (Abigail, 19, p.6)

It is a unique space that she enters on Friday and departs from on Saturday night. The realms of Shabbat and weekdays are experienced as separate entities, with distinct characteristics and differences. Abigail recognises that she can never inhabit both worlds simultaneously, as they are distant and distinct from each other. When she transitions from the realm of Shabbat, she becomes fully immersed in the other world, switched on to its demands and dynamics.

Shaul struggles to articulate the feeling and it's difficult to find the words for something so conceptual;

> 'Shabbat is like, it's set aside, there's no distractions, there's extra time, it allows us to do this, it's a state of mind...' (Shaul, 22, p.2)

He perceives Shabbat as a distinct mental space, separate from the ordinary realm of weekdays. In his mind, it holds a unique and sacred status, untainted by the routines and demands of regular days. It evokes a set of provisions and experiences that are distinct and separate from those encountered during weekdays.

Leah recognises that the act of disconnecting from technology also disconnects her from a separate world;

'...when you switch off before Shabbat specifically, you're massively stepping away from the outside world.' (Leah, 20, p.5)

In Leah's perspective, one world represents the realm of technology, while the other world is characterised by the absence of technology. The latter world narrows down her focus to her immediate surroundings, including her family, friends within close proximity, neighbours, and community members whom she can interact with face to face. This world is accessible through a conscious choice to step into or out of it. On the other hand, the world of technology is referred to as the 'outside world,' as she does not live within it but experiences it externally.

Leah describes how she embraces her world of Shabbat and imbues it with sanctity;

'...I make times for me to learn on Shabbat so that it really does bring in the atmosphere of the day.' (Leah, 20, p.17)

She consciously invests effort in enriching this world with knowledge, meaning, and values. This intentional cultivation sets it apart from her weekday world and the world of technology. By infusing her immediate surroundings with purpose and significance, Leah creates a distinct and cherished space that contrasts with the digital realm she engages with during the week.

In addition to Leah's intentional efforts to cultivate a sense of the divine, there is also a natural state of otherness that the family experiences together when technology is absent;

'I think actually that we all kind of naturally fall into this family time space, it naturally becomes a family space without technology.' (Leah, 20, p.11)

By actively setting aside their devices, a space becomes created that fosters a genuine sense of togetherness, giving rise to a separate world within a distinct zone;

Adina finds that Shabbat is contained in a different world, a sanctified space that is guarded;

'I also think that it translates to the rest of the week through creating like a protected space. I think that refraining from technology and whatever, like wearing nice clothes and eating nice food, I think it's the defining feature of Shabbat that makes it a different day to the rest of the week and that gives it a protection and a protected space when so many other things in our religion are not being protected and are merging into everything else. Ehm and also refraining from tech does make this boundary between like ourselves and the outside world.' (Adina, 19, p.8)

Adina perceives a clear contrast between her secular world and the realm of Shabbat. She acknowledges that entering this special world requires intentional effort and preparation, as indicated by the family's various rituals aimed at enhancing the Shabbat experience. These rituals hold significance for Adina as they contribute to the creation of a sacred sanctuary for Shabbat. As a guardian of Shabbat, she recognises the importance of disconnecting from technology and refraining from its use during this time.

Dov perceives Shabbat as a sudden shift from his regular world into a distinct and separate realm;

> 'I enjoy it, it brings in Shabbat nicely sort of a cut-off for something, sort of something cool is coming.' (Dov, 22, p.3)

The act of switching off his technology serves as a clear and abrupt transition, signalling the departure from one reality and the entry into another. This transition brings a sense of excitement to Dov, as he embraces the unique atmosphere and experience that Shabbat offers.

Dov also experiences Shabbat as having a special dimension to it, partly created through physical preparation;

> 'There was always like a special atmosphere in the house. Ehm it felt very pure, very calm, very my house Friday nights, we had the curtains down, the lights were on nighttime and nice cutlery out, guests, very warm, very cosy. Yeah also another dimension almost away from like news and gossip and films and like just calm and it's like atmospheric, very atmospheric. You know, good food, very focussed, nowhere to go, nowhere to be, no shops are open, no errands to run, no one to speak to.' (Dov, 22, p.20)

A warm smile lights up Dov's face as he fondly recalls his childhood memories of Shabbat. It brings forth a sensation of brightness and simplicity, a radiant yet unadulterated experience. The ambience of Shabbat is a blend of intentional planning and uncomplicated ease, resulting in a soothing, harmonious, and serene atmosphere. It exists as a distinct realm, beyond the reach of secular days, incapable of being replicated. Shabbat resides in a space that transcends the confines of weekday realities, offering a sanctuary untouched by their demands and pressures. Dov experiences a sense of uniqueness during these moments, where everyone is fully present without any desire to be elsewhere. There is a genuine sense of comfort and relaxation among family members, and Dov feels a deep sense of harmony within himself in this sacred world.

Active Engagement with Shabbat

Shaul discerns a clear distinction between having his phone and engaging in a digital detox. During his digital detox, he recognises the need to exercise patience and delay immediate gratification in order to pursue a higher purpose;

> 'And that instant gratification there isn't any of that suspense.' (Shaul, 22, p.10)

This requires considerable effort on his part as he learns to navigate the uncertainties that arise. Furthermore, in order to experience peace of mind on Shabbat, he must develop the ability to compartmentalise his thoughts, acknowledging the things he can address and setting aside those that are beyond his control. This inner strength is essential for maintaining a sense of tranquillity.

Shaul also grapples with moments of emptiness and boredom, which are unfamiliar experiences for many individuals of his generation who have grown up with smartphones;

> '…nowadays there's never that boredom: Oh I need something to do. There's always media to consume to – unless you dedicate some time away to really think, you're not gonna find, it's not gonna come on its own and I don't have the self-discipline to set aside time during the week so I use that time set aside on Shabbat…' (Shaul, 22, p.7)

Overcoming these challenges necessitates self-discipline and resilience to resist the temptation of technology. Shaul acknowledges that he cannot accomplish this on his own and recognises the need for external support and strength which comes only through Shabbat.

Dov discovers that engaging in religiously-oriented activities, such as attending Shabbat services, holds a much deeper significance for him compared to the distant and impersonal interactions he experiences on his phone;

> '…and the more you look forward to the Yiddishkeit (Judaism) itself, and the more you realise you sort of enjoy Shabbos, it's somehow less enticing the screen, you know – to sing in X (his synagogue) on Shabbos afternoon, to learn with your friends is somehow a lot more enjoyable than sitting texting someone.' (Dov, 22, p.16)

In these religious gatherings, he encounters familiar faces on a regular basis, meets friends, engages in study sessions, and receives guidance from his Rabbi and spiritual mentor. The songs and melodies that he has known since childhood also add to the meaningfulness of these experiences.

Dov is explicit when he notices that he will find fulfilment from finding activities on Shabbat;

> 'Yeah sure. I always try and do something on Shabbat, go out to people's houses, go out and learn ehm always try and do it.' (Dov, 22, p.17)

Unlike weekdays, where time is spent on technology, the activities he seeks on Shabbat will be active rather than passive. He will seek to visit friends or neighbours in the quest for connection and conversation and he will study to build his knowledge.

Mendel, like others, emphasises the significance of finding meaning on Shabbat;

> '...feeling fulfilled with yourself that you've volunteered and ehm whatever you went to shul (synagogue)...' (Mendel, 22, p.20)

He expresses a desire to avoid the feeling of missing his phone and instead focuses on engaging in activities that bring him a sense of pride and satisfaction. Mendel values making wise choices about how he spends his time and seeks to prioritise activities that contribute to his personal growth. Mendel emphasises that the fulfilment he seeks is an internal one where he says 'feeling fulfilled with *yourself*'. Mendel is driven by a desire to connect with himself. His motivation for engaging in meaningful activities on Shabbat is not to capture and share them on social media or messaging platforms. Instead, he pursues these activities altruistically, aiming to experience a sense of pride and accomplishment that fulfils his own emotional needs and gives purpose to his existence. Mendel finds personal satisfaction and fulfilment by focusing on activities that nourish his inner self, independent of external validation or recognition.

Mendel acknowledges that finding fulfilment on Shabbat is not an effortless task;

> '...sometimes I need to say the things that I'm doing are meaningful to the community or to myself and those things will become my substitute for my phone.' (Mendel, 22, p.22)

It requires an active effort on his part. He recognises the need to constantly remind himself that the easiest path is not necessarily the most fulfilling one. Mendel understands that he must exert significant effort and work hard to seek out activities that will truly satisfy him and leave him with a sense of accomplishment. It is through this conscious and deliberate approach that Mendel aims to discover meaningful experiences during his Shabbat observance.

Orly, like Mendel, recognises that finding meaning on Shabbat requires intentional and active engagement;

> '...it's such a waste of time to not value it, so once that's what I realised, so okay fine, if I'm wasting my

time thinking about tomorrow, like thinking about Sunday about the end of Shabbat, it's not making me feel happier, like it's not the distraction of thinking about when it's over doesn't actually make you feel better about it, like it doesn't make Shabbat any easier.' (Orly, 19, p.12)

She understands that simply letting the day pass by without purpose will not lead to a fulfilling experience. Instead, she takes it upon herself to seek out meaningful activities and actively build herself during Shabbat.

Leah discovers that Shabbat provides her with an opportunity for self-exploration and introspection in her quest for meaning;

'I definitely think more about, on Shabbat, so I'd say more ehm more difficult life things, difficult life questions. You actually have the time without having the distraction.' (Leah, 20, p.9)

During this sacred time, she delves deep within herself to better understand her own identity. Leah embraces the chance to explore her preferences, opinions, thoughts, and unique qualities that contribute to her individuality. Shabbat becomes a period of contemplation where she ponders the significance of life and the personal meaning she constructs for herself.

Time on Shabbat

The decision to choose this sub theme arose from the participants' recognition of the valuable gift of time that Shabbat provides. While the abundance of time can present challenges, as discussed in the previous sections, it also offers unique opportunities that are not typically available. Mendel, for instance, experiences a sense of openness during Shabbat, where he can engage in discussions on any topic of his choosing. This newfound freedom allows for deeper exploration and connection that may not be easily attainable during other times.

> '...supper during the week is 20 minutes, half an hour, because everyone's rushing off to do their thing ehm and then Shabbat it's like two hours and you talk about everything under the sun.' (Mendel, 22, p.2)

Mendel recognises a significant contrast in the duration of mealtimes between Shabbat and other days. During Shabbat, he experiences a sense of unhurriedness and ease. There is no pressure to rush or move quickly; instead, he can simply sit in the present moment and engage in conversation without the urgency and immediate demands that accompany weekday dinners.

For Orly, the expanse of time offers her an opportunity to think;

> 'It also gives you time to think like I think that like it kind of just... you're allowed to just kind of think about your own thoughts for that entire time.' (Orly, 19, p.6)

Orly observes that the nature of time on Shabbat enables her to think and not just any thoughts but her very own ones. It's not just for fleeting moments but for an extended period of a full 25 hours which will be renewed each week. Orly is noticing as she verbalises her feelings that Shabbat is a time just for thinking. She repeats the word 'just' twice as she contemplates the priority of this activity and she feels it's permissible to notice that this time is spent 'just' thinking without adding justifications. It's difficult for a Gen Z who is constantly online to contemplate 'just' thinking for an extended period, but Orly is reflecting that thinking is what she is doing for the entire duration of Shabbat and she feels endorsed to do so because it is approved.

The significance of thinking her own thoughts is interesting as it denotes that at other times she might be thinking the thoughts of others. Technology is a provider of sources of information gathered from other people and absorbed into our minds via our consumption of media. Sometimes information is depicted subtly and at other times digital communication is portrayed directly such as on social media when viewers' thoughts are shaped by influencers. On Shabbat by contrast, Orly feels that she is developing her own mind through thinking her very own thoughts, not just for a few minutes but the 'entire' time of Shabbat, which feels significant to Orly.

Another way that Orly perceives time on Shabbat is that she owns it;

> '...And like without my phone, without technology the time isn't taken away from me as much as it would be, with my phone, if that makes sense.' (Orly, 19, p.5)

Orly asks a rhetorical question whilst she makes sense of her experience. She's unsure as to the rationality of what she's just said. She is trying to make sense of the plausibility of the notion that time is being taken away from her as a grown-up person. Without technology, Orly notices that by contrast she would own and be in full control of her time.

Mendel discovers that the span of Shabbat provides a valuable opportunity to engage in meaningful discussions with his father;

> '...you have the time and space to properly talk through things and like explore all the options on the topic or, for example, if you have an idea and then like really get to the nitty gritty of it and whereas during the week like I need to do this task and this task or that and then it's like your decision process during the week becomes much quicker ehm which isn't always a good thing.' (Mendel, 22, p.9)

The availability of uninterrupted time along with the absence of external pressures allows him to delve deeper into ideas and concepts and reach solutions which require time to arrive at. Mendel realises that this extended period of contemplation enables him to make better decisions by thoroughly considering various perspectives and possibilities. As an aside, these opportunities to talk with his father at length connect and bond them.

Mendel finds that at other times on Shabbat he experiences a sense of blankness, like a vast vacuum devoid of activity;

> '...Personally, for me, it's just really good to have that sort of a couple of hours of just nothingness ehm and

I really look forward to it actually these days...'
(Mendel, 22, p.8)

These hours he describes carry a feeling of emptiness, as if there is nothing specific to fill them. However, he doesn't perceive this emptiness as a problem; rather, he anticipates it as a time for pure existence, where simply being in the moment is enough.

All participants found that time had a different meaning for them on Shabbat and have described their experiences of it in a way which feels meaningful to them. In the final reflection, Mendel encapsulated how time is experienced by him on Shabbat in a way that seems unfamiliar in our modern era as humans who are continuously engaged in a flurry of activity when even time spent winding down is justifiable and rational. The way that Mendel described his need for time as admissible 'nothingness' brings a different understanding to time on Shabbat where Shabbat gives him the permission to spend his time resting and still whilst also feeling valuable and being purposive. This symbolises the true meaning of Shabbat as for six days God worked in His creation of the world and on the seventh day He rested. Resting by just 'being' has become a rarer phenomenon in our age of technology, however Mendel has stated pleasure and anticipation of doing just that.

Feelings of Authenticity

This subtheme focuses on the participants' experiences of authenticity and the contrast they observed between what they considered 'real' life, where they consciously engage and make intentional choices, and 'not real' life, which occurs when they are unaware of how they spend their time, particularly when using technology. The participants recognise that during these 'not real' moments, valuable time is being lost from their lives, leading to a sense of disconnection from their authentic selves. They feel that true authenticity is found in consciously living and being fully present in their experiences, rather than being consumed by technology.

Leah recognises the importance of living a purposeful life with clear goals, values, and a meaningful life plan.

> 'I think without that it's very easy to let life pass by without giving it a thought.' (Leah, 20, p.10)

She believes that living authentically and in alignment with her vision is essential for her life to hold significance. However, she acknowledges that technology can hinder this authentic living by consuming hours of her day through mindless scrolling and distractions. This awareness prompts Leah to reflect on the time lost and the lack of fulfilment she experiences when her actions are not aligned with her authentic self.

Leah perceives technology as a simulated world, closely resembling her real life yet fundamentally distinct from it;

> '...It's a very powerful thing that I don't want to confuse with my life. It's very ehm addictive, I'd say.' (Leah, 20, p.5)

It persistently lures her to participate, but she consciously puts effort into distinguishing between the two. She recognises that while technology may mimic aspects of her authentic world, it ultimately falls short and fails to capture the essence of her true reality.

Leah recognizes Shabbat as a time of authenticity that stands in contrast to the busyness of weekdays;

> 'I work a lot with younger kids, let's say from 11-14, and I noticed that they don't, they're very, they're given a way of life where they don't actually have to think too much because they're given so much distraction and, even with older people, I think it's much easier just to let life slip by without giving it a real thought. And I noticed I was doing it a bit and I noticed that on Shabbat I actually could think about what I was doing in general.' (Leah, 20, p.10)

During Shabbat, many activities are restricted, such as work, exercise, and travel, allowing for a more focused and limited set of activities within a specific framework. For Leah, it is in these moments of rest, prayer, Jewish study, spending time with family, and being in the company of friends that she experiences authenticity. Shabbat provides a space for meaningful connections, spiritual reflection, and a sense of purpose that she finds lacking in the fast-paced nature of everyday life.

Leah later discerns a distinct quality of technology that fosters a sense of disconnection from real-life experiences when she consumes it;

> '...the issue I have with the news is that it gives me the illusion that I know everything that's going on

and really I don't. Really it's very biassed and very ehm, nothing's authentic nowadays, so it's it's not too bad but I don't find it benefits my life in any way.' (Leah, 20, p.20)

She perceives it as illusory, offering a false impression of awareness and information, while the transmitted content carries biases and prejudices. Leah must carefully evaluate its veracity and usefulness, ultimately realising that these virtual portrayals lack authenticity and hold no value for her.

Sarah finds herself immersed in the distorted world of social media;

'…probably better that I'm not always on technology and social media 'cause you see how people present their lives and it's not always the correct way… it's not that distortion that we sometimes get from social media where it's not the reality being shown.' (Sarah, 24, p.14)

Sarah has observed that she is closely following a world that is not real. She is spending time admiring celebrities and picture-perfect models that disseminate an existence that she could never hope to achieve. She is aware that the reality of their lives is not the one that they portray to their followers and that none of it is real. For Sarah, the digital detox is about having distance from this lack of reality.

Dov struggles to find the right words to express himself, as he grapples with the challenge of describing his experience;

'On Shabbat, it's a bit more eh it's like a bit more whole – I can't describe it to you without sounding like a hippie. Shabbat is a bit more whole, a bit more built. Yeah whole, built, real, all those kind of words.' (Dov, 22, p.23)

Shabbat fills him with a sense of completeness, integrity, and self-sufficiency. He finds it difficult to convey this feeling without sounding too whimsical, fearing that it might undermine the seriousness of his perspective. However, the emotions he experiences are truly genuine and sincere, and he finds it challenging to communicate the sense of authenticity without appearing ungrounded in reality.

Sarah finds that during her digital detox she isn't lacking anything real;

'...it doesn't make such an impact that you are missing on something, it's more, it's a time filler, it's something to do.' (Sarah, 24, p.5)

Sarah pondered the impact of disconnecting from technology during the 25 hours of Shabbat and came to the realisation that the time spent on her phone is devoid of realness or authenticity. 'Missing on something' denotes missing out on life as she notices that it merely serves as a means to pass the time, lacking meaningful and genuine engagement or activity.

Adina notices a distinct difference between the time spent as a family on Shabbat and other occasions, which she finds difficult to label as genuine moments;

'So, it makes people just actually spend time with each other when a lot of the time when we're spending time with each other is not real time spent together, if that makes sense?' (Adina, 19, p.9)

As she verbalises this observation, it sounds peculiar to her, causing her to question the plausibility of such a notion. She grapples with the concept of time existing in different ways, realising that a significant portion of her time spent with her family lacks authentic qualities that she only experiences on Shabbat.

Orly finds herself feeling in sync with the universe on Shabbat;

'…so, it's that sort of thing where okay I'm one with the world I'm not me and phone alone.' (Orly, 19, p.19)

Orly comes to the realisation that on Shabbat, she experiences a sense of independence, feeling self-sufficient without the need for external tools or aids to navigate life;

'it's kind of like I get to kind of just it's like a survival tool but not a survival in that way you feel you are okay like stranded in the desert. You only have everything that really is part of you and that you basically have to figure out like.' (Orly, 19, p.7)

She embraces a genuine and profound sense of legitimacy and completeness, where she feels truly authentic and whole.

5.2.4 *Group Experiential Theme 4*

4. MAINTAINING AND BREAKING THE DIGITAL DETOX

This GET covers the experiences of participants in maintaining a digital detox, particularly in the context of parenting. The interviews revealed that the participants' engagement with digital detox began at an early age and was instilled and exemplified by their parents at home. The theme of parenting emerged frequently, as participants reflected on the challenges they faced in upholding their digital detox, especially during their teenage years. Some participants acknowledged that they occasionally struggled to adhere to their commitments during this period. Moreover, the participants' feelings towards their digital detox on Shabbat evolved as they matured and went through different life stages.

Impact of Parenting

In the current era of incessant technology usage, maintaining a digital detox has become increasingly challenging. This sub-theme aims to delve into the impact of parents in navigating this difficult task.

Abigail observes that there was deference for Shabbat in her home;

> 'I think that the way that my parents raised us, it would be disrespectful if it wasn't that environment in the house and they put an emphasis on always having a Shabbat environment.' (Abigail, 20, p.15)

Abigail did not actively choose to embark on a digital detox; rather, it was an inherent aspect of her upbringing. Growing up in a home that valued the sanctity of Shabbat, Abigail was immersed in a home where the atmosphere and boundaries surrounding Shabbat observance were deeply respected. This reverence for Shabbat was instilled in her from a young age, shaping her understanding of how this sacred day should be honoured.

Later, Abigail gives a clue as to how her parents raised her to respect the Shabbat;

> 'I do think that the way my parents made Shabbat largely affected why I enjoy Shabbat so much.' (Abigail, 20, p.19)

The inclusion of the word 'made' when referring to Shabbat highlights the active role that Abigail's parents play in facilitating the observance of Shabbat. It suggests that Shabbat doesn't happen spontaneously or naturally but requires intentional effort and preparation. Abigail's parents are responsible for creating the necessary conditions and arrangements to ensure that Shabbat can be observed properly. Their active involvement is crucial for the establishment and maintenance of the Shabbat experience.

Abigail provides further insight;

> 'I think that the way my parents raised me and my siblings is that they taught us their values and then, once we reached a certain point, like whatever we determined from there we could do... but always in

our house there was a Shabbat environment like a frum (observant) environment ehm, but I think that the way that they raised me was with a lot of leeway which didn't make me want to rebel because there was nothing to rebel against.' (Abigail, 20, p.18)

Growing up, Abigail had the privilege of witnessing a seamless integration between beliefs and actions. Her parents embraced their values with confidence and imparted their traditions to their children, fostering an atmosphere of respect and enjoyment. As the children matured, their parents recognised their autonomy and granted them the freedom to shape their own values and choices. This unconditional acceptance and trust minimised any inclination in Abigail to rebel against her parents' traditions, as she knew that her decisions would be respected and supported, regardless of the path she chose in life. Abigail's brother no longer keeps Shabbat but when he's home he respects the environment at home.

'Yeah, two of my siblings keep Shabbat, one of them doesn't, but when he's home he does.' (Abigail, 20, p.20)

In the household, an implicit code of respect towards parents and the observance of Shabbat permeates the atmosphere. One of the adult siblings lives away from home. However, the bonds with the family remain strong, and there is a mutual understanding and acceptance of individual choices. When this sibling returns to spend Shabbat at home, they willingly embrace the environment of digital detox, honouring and respecting the family's way of life.

Shaul makes a distinction between himself and his peers in regard to how they grew up differently;

'...Yeah, I think maybe the way I was brought up, like I said, was a very positive experience of Shabbat, but I can understand why so many of my friends struggle in this area who didn't have that experience.' (Shaul, 22, p.11)

Shaul feels that maintaining the practice of a digital detox on Shabbat is closely intertwined with childhood experiences of Shabbat. If memories of Shabbat involve a loving and warm atmosphere, filled with joyful moments, individuals are more likely to carry forward these traditions into adulthood when making their own life choices. On the other hand, if their recollections of Shabbat are marked by negativity, with a lack of harmony and effort to create an uplifting experience, the younger generation may choose to break away from these traditions.

Leah also puts a lot of responsibility on parents for creating an atmosphere in the home on Shabbat;

'I think a massive role is to parents cause they set the tone, for, for Shabbat, so I'd say making an active effort to make Shabbat as exciting as the week, 'cause the week is full, it's very difficult to compete because how are you supposed to compete with the online world? But really making effort to make it exciting, enjoyable, making activities, keeping kids busy 'cause boredom is such a massive problem for kids on Shabbat, you know. They have to come away from their screen and what are they going to do? They might build some resentment towards it so they're just keeping everything busy, keeping everyone going and just building a happy atmosphere so that's one of the most important, making sure everyone's calm in a good mood and trying to avoid conflict at all costs, especially 'cause it's it will just get more irritable with the boredom that sort of thing.' (Leah, 20, p.18)

Leah bears witness to her parents' diligent efforts in creating a serene home environment, free from the distractions of screens. They wholeheartedly understand the importance of this responsibility in instilling a deep appreciation for the traditions of Shabbat in their children. Leah recognises that her parents exert considerable energy to ensure that the family is engaged and entertained, addressing the potential hurdle of boredom during Shabbat. They actively curate activities that match the excitement experienced on weekdays, acknowledging that children are often captivated by screen-based stimulation. They are keenly aware that failure to provide engaging alternatives could lead to waning interest and a potential departure from observing Shabbat. Leah perceives this as a significant challenge faced by both parents and children, as they strive to uphold the spirit of Shabbat in a screen-dominated world.

Orly's upbringing was characterised by a harmonious blend of parental guidance and personal freedom;

'I think the good thing about my parents is that they are very much people who want you to explore the religion by yourself. Ehm they're happy to help obviously… they're also very much, you need to figure out for yourself like, if you don't have that sense of independence and if you don't have that space, like if you don't build up your own belief system, then it's much like if you have your own belief system – it's harder to break down than if you don't.' (Orly, 19, p.13)

Orly recognises the strength of her parents as they imparted their way of life and remained a constant source of guidance and support. However, they also believed in the importance of personal responsibility and understanding. They encouraged their children to make their own choices based on their learned beliefs, rather than simply imitating their parents' practices. This freedom allowed for individual growth and, in their view, would foster a stronger faith in the long run.

Similarly, Adina discovered that her parents granted their children a great degree of freedom, and it had positive outcomes;

'Honestly, it's like a bit controversial but the ones who did it and then stopped doing it are the ones whose parents were stuffing it down their throats because like, I don't think it's a coincidence that the three friends I can think of who don't do it anymore all have Rabbi's as parents, all of their friends are Rabbis and Rebbetzens, but I think it was a part of their parents being quite image focussed. I know it sounds really bad, but I think it's like my parents always taught me to love it and to understand the root of it, and they also told me that it's completely my free choice and if I don't want to do it they'll be disappointed but I don't have to do it, which obviously made me want to do it. But I think it happens to be the friends who were told you have to do it, and we're taking you're phone away on Shabbat, who ended up buying other phones and just not doing it because they weren't given that choice.' (Adina, 19, p.20)

Adina contemplates the key factors that contribute to children maintaining their digital detox as they mature. She realises that the essence of Shabbat needs to be deeply internalised and embraced. It cannot be enforced through pressure, social expectations, or external influences. True observance of Shabbat can only emerge when children are given the freedom to make their own choices, even if the outcome may be unpredictable or challenging. She considers this observation to be somewhat 'controversial', as it challenges common expectations. Traditionally, one might assume that the children of Rabbis, who grow up in homes deeply rooted in faith, would be the most devout. However, in her experience, as these children have matured, many have chosen to relinquish the strict responsibilities of an orthodox lifestyle. Adina believes that this outcome is a consequence of teaching Judaism with misguided intentions or improper focus.

Adina highlights another issue, where parents or other adults in the community tend to label or categorise children;

'It would help them do it. I think it would help them do it because also, like, if people, like adults are looking at them and thinking they're rebellious, they're this, they're that, they're just going to act more like that, so that's really damaging.' (Adina, 19, p.21)

Adina has noticed that teenagers as young as fourteen are often subjected to negative labels by elders in the community, branding them as problem children. She strongly feels that such cruel attitudes not only tarnish the reputation of these young individuals and their families but also exacerbate the situation. Adina believes that if adults truly understood the challenges faced by young people in maintaining a digital detox, they would refrain from passing judgment. This judgment only serves to push the children further away from embracing traditions. According to Adina, if children were not singled out or stigmatised for not observing Shabbat, they might discover their own path back to embracing it.

Mendel found that parents who grew up in a different generation don't understand the pull of technology;

'...because their parents didn't grow up with a phone, so they don't understand the sort of relationship that maybe someone who's slightly younger than me would have with their phone, so they won't get that it's not a big deal for the kid to leave it in their room.' (Mendel, 22, p.6)

In Mendel's family, there was a practice of having all the children put their phones away in a designated place before Shabbat.

'I think the self-control that people have, 15-year-olds have, not to go on their phones is underappreciated by adults.' (Mendel, 22, p.22)

Mendel believed this was necessary because the temptation of the phone is so strong that children would find it difficult to resist using it during Shabbat. However, as Mendel reached a level of maturity, this practice ceased, as he was able to exercise self-control without external enforcement. Mendel recognises the generational differences, where parents who grew up without technology may struggle to fully understand the significance of technology in their children's lives.

Dov remembers an otherworldly atmosphere that was prepared by his parents;

'For me, it was beautiful, warm colours, a lot of warmth, warm house. It was nice.' (Dov, 22, p.21)

Dov reminisces about the enchanting and cozy memories of Shabbat. It evokes a sense of magic and warmth, creating a soulful and inviting atmosphere that feels safe, secure, and filled with love. Dov believes that his parents, driven by their love of Shabbat, lovingly prepared these surroundings to instil in him a deep sense of serenity and a feeling of being truly special.

Breaking the Detox

Over half of the participants in this study recollected instances where they broke their digital detox on Shabbat during their younger years. The reasons behind these breaches varied and included factors such as boredom, curiosity, and a lack of understanding regarding the significance of resisting temptation for a greater purpose.

Abigail contemplates various reasons for her attraction to technology on Shabbat, considering boredom and teenage rebellion as potential explanations;

> 'I don't know. I think I was just bored. I think I was minorly rebelling, but I don't know against what because I don't think that my parents really cared that much. I was just bored.' (Abigail, 19, p.17)

Ultimately, she concludes that boredom is the most likely cause for her breaking digital detox on Shabbat. Abigail demonstrates that her primary drive is to achieve overall happiness;

> 'I didn't feel that it was bringing me extra joy, so I just stopped. I think I just grew out of it.' (Abigail, 19, p.17)

Abigail reached the conclusion that using her phone on Shabbat did not bring any significant benefits. Having tried it and realising that her parents were indifferent to it, she determined that it wasn't worthwhile. She believed that there was more to be gained by observing Shabbat properly and engaging in meaningful activities.

Similarly, Leah, driven by curiosity like any normal teenager, discreetly used her phone without her parents' knowledge to see if she was missing out on anything;

> 'Shabbat, when I was younger, I found it more hard to keep because I was, there was a period, there was a very short period where I felt like it wasn't something I wanted to do ehm and I don't remember it adding anything to my life.' (Leah, 20, p.14)

However, her experiment didn't last long, as her curiosity was swiftly satisfied. Like Abigail, Leah also came to the realisation that there were no benefits to using her phone on Shabbat.

Orly encountered challenges in deviating from her family's practices and traditions. She grappled with the discrepancy between her own difficulties in embracing something that seemed to come effortlessly to her family. This internal struggle left her with a sense of isolation and a feeling of being misunderstood.

> 'I think that also, like when I was younger, I didn't really keep Shabbat properly. Like my whole family did and I found it really difficult and like it was something that really didn't come easily to me.' (Orly, 19, p.12)

Orly reflects on her motivation behind breaking her digital detox on Shabbat and links it with a sense of boredom and the need for stimulation;

> 'I just genuinely found it very difficult to not have that distraction, like so I would just use it to like watch things which like now I wouldn't do but then obviously that's what I needed. I was obviously in not the best mindset...' (Orly, 19, p.14)

As a young teenager, she found it challenging to resist the temptation of constant engagement with technology, and that led her to break her detox. Upon further reflection, Orly self-critically ponders the factors that might have led her to succumb to that temptation. In her analysis, she comes to the realisation that there must have been underlying issues or challenges she was facing at that time, which compelled her to engage with technology despite the established boundaries of Shabbat.

As Shaul reflects on his past actions of using devices on Shabbat during his teenage years, he ponders the underlying motivation behind his behaviour. Struggling to find the precise word to describe it, he checks for confirmation and clarity;

> 'Yeah, it was me wanting to play games on my PSP. Ehm what do we call that, desire?' (Shaul, 22, p.5)

Upon introspection, Shaul realises that the word he was searching for is 'desire', as he recalls being strongly attracted to playing video games during his younger teenage years on Shabbat. At that time, he acknowledges that there was no compelling enough reason for him, as a 12 or 13-year-old boy, to resist the allure of his PSP. It was only with maturity and a deeper understanding of the importance of digital detox that he was able to withstand the temptations.

Adina reflects on reasons that make it harder and easier to maintain a digital detox;

> '...definitely being around people who are doing it, I think that's massive... Ehm I also think that like

understanding the reason for it is really important... also how it adds value to our life, and I don't mean that just religiously I mean literally understanding how stressful going online is... I think like being very honest with yourself and recognising how like deeply stressful like technology really is, is probably very helpful to make people want to refrain from it.' (Adina, 19, p.7)

Adina firmly believes that being in the company of others who observe the digital detox on Shabbat makes it easier for her to adhere to it as well. Additionally, she emphasises the importance of having a clear understanding of why she chooses to engage in this detox. Recognising the potential dangers of constant technology use further reinforces her desire to detox from it.

Drawing from her own experience as a teenager who once struggled with breaking the digital detox, Adina provides valuable advice for fellow teens facing similar challenges;

'By going out of your way to learn it so, from a religious perspective, you can listen to podcasts and shiurim (Talmudic study sessions), ehm you can talk to people who know more than you about it. Ehm from like an emotional perspective, I'd say like learning from others is the key, so I'd say like talking to people who are older than you who do it and like talking to them about why they do it and maybe I'd say maybe one most useful thing for younger teenagers who are struggling is maybe talking to, talk to people who are exactly the same as that 'cause

I know for them a lot of the time it feels that everyone else finds it so easy and they don't. Ehm and no one understands that they don't find it easy and they're branded as bad or rebellious or whatever but when actually they're not. They're just finding it really difficult 'cause it is really difficult. Ehm and like to speak to someone who's got more knowledge and more life experience than them and to ehm like be spoken to about why and the benefits of doing it and ehm and also just understand, acknowledgement of just how difficult it is and like acknowledging them and understanding them if that makes sense.' (Adina, 19, p.20)

Adina, having successfully overcome her own challenges, exudes enthusiasm as she shares valuable ideas and tips on how to avoid falling into the trap of breaking a digital detox on Shabbat. Her passion is palpable as she articulates her insights into the detrimental effects that certain community attitudes can have, as well as practical advice that any teenager can benefit from in order to resist the temptation of using technology on Shabbat. Adina takes pride in her personal growth and the positive impact it has had on her life, and she is eager to share these benefits with others.

Keeping the Digital Detox Across Time

This sub-theme conveys the continuity of the digital detox practice over time. Sarah's experience illustrates a shift in her approach to Shabbat as she transitioned from her pre-smartphone youth to her adolescence. During her earlier years, there was a strong focus on keeping Shabbat without any distractions. However, once she obtained a smartphone as an adolescent, she noticed a notable change in her perspective;

> 'Technology didn't play such a big part when I was younger. It wasn't something like, you know... it wasn't even something I thought about because when I was a young kid we were so focussed on playing outside because there were books and always something to do.' (Sarah, 24, p.12)

In Sarah's experience, as a young child, the observance of Shabbat was never in question. She was fully absorbed in play and immersed in reading, completely unaware of the significance of technology. Throughout her primary school years, technology had no relevance or significance in her life, thus eliminating any potential conflicts regarding its use on Shabbat.

Upon entering high school and the onset of adolescence, Mendel became aware of the presence of technology in his life;

> 'I don't even think about it anymore. I think it was probably, it bit more of an occasion when I was younger and I think I've sort of matured into that.' (Mendel, 22, p.1)

Reflecting on those years, he recalls that refraining from using his devices on Shabbat felt like a significant event, indicating a conflict between his desire to use technology and the accompanying feelings of guilt and fear of being caught. However, as Mendel progressed through adolescence, his commitment to Shabbat evolved, and it no longer became a noteworthy occasion. It has now become a natural part of his life, devoid of inner conflict.

By contrast, during Mendel's younger years, he vividly recalls the sensations he experienced while using his phone;

'It's literally flutters in, in my chest.' (Mendel, 22, p.15)

The anticipation of something exciting would create a bodily response within him, heightening his senses and generating a sense of anticipation.

Shaul provides insights into the development of his own personal journey and transformation;

'Ehm I think just at some point in my life ehm I had a decision to make like I was at that point doing it cause I was told to do it and I had to decide for myself do I do it because I'm ehm, do I do it because I want to, because otherwise it's not worth doing.' (Shaul, 22, p.6)

During Shaul's younger years, he recalls a sense of coercion, where he felt obligated to engage in certain practices simply because it was the established family tradition, without questioning or understanding the reasoning behind it. As Shaul grew older, he realised that he had to take ownership of his decisions and understand that he alone would face the consequences of his actions. This led him to contemplate the purpose and meaning behind his family's practices and traditions.

He questioned whether it was beneficial for him to continue following them or if he should break away and pursue a different path that resonated with his own beliefs and values.

Dov underwent a similar process of questioning the practices that had been handed down to him as unquestioned norms;

> '...also you mature a little bit, there's a lot more to life than you know. You start figuring out, I guess, what ehm what is this phone really doing for me?' (Dov, 22, p.16)

As he matured, he began to reflect on the deeper meaning of life and the values that held significance for him. Curiosity led him to contemplate the role of his phone and the impact it had on his overall existence. He delved into the nature of his device and its influence on his sense of self.

Orly observes a connection between her personal journey of maturation and the accompanying cognitive development that unfolded during her adolescence;

> '...I think a lot of people become more religious when they become older, or you feel more comfortable just having that uncertainty. Whether it's your own thoughts or whether it's faith as a whole, you aren't able to handle it.' (Orly, 19, p.15)

Orly perceives this progression as a natural and inherent aspect of growing up. The confusion she experienced during her younger years gradually gave way to a deepening belief in God, which brought a sense of reassurance. Rather than grappling with the uncertainties and complexities of life, particularly during adolescence, her growing faith in God provided a foundation of trust that led to increased religious observance. For Orly, belief in God became a way of navigating life's anxieties and finding solace.

Adina recalls a time in her youth when she felt subject to external forces of power that exerted control over her decisions;

> 'I've also gone through points in my life where I've felt forced into it just because I was 14, 13, whatever. Ehm a lot of people go through like a feeling of being forced into it and then ehm have a meaningful rephrasing perspective, if that makes sense, and review how they see it and learn more about it, so I think knowledge is also definitely a factor.' (Adina, 19, p.19)

As Adina matured and gained independence as an adult, she became less reliant on these dominant influences and began to reflect on her own desires and aspirations separate from the values imposed upon her. She recognises that her experiences resonate with those of many teenagers who grapple with similar challenges. Taking responsibility for her choices as a grown-up has involved developing heightened cognitive abilities that enable her to critically examine her wants and needs in light of her education and the knowledge she has acquired through reading and learning.

This section has explored the evolution of maintaining a digital detox throughout different stages of life, starting from early childhood, progressing through adolescence, and reaching young adulthood. It becomes evident that the transition from adolescence to young adulthood is a profoundly transformative period in a young person's life. During this transition, individuals undergo a metamorphosis, moving from being followers of their parents' values to engaging in personal introspection and contemplating their own beliefs and aspirations. It marks a quest for independence and a search for individual identity and future goals.

5.2.5 *Group Experiential Theme 5*

5. LIVING WITHOUT TECHNOLOGY

This GET emerged from the exploration of how participants spend their time during a digital detox on Shabbat. It covers the powerful influence of technology and the subsequent decision to abstain from it. Within this context, themes of meaning, time, and authenticity also emerged and are integrated into this GET. The focus is on understanding how participants navigate their time and find purpose during the absence of technology, while recognising the broader implications and significance of their choices.

Experiencing the power of technology

This sub-theme conveys the participants' accounts highlighting the powerful allure and attraction they experienced towards their phones. For many of them, the use of technology was described as akin to addiction.

Leah, in particular, was profoundly captivated by technology, to the extent that simply observing Shabbat alone did not provide a satisfactory digital detox. Recognising the need for stricter boundaries, she took proactive steps to implement additional measures and set controls on her phone, allowing herself a daily respite from the constant digital distractions;

'I do have things on my phone to prevent me from, I have to actually put measures on my phone to make sure that I'm not so, so I have filters, I have timers, I have periods of time where I can't turn on my phone that I've put on myself...' (Leah, 20, p.5)

Leah experiences a moment of hesitation as she searches for a word to express her relationship with her phone, perhaps reluctant to acknowledge the addictive nature of her attachment. Instead of finding the word she seeks, she moves forward and begins describing the specific controls she has implemented. These controls are pre-established and she has deliberately set them up to exert authority over her phone usage. By implementing these commands, she feels that she has introduced a necessary controlling power that helps her regulate her technology use. The phrase 'I have to actually' used by Leah indicates her difficulty in fully acknowledging her dependence on technology. It reveals a sense of disbelief that she has reached a point where she feels the need to exert control over herself. By using those words, she subtly expresses her realisation that she has had to take proactive measures to be in charge of her own actions and limit her technology usage. It signifies a recognition of the extent of her dependence and the efforts required to regain control.

Leah is acutely aware of the distinction between having unrestricted access to a smartphone and not having one at all;

> '...having that year of not having too much interaction with social media and having a smartphone and, especially on Shabbat, it made, I realised the change that it made in me. I was much more present. I spent my time a lot better. I actually felt happier, so coming back and having my smartphone again, which was a choice, I felt myself reverting again, reverting back to all my old habits, so I was mindlessly scrolling on my phone every day. I was wasting so much time. I wasn't so sociable as I used to eh and I think just having that difference for over a year especially it really opened me up to this is really controlling my life.' (Leah, 20, p.6)

During her gap year in a seminary in Israel, she experienced a transformative period dedicated to spiritual growth and development, where she immersed herself in studying Torah without the presence of a smartphone. This time allowed her to reflect on the stark contrast between the focused, enriching experience in Israel and the challenges she faced upon returning to the UK and falling back into old patterns associated with smartphone usage.

Similar to Leah, Sarah has also taken steps to control her device usage during weekdays;

> '...what I've done with my phone is I have a like a time limit for all my apps, so I've already set it...' (Sarah, 24, p.19)

Both participants have recognised that limiting their digital engagement to just one day a week leaves them susceptible to the temptations of technology on the remaining six days. They have found that exercising greater control over their device usage throughout the week is necessary to maintain a more balanced and mindful approach to their digital lives.

Sarah contemplates the idea that, apart from Shabbat, she lacks the willpower to voluntarily separate herself from her phone;

> 'I think, in many ways, it has to be if someone's taken it away and locked it up...' (Sarah, 21, p.4)

She acknowledges that unless someone were to physically take her phone away and lock it up, she would be unable to resist its pull and would feel compelled to be constantly connected.

When she disconnects from her phone, she experiences a sense of freedom and liberation;

> '...it's a time when I'm not using technology. I just have that almost like an escape.' (Sarah, 24, p.8)

Without the constant presence of her technology, she feels unencumbered and unrestricted, as if the chains that bind her have been released.

Mendel discovers that his phone provides a constant source of busyness and distraction irrespective of whether he is truly occupied;

'I'd never go on a walk with my family on a random Tuesday ehm, you know, because naturally the phone sort of makes you busier, even if you don't have anything to do, and the phone makes you do one thing after the other and then you wouldn't do I'd say very basic things like, for example, go on a walk or, you know, like go to your neighbours.' (Mendel, 22, p.2)

The mere presence of his phone creates a perception of busyness in a never-ending cycle as one task leads to the next without stopping. This reaches the extent that there is complete neglect of what he considers 'basic things' as his time and attention is completely consumed by his phone.

Later, Mendel thinks of the right word for how his phone relates to him;

'...It's more of a stimulant so you get stimulation or like your brain sort of gets, mine lights up way brighter than if you were just having a very mundane conversation. Ehm well, it's it shouldn't be considered mundane, but you know, in relation to ehm whatever's going on in your brain, it I think I would use that word a stimulant probably ehm, but yeah.' (Mendel, 22, p.3)

Mendel has searched his mind for a suitable description of the experience he undergoes when his phone is within reach. He sought to articulate the phenomenon of neglecting fundamental and vital activities while being engrossed with his phone. He arrived at the word 'stimulant' and, by reaching this term, Mendel draws a parallel to the effects of substances that flood the brain with dopamine, a pleasure-inducing chemical known to have addictive properties. By contrast, Mendel finds conversations with his family to be 'mundane', as they fail to elicit the same level of excitement in his brain as his interactions with technology. However, upon reflection, he realises that these conversations are not inherently dull, but rather seem that way in comparison to the stimulating experiences he has with his devices.

Whilst on Shabbat, Dov's phone serves solely as an alarm. During the week, he feels the need to check his phone 'every 20 minutes' despite it giving him a headache;

> 'Youtube, BBC News or BBC Sport, that's what I, always checking BBC Sport every 20 minutes, every half an hour and the news or something. It gets quite, you know, a headache even, watching screens and checking things.' (Dov, 22, p.6)

Dov checks his phone for news or sport more frequently than the news is updated and will withstand physical discomfort in order to do so.

Later, Dov explains how he could survive a headache to be on technology;

> '...somehow the addiction of it somehow pulls you in and yet you are like at the same time I don't want to be here, kind of. Trapped by it in a sense, kind of. That's part of the need you have to get out of it.' (Dov, 22, p.16)

Dov feels a sense of helplessness as technology exerts control over him, against his own desires. He finds himself held hostage, unable to escape its grip. Despite his reluctance, he sees no viable means of breaking free from its influence. The enticing nature of technology is so strong that it overwhelms his ability to resist.

Dov's remarks allude to the constant pursuit of pleasure, akin to what Shaul in the excerpt below describes as the seeking of 'dopamine'. Dov implies that he, like many others, is enticed by the allure of instant pleasure and gratification provided by his phone. This behaviour reflects the prevalent desire for dopamine-induced experiences, which can have addictive tendencies and hinder the pursuit of more substantial and fulfilling endeavours.

> '…always having that dopamine eh, so not having that it's almost like a reset, so that's very beneficial and healthy.' (Shaul, 22, p.4)

Shaul acknowledges the impact of his phone on his well-being by referring to the release of 'dopamine', a chemical in the brain associated with pleasure and reward. This choice of words indicates that Shaul perceives his engagement with technology as an addictive activity. However, he also recognises that Shabbat serves as a crucial 'reset' for him, allowing him to restore equilibrium in both his body and soul. This implies that the dopamine rush he experiences from his phone is detrimental to his overall balance, and Shabbat provides him with an opportunity to regain that balance.

Leah experiences a sense of helplessness and lack of control over her phone;

'It's a shame to feel there's something you feel obligated towards when you're in a period when you shouldn't be...' (Leah, 20, p.4)

She expresses sadness as she realises that her phone has become an 'obligation' that she feels she should have power over. This feeling of obligation seems to overpower her, leaving her with a sense of powerlessness and a lack of autonomy. The phone exerts control over her instead of her having control over it.

All participants shared a common experience of feeling that their phones represented a power greater than themselves, something they struggled to control. Some recognised that the digital detox on Shabbat alone was not enough to address this issue and, as a result, they chose to implement self-imposed digital detoxes during weekdays by using phone controls and limitations. The success of these measures varied among participants.

The decision to introduce these limitations stemmed from a realisation that their phones were negatively impacting their lives. They felt they were wasting valuable time and losing control over the influence of their phones. In addition to the loss of control, some participants also experienced anxiety related to their phones, fearing misrepresentation or negative consequences.

Routine During Shabbat

Maintaining a digital detox is challenging. This sub-theme covers how the participants from Generation Z in this study spend their Shabbat. The aim is to gain insights into how they occupy their time and explore the activities they engage in as alternatives to spending time on technology. By examining their chosen pursuits, we can gain a better understanding of the meaningful experiences and endeavours that take precedence during this technology-free period.

Abigail emphasises the significance of having structure in her day, particularly during Shabbat;

> '...having my friends come round or going to see my friends, or like, even having a book, having a proper Shabbat lunch and Friday night dinner, so I'm not waking up and then being like, now what? Like a routine to my day, kind of.' (Abigail, 19, p.20)

Certain aspects of this structure are predictable and well-prepared, such as the planned meals. However, there are other elements that are less predictable, such as the availability of friends or an engaging book to read. These factors require weekly planning to ensure a fulfilling experience. On the other hand, the Shabbat meals are inherently connected to the routine of the day and may vary in terms of hosting or being hosted by guests, but Abigail is certain that they will always be part of the Shabbat experience.

For Abigail, one of the notable aspects of her Shabbat routine is shared mealtimes;

> 'Yeah, my entire life Friday night dinner has been with my extended family – my grandparents, my cousins, my aunts and uncles – every single week,

so it is very much like family time.' (Abigail, 19, p.13)

This holds particular significance because, despite living nearby, their interactions during weekdays are often hindered by distractions like technology. If they were to gather on regular days, the presence of technology would divide their attention, preventing them from fully experiencing and engaging with one another. However, Shabbat offers a distinct contrast. During this time, not only do wider family members come together to dine, but they also have the opportunity to genuinely connect and experience one another's presence.

For Orly, incorporating extra sleep into her Shabbat routine holds great significance;

'it's really, really good to just catch up on sleep.' (Orly, 19, p.7)

The repetition of the word 'really' emphasises just how important this additional sleep is for her. The phrase 'catch up' suggests that Orly is unable to get sufficient sleep during the weekdays, possibly due to the distractions of her phone keeping her awake at night. However, during Shabbat, when she is free from the grip of technology, she can make up for these lost hours and recharge her energy levels.

Shaul also identifies the need for sleep as part of his routine on Shabbat;

'I do not get enough sleep during the week, ehm but Friday night I'm getting at least eight hours plus a

nap on Shabbat afternoon, so I get a lot more sleep.'
(Shaul, 22, p.3)

Shaul, like Orly, acknowledges that he often experiences insufficient sleep during weekdays, and he utilises Shabbat as a period of rejuvenation to replenish the lost sleep from the week. These accounts highlight the notion that time away from technology presents an opportune moment to prioritise one's bodily needs and engage in rest when it is necessary. On Shabbat, there are no competing obligations that overshadow self-care, allowing ample time to attend to personal well-being without the constant pressure to be occupied with other tasks.

The importance of having structure on Shabbat becomes evident when considering the challenges of maintaining a digital detox. Without a framework, it would be significantly harder, if not impossible, to resist the magnetic pull of technology. In order for the replacement activities to be effective, they must be predictable, meaningful and enjoyable, providing a sense of respite and fulfilment that can rival the allure of technology.

Attitudes Towards Shabbat

In this sub-theme, participants provide their perspectives on their digital detox and the significance of Shabbat.

Abigail acknowledges that she is only able to maintain her digital detox because of the observance of Shabbat, she cannot imagine doing so otherwise;

'I think, if it was a random day and I knew that I could, I don't know that I would be able to do it.' (Abigail, 19, p.12)

This observation suggests two things: firstly, that phones and digital devices hold such a strong allure that it requires a significant force to disconnect from them, and secondly, it emphasises the power of Shabbat in enabling Abigail to separate herself from her devices in a way that nothing else could. Shabbat holds a unique and powerful influence in enabling Abigail's digital detox which would otherwise be impossible.

Abigail recognises the magic of Shabbat and understands that there is a significant reason behind her ability to abstain from phone usage for a full 25 hours;

'I like the break, I like the family time, I like the tradition of it. I think that if I didn't enjoy Shabbat, I probably wouldn't keep it. And so the fact that I do enjoy it makes me not want to do any of these things.' (Abigail, 19, p.12)

Shabbat offers a highly positive and fulfilling experience that encompasses precious moments and carries deep meaning through the continuation of a family practice that has endured for generations. Abigail is clear about one crucial factor: she enjoys Shabbat, and it is this enjoyment that enables her to maintain her digital detox. While being a link in a chain that preserves old family traditions holds meaning, it alone would not be enough to overcome the temptation of her technology. It is the personal benefit and fulfilment she derives from observing Shabbat that serves as her motivation to disconnect from her devices.

Abigail further emphasises this point by reflecting on an older sibling who is no longer observant of Shabbat;

> 'I do think that the main reason I keep Shabbat is because I enjoy it and if he wasn't enjoying it then I'm sure that that is what led to him not keeping it.' (Abigail, 19, p.15)

In her observation, she firmly believes that for young adults, the pursuit of pleasure holds primary importance. While tradition, spirituality, the search for meaning, and personal well-being may play smaller roles, the dominant factor is the hedonistic pursuit of pleasure among Gen Z individuals. Abigail is certain that if Shabbat did not bring enjoyment, it would lead to disconnection and disengagement.

Shaul acknowledges multiple reasons for his commitment to observing Shabbat, including the spiritual aspect and a sense of fear;

> '…there's the religious side of it as well that I, I don't want to be breaking any of the laws of Shabbat, so to keep the laws of Shabbat is inherently to be happy with your digital detox.' (Shaul, 22, p.5)

As a religious individual, he experiences a reverent fear of the consequences that may arise from not observing Shabbat. For Shaul, the fear and happiness associated with Shabbat are intertwined and inseparable.

The fear of breaking Shabbat is ingrained in him, and it brings him a sense of tranquillity to abide by its laws. He sees the decision to keep Shabbat as one that is commanded by God, and the fear he feels of breaking it is accompanied by a sense of pleasure in fulfilling God's commandment.

Leah expresses her perspective on Shabbat, viewing it as a sanctuary where she can truly be herself, liberated from the overpowering influence of her phone and the digital world it represents;

> 'I guess it is just what Shabbat is, it really is just a, a sense of freedom from everything. There's a massive relief when it comes in cause I know there's nothing else, nothing I have to do that, nothing I have to, you know, keep up with. I just have to be and function and see the people that I love and that's really just in itself a massive weight off my shoulders.' (Leah, 19, p.13)

Shabbat provides her with a profound sense of peace, as she no longer feels the need to engage in activities such as shopping, running errands, or utilising transportation. Everything she requires is already present in her immediate surroundings, and preparations have been made in advance, including meals that require no cooking. This self-contained environment allows Leah to be in the company of her loved ones, experiencing a sense of fulfilment and self-sufficiency.

Leah succinctly captures her sentiments about Shabbat, encapsulating the shared experiences of all participants.

Despite the acknowledged difficulties and withdrawal symptoms associated with their digital detox, Leah offers insight into the wellspring of her resilience. She finds solace and empowerment in the sense of liberation and lightness that Shabbat brings, enabling her to successfully navigate the digital detox period. Moreover, she recognises the inherent importance of this experience in nurturing a healthy sense of self, eagerly anticipating its arrival throughout the week.

Discussion and Conclusion

Introduction

This study aimed to gain a rich, in-depth understanding of the lived experiences of a weekly digital detox every Shabbat for young Jewish adults. Semi-structured interviews with five women and three men aged between 19-24 were used to gather data which was then analysed using Interpretative Phenomenological Analysis. Five Group Experimental Themes arose, containing a total of 18 sub-themes. In this chapter, the main findings from these themes will be summarised through the lens of current research and supported within the framework of existential theory. This chapter will then discuss the Four-Dimensions Criteria within the research context, followed by the implications of this study for counselling and therapy and also for society. The strengths and limitations of the study are then considered and areas for future research are recommended. Finally, this chapter ends with a closing reflexivity and a conclusion.

It is important to acknowledge that the inclusion of references to literature not initially covered in the initial literature review is a direct outcome of unexpected themes that emerged during the interview process. This occurrence can be attributed to the inherent nature of Interpretative Phenomenological Analysis (IPA), as highlighted by Smith et al. (2009, p.113) who states that "the interview and analysis process often lead researchers into previously unexplored and unforeseen areas."

5.3 Summary of Main Findings

5.3.1 Main Findings – Detox and Relationships

1. Detox and Relationships

This Theme conveyed the difference between physical presence and a genuine sense of presence within families. Participants in the study only experienced actual presence during Shabbat due to the absence of technological distractions. The lack of technology created spare time, fostering genuine listening and communication among family members and between friends. Participants in the study noticed positive aspects to their relationships with friends and family during Shabbat due to face-to-face interactions without technology. Bonds were strengthened, and families reconnected on Shabbat without distractions from competing interests on digital technology.

It was found that participating in a digital detox on Shabbat is widely supported by both family and community. This engenders a sense of togetherness, as participants can share their experiences with those around them. Engaging in a digital detox on Shabbat within a like-minded community provides a respite from technology without the associated anxiety of missing out and creates opportunities to engage in alternative activities together. This fosters a sense of unity and shared purpose, as everyone within the community is observing Shabbat simultaneously. Furthermore, opportunities for activities such as volunteering are facilitated and encouraged. The attitudes of others outside the Jewish community contrasted with the experience of maintaining a digital detox within a community, as participants had to navigate the challenge of explaining their detox while having non-Jewish or non-Shabbat-observant associates.

The discovery of "real presence" is substantiated by research conducted by (Misra et al., 2014) who found that the mere presence of a silent mobile device on a table influenced conversations, making them feel more fulfilling, compared to situations where mobile devices were absent. Additionally, Misra et al. (2014) discovered that relationships devoid of mobile devices exhibited higher levels of empathic concern, further supporting that computer-mediated usage competes with genuine social interaction and intimacy, as Turkle (2017) discussed. Dwyer et al. (2018) found that people enjoyed meals with friends significantly less when they had access to their phones compared to when their phones were kept aside. These findings are in line with Navon and Gopher (1979), whose research revealed the limited nature of attention as a cognitive resource. Furthermore, Hiniker et al. (2016) found in their study that parents who frequently used their phones often missed their children's attempts to seek attention. In a study conducted in the USA and Israel, researchers (Ellis et al., 2019) observed that parents who were absorbed in their phones were emotionally and mentally unavailable for their children in the locations of playgrounds and eateries, regardless of their children's requests for attention, help, or to give praise. These parents displayed little or no communication with their children, turned away from them, and rarely made eye contact. The researchers suggest that this phone-related disengagement could potentially compromise children's safety and emotional well-being. The findings are consistent with this study's adult participants, who similarly observed that their parents were tuned out to them on weekdays in the presence of their phones compared to Shabbat, where they felt they could engage in conversation and attunement.

Participants discovered that Shabbat was not a time to address utilitarian needs or engage in discussions but to be present at the moment and connect without requesting favours. Buber referred to the profound engagement with and recognition of another person's essential nature as "confirmation". He held that our inherent ability to confirm others, and to receive confirmation of our own individuality from others, is the foundation of our humanity. At the core of the I-Thou encounter and human flourishing lies confirmation. This concept is akin to the idea of avoiding "conditions of worth" in a relationship. Buber contrasted this I-Thou relationship with an I-It relationship in which the other person is viewed as an object to be manipulated or utilised as a means to an end (Buber, 2012; Martin & Cowan, 2019). Confirmation goes beyond a mere social or interpersonal interaction and involves a genuine appreciation, understanding, and knowledge of the other person's perspective, emotions, and desires. This requires a leap into the other person's life, where they are fully present and appreciated for their unique qualities and individuality. Any confirmation that is not experienced in this manner is superficial and lacks authenticity (Friedman, 2008).

Philosopher Martin Buber detailed the qualities that characterise a real "encounter", or I–Thou meeting, between two people. During this interaction, a novel aspect of human connection that Buber referred to as "the between" is made evident. When this between dimensions exists, the relationship transcends the individual contributions of those involved. Buber referred to this type of encounter as an I-Thou relationship. The I-Thou relationship is marked by reciprocity, immediacy, presence, intensity, and ineffability. Buber characterised the between as a courageous leap into the other person's experience while remaining open, present, and accessible. He used the term "inclusion" to describe this heightened form of empathy. This is a far cry from the typical scenario of a group of friends gathered around a table at a restaurant, all fixated on their smartphones (Buber, 2012; Martin & Cowan, 2019).

According to Buber (Buber, 2012; Martin & Cowan, 2019), the encounter between the I and Thou is the most significant aspect of human experience because it is through relationships that we attain our full humanity. When we encounter another person as Thou, we recognise their uniqueness and separateness without losing sight of our shared humanness and connection. The I-It world may be orderly and efficient, but it lacks the vital elements of human connection and completeness that are intrinsic to the I-Thou encounter.

Researchers have found that technoference (shorthand for technology-based interference) and phubbing (phone snubbing) can have adverse effects on relationships since a partner may view attention to one's phone as a sign that they are not the primary focus or that expectations within the relationship are being breached (Halpern & Katz JE, 2017; Krasnova EL et al., 2016; McDaniel BT & Coyne SM, 2016a; McDaniel BT & Coyne SM, 2016a; McDaniel BT et al., 2018; Roberts JA & David ME, 2016). McDaniel and Drouin (2019) further contribute to the existing body of empirical research by demonstrating that, from an individual's perspective, perceived technoference on a daily basis is linked to higher levels of conflict, fewer positive face-to-face interactions, negative mood, and poorer relationship quality. Our ability to assess these outcomes on a daily basis indicates that each potential pathway from technoference to negative relationship consequences has immediate and potentially cumulative impacts.

The absence of technology during Shabbat allowed participants in this study to have more meaningful and personal conversations where they felt valued and heard. It also gave them the opportunity to spend quality time with their families and choose their social interactions more thoughtfully. Without distractions, people were able to appreciate the present moment and connect with others on a deeper level.

Previous studies on digital detox have demonstrated limited success when individuals attempt to observe it in isolation. Thommee et al. (2011) highlighted the negative consequences of constantly being accessible and reachable through mobile phones. Their research indicated that participants experienced stress, depression, and sleep problems due to the perception that everyone else was readily available while they felt the need to be constantly accessible. In contrast, the present study suggests that the sense of keeping a digital detox within the context of a family and community may serve as a protective factor against stress. This finding aligns with Thomas et al. (2016), who examined the costs and benefits of constant digital connectivity across different age groups. Their research identified significant challenges to unplugging, particularly when individuals were the only ones disconnected from devices in social settings among friends and family members who were habitually engaged with technology. Fear of missing out (FOMO) has recently emerged in the literature as people feel the need to be constantly connected with one another and up to date on each others' lives (Przybylski, 2013).

This sentiment is exemplified in a quote from a college student in the study by Thomas et al. (2016), who expressed a desire for those around them, including their spouse, family, and friends, to occasionally take a break from digital devices during their shared time together. "However, I often wish those around me (spouse, family, friends) would sometimes take a break when we are together". This finding is consistent with Hiniker et al. (2016), whose study showed that both parents and children believed that parents should disconnect from technology when spending time with family.

Participants in the present study recognised the stress that came with disconnecting from their technology, but unlike participants from Thomee et al.'s study (2016), they did not feel a sense of fear or anxiety associated with missing out on anything. This was due to the fact that they kept their technology detox within a larger community and found support from others within it. By doing so, they were able to alleviate any negative feelings and remain focused on their overall goal of disconnecting.

Sartre's famous description of peeping through a keyhole highlights how humans consider their actions in view of others (Sartre, 2021). Initially, we are pre-reflectively absorbed in the scene on the other side of the door, with minimal self-awareness. However, when we hear footsteps, we suddenly become aware of ourselves as an object in the eyes of another. This involuntary apprehension of ourselves as an object produces a "pre-moral" experience of shame without any cognitive processing. Sartre suggests that this ontological shift is triggered by the presence of another person, adding a significant and distinctive dimension to our experience of others as both objects and subjects. The experience of participants in their digital detox is comparable to Sartre's description of how humans view their actions in the presence of others. When participants engaged in the detox within their families, negotiation was unnecessary as it was a shared experience. However, when they reflected on their detox in view of peers who were not observing it, participants had to apply reflexive thought to consider how they might be perceived and judged by others. In this context, "the other" refers to those who do not share the digital detox experience. This highlights how the presence of others brings a different consciousness of ourselves as objects in the eyes of others.

5.3.2 Main Findings – Detox and Impact of Self

2. Detox and Impact of Self

This theme elucidated the effects of participants' digital detox on their sense of self. It encompassed various aspects, such as an increase in reading time, the experience of anxiety related to digital technology, enhanced feelings of well-being, and their perspectives on who else could benefit from a digital detox.

All the participants in the study shared their unique experiences of how Shabbat provided them with an opportunity for reading or learning, where they experienced the joy of immersing themselves in books. They found that the absence of technology during Shabbat made reading more appealing as they admitted to being constrained by distractions that limited their reading time to Shabbat. Some participants reflected on how reading was an activity they cherished during their younger years but gradually neglected as teenagers when smartphones entered their lives.

This finding aligns with other studies. For example, Morris and Pickens (2017) analysed 39 stories found on websites and found that participants reported a number of positive experiences during their unplugging period, especially in the realm of personal growth. As people recognised the extra time they had, they sought out new ways to spend it or to re-engage in activities that they had previously neglected, such as reading. Aligning with accounts from this study, one participant shared their experience, which involved finishing a book that they had been intending to read for a long time and taking an early morning walk. They mentioned that they often took walks, but this time, without their phone distracting them, they noticed new things that they had never seen before (Morris & Pickens, 2017). Similarly, Loh and Sun (2022) found that data from interviews with adolescents supported a common theme that the adolescents in the study had less time to read as they got older because of the competing demands of schoolwork and other activities, resulting in less leisure time. Moreover, some adolescents reported that having greater access to their own smartphones was a hindrance to reading. This discovery corresponds with the participants in this study, who noted that they ceased reading when they acquired their initial smartphones and now only read on Shabbat.

This theme highlighted how, on the one hand, phones bring about anxieties for their users, while on the other hand, being disconnected from their technology during Shabbat introduces a different set of anxieties, and participants experienced both simultaneously. They found relief from the anxiety of being constantly connected to their phones, yet they also felt a desperate longing to be back on their phones. Some participants also experienced a heightened awareness of feelings of lack of control and anxiety associated with being present with themselves without the distraction of their phones. Abigail found that her anxiety increased during the COVID-19 pandemic because of constant access to the news and that these feelings subsided during her digital detox. This is supported by Hoyt et al. (2021), who found in an online survey of 480 adults that increased exposure duration to the news predicted greater anxiety.

Studies on nomophobia found that there are feelings of anxiety and fear associated with being unable to communicate via mobile phone or the internet, which is common in the technical world (Adawi et al., 2019; Sun et al., 2022). Nomophobia (No Mobile Phone Phobia) has been found among young generations aged 18-24, delineating complex impacts on personal well-being (Essel et al., 2022).

Yao and Wang (2022) analysed the responses of 540 university students to a survey and found that technostress related to smartphone use was positively associated with compulsive smartphone use and information overload and that technostress was also associated with poor sleep quality. The predictive effects of compulsive smartphone use and information overload on technostress suggest that controlling these stressors may help alleviate technostress among students. The current study revealed that sleep quality was enhanced on Friday nights, supporting the negative effects of technology on sleep. However, the findings also suggest that a certain level of anxiety related to mobile phone usage may persist despite efforts to limit or avoid technology use.

This theme also found that embracing short-term difficulties can lead to a sense of well-being in the long run. In a 14-day diary study conducted by McDaniel and Drouin (2019), participants recorded their daily experiences and emotions, providing valuable insights into their own and their partner's daily behaviours and emotional states. The fluctuations in technoference on a daily basis were found to predict conflict arising from technology use, the quality of face-to-face interactions, negative mood, and daily assessments of relationship quality. Furthermore, technoference was found to be correlated with depression and attachment anxiety, both of which were linked to relationship satisfaction. The daily use of phones was found to have a significant impact on mood, quality of interactions, perceptions of relationship quality, and couple conflict beyond general relationship dissatisfaction and any feelings of depression or attachment anxiety. These findings suggest that, regardless of an individual's or a couple's current level of well-being, the perception of technology interfering with interactions with one's partner can have negative effects. Smith-Gabai's (2011) research supports the notion that observing Sabbat can have positive effects on well-being and alleviate burnout. However, this study found that this does not necessarily translate to immediate feelings of well-being or satisfaction in relationships or other areas of life.

Findings from Dein, and Loewenthal (2013) with regards to unplugging on Shabbat are mixed when it comes to feelings of well-being and align closely with participants from this study. Dein and Lowenthal reported that Shabbat can be a paradoxical experience as it offers positive psychological benefits, but sometimes it can exacerbate worries. While the freedom from work and weekday concerns may create a sense of relief for some, it can also create a void that may be filled with worries and preoccupations, leaving people feeling helpless to take action. Although the lack of distractions may make individuals feel better, it can also lead to increased depression as they become more aware of their everyday thoughts and feel powerless to address them. While Shabbat offers a reprieve from daily tasks and responsibilities, it also means that any forgotten tasks cannot be addressed until after the day of rest. Furthermore, since electronics are prohibited, individuals have more time to think, which may cause negative thoughts to escalate. Therefore, while Shabbat can provide a much-needed break from the stresses of daily life, it can also amplify worries and negative thoughts.

Shaul views his weekly detox as a similar undertaking to therapy, where it feels difficult in the short term but is an investment for the long term. Although he experiences mixed emotions during Shabbat, he is certain that his overall health would suffer if he did not adhere to his digital detox routine. By taking a break from technology on Shabbat, Shaul can regulate his emotions and order his thoughts. He acknowledges that enduring the discomfort and pain in the short term will yield long-term benefits for his well-being. This finding was a shared experience among all participants, who recognised that the challenges and stress of disconnection from technology were ultimately beneficial for their overall well-being. Despite the difficulties that came with the digital detox process, they all believed that the benefits of taking a break from technology outweighed the inconveniences. In essence, they viewed the temporary discomfort as a worthwhile investment in their long-term health and happiness.

This theme conveyed the belief indicated by all participants that a digital detox would have positive effects on others. They acknowledged the significance of sharing the valuable experiences they gained from their own detox and recognised that various groups of people could particularly benefit from taking a break from technology. According to the participants, adolescents and young people would experience positive outcomes by engaging in a digital detox and reducing mindless and constant scrolling through social media. This aligns with research indicating a correlation between continuous usage of social media and heightened levels of stress. Beyens et al. (2016) studied 402 adolescents' Facebook use and perceived stress as a result of FOMO associated with its use. Results found that adolescents' need to belong and need for popularity were related to increased FOMO associated with constant access to social media, increasing feelings of stress. This stress increased when adolescents perceived themselves as being unpopular on Facebook.

Through three studies, Sagioglou and Greitemeyer (2014), investigated the proposition that engaging in Facebook activities has an adverse impact on individuals' emotional state. The first study revealed that the longer individuals spent on Facebook, the more negative their moods became afterwards. The second study offered causal evidence for this outcome by demonstrating that Facebook use led to a deterioration in mood compared to two distinct control conditions. The study indicated that this effect was mediated by a sense of having accomplished nothing meaningful. Despite such negative consequences for its users, the question remains as to why many people continue to utilise Facebook daily. A third study proposed that this may be due to an affective forecasting error, wherein individuals anticipate feeling better after engaging with Facebook, whereas, in reality, they feel worse. The results of this study are in line with the recommendations made by participants in this research, who believed that all individuals would benefit from decreasing their time spent on social media. They also felt that young people, in particular, should take a step back and become aware of what they may be missing out on. Constantly being immersed in social media can lead to negative feelings that are beyond an individual's control, resulting in a situation where they become passive and mindlessly enslaved to media.

Abigail, Adina, Sarah and Shaul found that teens would benefit from disconnecting from social media to help them shift focus to the real world and the people in their everyday lives who represent more realistic notions of appearance, behaviour, and eating habits. Myers et al. (2012) found in a questionnaire survey of 91 undergraduate women that there is a relationship between social comparisons and body image disturbance. Findings revealed that women who internalised the thin ideal more frequently compared themselves to others in terms of their appearance. This internalisation also made them more likely to feel bad about themselves when they made these comparisons.

The widespread use of social media and the rapid growth of Internet usage among teenagers create novel dynamics and hazards for the emergence and perpetuation of eating disorders. Recent studies elucidate the correlation between the use of the Internet and social media and the risk of developing eating disorders, with the most significant links observed among young individuals who heavily participate in photo-based activities and platforms (Saul et al., 2022).

The results align with those of Fardouly et al. (2015) indicating that individuals who utilised Facebook reported feeling more negative compared to those who utilised the control website. Additionally, women with a greater tendency for appearance comparison reported experiencing more disparities in facial, hair, and skin-related aspects following exposure to Facebook than the control website (Fardouly et al., 2015). The situation is less certain for boys as the links between social media and body satisfaction and overall well-being are still not fully comprehended (Jarman et al., 2021).

5.3.3 Main Findings – Meaning of Shabbat

3. Meaning of Shabbat

Shabbat presents a distinctive realm in time and space. Participants perceive Shabbat and weekdays as separate entities with distinct characteristics and disparities. They acknowledge that it is impossible to exist in both worlds simultaneously, as they are distant and distinct from each other. Upon transitioning from the realm of Shabbat, they fully immerse themselves in the other world, becoming attuned to its demands and dynamics. Smith-Gabai (2011) writes that the practice of Sabbath keeping remains pertinent in contemporary times due to its function as a restful refuge or counterweight to the fast-paced nature of modern life, which involves constant exposure to stimuli, technological advancements, and our dependence on electronic gadgets.

The Sabbat has been likened to an "island in time" (Donin, 2019; Weiss & Levy, 2010) due to its potential to alleviate the pressures of the workweek. By offering distance from the source of stress, the Shabbat can serve as a useful coping mechanism for managing and recovering from stress (Eden, 2001). Shabbat keeping is rooted in temporal context, as a crucial aspect of the Sabbat is the demarcation of the week into sacred time versus mundane time. Mundane time encompasses daily activities such as work, self-care, and recreational pursuits, while the Sabbat serves as the focal point of the week, incorporating religious practices that imbue holiness and spirituality into rest, contemplation, and family time (Diamant & Cooper, 2009; Frank et al., 1997).

This theme illustrates how participants use Shabbat as a time to search for meaning. Unlike weekdays, where time is often spent on technology, they engage in active rather than passive activities on Shabbat, prioritising those that contribute to their personal growth. Participants sought fulfilment through connecting with themselves and pursuing activities that brought them a sense of pride and satisfaction without the need for external validation or recognition. They recognised the need to put in the effort to seek out activities that truly satisfied them, leaving them with a sense of accomplishment. Leah, for instance, has discovered that Shabbat provides her with an opportunity for self-exploration and introspection in her quest for meaning. Observing the Sabbath allows individuals to contemplate the significance and aim of their lives, enabling them to express their religious beliefs and cultivate a stronger connection with a higher power (Gurock, 2006). The concept of physical, mental, and emotional rest and rejuvenation is one of the most essential components of the Sabbath, according to Gabai-Smith, who illustrates how the structure, purpose, and significance of a religious practice can yield beneficial outcomes for its participants. (2011).

> "Are we really justified in diagnosing a sociogenic neurosis? Consider today's society: it gratifies and satisfies virtually every need – except the one, the need for meaning!" (Frankl, 1963)

This quote relates to the participants who recognise the value of engaging in meaningful activities during digital detox rather than letting time slip away mindlessly scrolling on their phones, as they do on weekdays. By engaging in activities that feel meaningful to them, they fulfil their need for purpose and significance, which may not be adequately met in their daily lives. This highlights the importance of seeking out activities that provide a sense of fulfilment and purpose, particularly in a society that may not prioritise this need.

Heidegger (2008) emphasises that Time is synonymous with Being, and Being is synonymous with Time. The prevalence of clock time in modern society, driven by money and technology, can lead us to equate time with mere exchange values that lack genuine significance in our daily lives. Genuine, authentic time is always non-negotiable, and it reminds us of our finite existence. Each participant perceived time differently on Shabbat and expressed their experiences in a manner that felt significant to them. The Jewish Sabbath establishes a tempo and structure to the week by emphasising time through its prescribed rituals and activities (Smith-Gabai, 2011). Diamant and Cooper (2009) observed that the Sabbath is perceived as a day that distinguishes itself from the other weekdays. Zerubavel (1982) noted that the Jewish people were the pioneers in organising their lives according to a weekly cycle of time. Distinguished from other time measurements in Western society, the week is not tied to nature. The notion of designating one day out of seven for rest and contemplation was a revolutionary idea, as leisure and introspection were previously reserved for the affluent and ruling classes only. (Heschel, 2005, p.8) stated that "Judaism is a religion of time aiming at the sanctification of time" and "Judaism teaches us to be attached to holiness in time" and referred to the Sabbath as a "palace in time" (Heschel, 2005, p.15).

Morris and Pickens (2017) conducted a study that analysed publicly shared stories on blogs, websites, and news articles detailing experiences of disconnecting from media. The study found that participants reported a sensation of reclaiming time and vitality as they continued their experience of unplugging. This was manifested in two key domains: devoting time to personal growth and reconnecting with family and friends. This supports participants' experiences of finding that they reclaimed time on Shabbat.

Muller (2000) observes that the Sabbat provides an opportunity for deep rest and mindfulness, allowing us to ponder the actions we must take in a complex and ever-evolving world. This finding concurs with participants in this study, who found that having uninterrupted time, without external pressures, allows them to delve deeply into ideas and concepts and arrive at solutions that require time and reflection. Participants realise that this extended period of contemplation enables them to make better decisions by considering various perspectives and possibilities thoroughly. Other participants recognised that uninterrupted time to think without distractions was beneficial enough. The opportunity for contemplation during Sabbat can serve as a reminder of our interconnectedness with both each other and nature. This reflection can inspire us to pursue change in the world during the rest of the week (Speedling, 2019).

This theme centres on the participants' encounters with authenticity and the distinction they perceived between what they regarded as "real" life, where they engage deliberately and make intentional choices, and "not real" life, which occurs when they are unaware of how they spend their time, particularly when using technology. The participants acknowledged that during these "not real" moments, they lose valuable time from their lives, resulting in a sense of disconnection from their authentic selves. They believed that genuine authenticity arises from living consciously and being completely present in their experiences rather than being consumed by technology. This aligns with the findings of Syversten and Enli (2019), who stated that digital detox is a way for individuals seeking authenticity to counter the artificial communication often associated with online experiences. It taps into a phenomenon where individuals desire an experience that is more genuine than what they find online.

Dov notes that when he is surrounded by people using devices, he feels disconnected and believes that basic human qualities are lost. Dov perceives interruptions on phones, where information is shared, as having a non-human quality, and he described it as an inhuman experience that feels disconnected from his authentic self. In a similar experience by Morris and Pickens (2017), one participant experienced a sense of dehumanisation due to their mindless use of technology and disconnection from the world, leading them to feel like "robot-like humans" who primarily acquire knowledge by accessing the vast "hive mind" of the Internet.

Sartre's notion of bad faith provides an innovative and productive explanation of human self-deception. According to Sartre, our capacity to deceive ourselves stems from the fact that we are always free to be something other than what we are. This freedom can be a source of both comfort and anxiety, making it tempting for us to deceive ourselves (Weberman, 2011). Participants observed that technology served as a tool for this deception, making it effortless for them to evade their freedom, opportunities, and the resulting consequences. Mindless scrolling took over their minds, allowing them to avoid facing their authentic selves. However, when they attempted to sit with their genuine selves without any distractions, it often triggered feelings of anxiety, suggesting that this freedom can also become an enormous burden. Mussar, a Jewish spiritual-ethics tradition, places great emphasis on the significance of not settling for thoughtless actions by highlighting the importance of cultivating one's inner life (Schiffman et al., 2023).

5.3.4 Main Findings – Maintaining and Breaking A Digital Detox

4. Maintaining and Breaking A Digital Detox

This theme highlights the participants' sense of responsibility towards their parents in instilling a love and respect for Shabbat. The practice of digital detox on Shabbat is closely connected to their childhood experiences of the day. If their memories of Shabbat are of a warm and loving atmosphere, filled with joyful moments, they feel more likely to continue these traditions into adulthood when making their own choices. Conversely, if their recollections of Shabbat were marked by negativity, with a lack of effort to create an uplifting experience, participants felt that the younger generation may choose to break away from these traditions. Participants observed that, even though their parents created a warm and loving atmosphere during Shabbat, they did not impose their traditions on them as they grew into adulthood. Instead, their parents respected their autonomy and granted them the freedom to shape their own values and make their own choices. This unconditional acceptance and trust minimised any inclination to rebel against their parents' traditions. For instance, Abigail knew that her decisions would be respected and supported, regardless of the path she chose in life, which contributed to her willingness to continue observing Shabbat. On the other hand, although Abigail's brother no longer observes Shabbat, he still respects the family environment during those times, whilst his parents continue to respect his choices regarding his religious observance.

This aligns with a standard English translation of Proverbs (22:6): "Train a lad in the way he [she] ought to go…" A question may be asked why not translate it as "Educate according to his [her] own way," as written in the original Hebrew? The phrase "the way he or she ought to go" implies that someone, typically an adult, knows the appropriate path and has the authority to guide the younger generation. This approach grants power to adults, making them essential and requiring their active control over the process of "training up". However, there is a significant difference between training and educating. The primary responsibility of adults is to establish suitable educational settings that facilitate the growth and development of young individuals as they navigate their path towards becoming well-educated (Raviv, 2000). This is in line with what Abigail and other participants have described. Parents of the participants had predetermined the path they wanted their children to take and had been preparing them for it since birth, leading them on the path that 'they ought to go'. Ultimately, when their children grow up and leave home, they will claim their own way of observing Shabbat, so the best thing that participants felt their parents could do was to provide the atmosphere, lead by example and then step back.

More than half of the participants recalled instances where they violated digital detox on Shabbat during their youth. The reasons for these transgressions included boredom, curiosity, and a lack of appreciation for the importance of resisting temptation for a higher purpose. This finding is consistent with the discovery that half of the Modern Orthodox teenagers text on Shabbat, a phenomenon known as "Half Shabbos" (Lipman, 2011). It involves observing Shabbat in every aspect except for using digital communication, which teenagers often justify by claiming addiction or boredom. This indicates that observing Shabbat alone may not be sufficient to prevent youth from resorting to their digital devices in the face of addiction and boredom (Schiffman et al. 2023). The discovery is further consistent with the findings of Thomas et al. (2016), which examined the perspectives of non-Jewish participants on disconnecting from technology. The study revealed that adolescents were considerably less inclined than other age groups to perceive any advantages from unplugging, whereas emerging adults acknowledged a greater number of benefits in comparison to adolescents.

Even within a religious framework, adherence to external rules is always a choice. As is the case with all existential thought, individuals are persistently conscious of decisions related to faith and religion. Tillich wrote about the struggle of choosing to be accountable to God, while not relinquishing one's self. This idea is a fundamental principle of many faiths, following the concept of "surrendering" oneself to a Higher Power. This notion aligns with Jewish parenting principles and with participants' insights that they needed personal life experiences. While they are taught the values of the Sabbath, the discipline to disconnect from their pervasive technology must ultimately come from within (Wyatt, n.d.).

As the participants transitioned from childhood to adulthood, they found that they underwent a transformation, shifting from adhering to their parents' values to engaging in self-reflection and pondering their own beliefs and ambitions. This transition marked a journey towards independence, a search for personal identity, and the setting of future objectives.

During the era of Spinoza and Newton, the Path of the Just (Ibn Paquda, 1996) was created with the aim of developing a unified religious philosophy that harmonises faith, intellect, and emotions (Bloch et al., 2018). Rabbi Bachya ibn Paquda, a medieval scholar, acknowledged the significance of introspection in attaining coherence between an individual's convictions and sentiments. If acknowledging introspection as a valid means of addressing existential distress is the initial stage in bridging the gap between psychological endeavours and religious principles, then integrating emotional labour into religious beliefs could be the next step. These results corroborate the findings of the participants, indicating that when adolescents initially received smartphones and had to detach from them on Shabbat, they experienced existential anguish. However, as they grew older and more knowledgeable about their Jewish identity, they utilised Shabbat as an opportunity for introspection, contemplating its significance and their religious ideals and values.

5.3.5 *Main Findings – Living Without Technology*

5. Living Without Technology

The findings of this section emphasise the importance of established routines during Shabbat, particularly the significance of rituals that are integral to the day's structure. While some participants recognised the significance of religious rituals, such as studying sacred texts and attending synagogue services, all participants acknowledged the relevance of rituals associated with mealtimes, spending time with family, and socialising as crucial components of the Shabbat experience. These rituals facilitate the process of digital detox by providing alternative activities to replace the time spent on technology. According to Fishbane (1995), the appropriate inner state can only be developed and realised through ritualised actions. These actions should be performed with joy and should also generate joy.

The observance of Shabbat, a weekly religious practice/ ritual among observant Jews on Friday evenings, is one of the oldest continuing family traditions. Scholars have argued that the practice of Shabbat is a contributing factor in the resilience of Jewish families in the face of repeated anti-Semitic attempts to dismantle Judaism and the Jewish people (Marks et al., 2017b). In her interviews with 30 families, Marks et al. (2017b) further supports the notion that family meals are instrumental in creating a unique and meaningful Shabbat experience.

According to religious existentialists, the purpose of faith is to foster a sense of unity among individuals through the use of rules, rituals, and doctrines.

These elements provide followers of a particular faith with a means of connecting with one another, and through these connections, they are also connecting with the wider world – coming as close to the Creator as possible within the bounds of human existence (Wyatt, n.d.).

In a study by Roberts and Koliska (2014), 891 students were subjected to a 24-hour digital detox, which revealed that many of them struggled to function without ambient media, as it had become an integral part of their daily lives. Participants specifically struggled with managing their routines without the use of technology, such as music, alarm clocks, and asking for directions. However, the participants in the present study have become accustomed to their weekly digital detox, having practised it consistently each week. As a result, they have learned how to live both with and without technology and have developed strategies for managing their daily routines during the detox. Participants did not report any difficulties with tasks such as waking up or asking for directions, as these aspects of their routine were not perceived as problematic. Another possibility might further suggest that the Shabbat day is structured differently than weekdays, with distinct routines and requirements that do not rely on technology in the same way as other days.

This theme portrays the participants' narratives with regard to their feelings of addiction towards their phones. Researchers have been actively investigating whether Internet or technology addiction meets the criteria for a clinically significant condition that merits inclusion as a diagnosable disorder in the Diagnostic and Statistical

Manual for Mental Disorders (DSM-5) (*Association, 2013*). Although the latest version of the DSM does not acknowledge Internet addiction as a mental health disorder, Internet Gaming Disorder was identified as a condition requiring further examination. Despite not being recognised as a diagnosis, participants in a study by Morris and Pickens (2017) exhibited classic symptoms of addiction, such as cravings, withdrawal, and dependence. The author summarises that, regardless of whether it is classified as a diagnosis, the study's participants reported exhibiting classic symptoms of addiction, similar experiences to those found in this study.

When it comes to behavioural addictions in digital domains, it can be challenging to determine where to draw the line between typical, excessive, and problematic usage (Ellis et al., 2019). Problematic usage should negatively impact normal functioning and cause distress. For instance, abstaining from addiction-related behaviours, such as drinking for heavy drinkers, can lead to changes in mood, anxiety, and craving (Kardefelt-Winther et al., 2017). If abstinence results in changes across all three measures, it may reveal similar symptoms required for a new phenomenon to be considered a genuine behavioural addiction.

In this study, participants experienced some addictive symptoms. However, during their digital detox, their normal functioning improved rather than being negatively affected. This supports that excessive technology use cannot alone be classified as an addictive disorder.

This theme brought to light diverse experiences of Shabbat that influenced participants' choices to uphold their digital detox. This underscored the notion that attitudes towards Shabbat observance and the commitment to maintaining the detox are subjective and individualised. Merleau-Ponty's observation was that we experience the world through our bodies and that our consciousness is embodied and perceptual (Moya, 2014). Our perception of the world is grounded in our own individual interpretation and construction of it. Abigail, for instance, enjoys Shabbat, and it is this enjoyment that motivates her to maintain her digital detox. She believes that pleasure-seeking is a top priority for young adults, particularly among Gen Z individuals. Shaul, on the other hand, is committed to observing Shabbat due to the spiritual aspect and a sense of fear. For Leah, Shabbat is a sanctuary where she can be herself, free from the overwhelming influence of her phone and the digital world it represents. Schnall (2006) highlights that, even within a specific denomination, such as Orthodox Jewry, there exists a diverse group with many subgroups. Members of these subgroups vary in their language, diet, worldview, dress, and even religious practices to a greater or lesser extent. Jewish teachings throughout the ages are vast and the lived experiences of Jews varied.

Serving God can be accomplished in different ways, including personal prayer, religious motivations, attachment to God, and social support (Schiffman et al., 2023). Among 1,849 Israeli Jews, Levin (2013) found that personal prayer was associated with elevated life satisfaction and well-being, while synagogue attendance and formal prayer were not. In a cross-sectional study, Lazar (2015) reported that the quality of prayer predicted elevated life satisfaction more than attending formal prayer did. For non-Orthodox Jews, religiosity was found to be associated with coping with health difficulties through social support (Pirutinsky et al., 2011). These studies suggest that individuals find varying satisfaction in their ways of serving God, with internal components of religiosity being more reliable predictors of flourishing for some but not others.

Positive psychology literature generally incorporates two types of happiness, each rooted in Greek philosophy: hedonism, concerned with pleasure, comfort, and enjoyment, and eudaimonia, focused on pursuing complex goals that are meaningful to self and society (Fave et al., 2010). The Hebrew Bible, rabbinic works, and later Jewish philosophical writings reflect different paths to happiness (Pelcovitz & Pelcovitz, 2014). Sacks (2014) notes that Judaism involves pursuing holiness rather than happiness. While happiness may result from living according to God's will, it is not the ultimate aim. These Judaic notions of happiness provide a counterbalance to the dangers of self-absorbed, hedonic happiness. Research and practice in this area is likely to be most fruitful when acknowledging the individual and contextual nature of happiness, along with its varied sources and expressions. The diversity within the Jewish conceptualisation of happiness incorporates elements of pleasure and enjoyment and integrates them into a larger framework of meaning and self-transcendence (Schiffman et al., 2023).

5.4 The Four Dimensions Criteria

To ensure trustworthiness, Lincoln and Guba (1986) developed a rigorous set of criteria in qualitative research referred to as the Four Dimensions Criteria (FDC). These criteria, namely credibility, dependability, confirmability, and transferability, are integral to maintaining the quality and validity of qualitative research (Forero et al., 2018). Guba and Lincoln (1989) later introduced the concept of authenticity in their subsequent work.

Several researchers have recognised establishing credibility as a fundamental indicator of robust qualitative inquiry (Lincoln & Guba, 1985; Lincoln et al., 2011; Bean, 2007). Credibility can be enhanced by providing thorough details about the study, such as its methodology, data collection procedures, and participant characteristics, along with offering contact information for the researcher (Saylor Academy Open Textbooks & Saylor Academy, 2022). Participants in this research were provided with detailed explanations of the research, accompanied by comprehensive participant information forms that contained all relevant details about the study and the data collected. Additionally, participants were given a debrief form to ensure clarity and transparency throughout the research process. Credibility is additionally enhanced by findings representing participants' experiences and also include prolonged engagement with participants and with the study (Forero et al., 2018). This was done in the interviews by regular checking in with interviewees and regular, ongoing engagement with the data.

Dependability ensures that the findings of the qualitative inquiry can be replicated (Lincoln & Guba, 1986). To achieve this, a detailed description of the study methods was provided, and an audit trail was established to facilitate stepwise replication of the method. Qualitative researchers strive to develop and implement methodological strategies to ensure the trustworthiness of their findings (Roberts & Priest, 2010). Reviewing interviews and transcripts many times and paying attention to detail, which is part of organic inquiry, helped improve dependability. A way to ensure the dependability of one's research is to organise all data in a manner that allows someone to follow a clear and coherent chain of evidence, leading from initial documentation to the final report (Yin, 1989). In this study, the methodology and method are outlined in a step-by-step process. They are appropriately ordered and easy to follow, enabling others to verify the chain of processes. This was done through regular reflection to ensure they were carried out in line with requirements.

Confirmability pertains to the assurance that both the data and interpretations of the findings are not mere products of the researcher's imagination but rather derived directly from the data itself. Enhancing confirmability becomes more manageable through a transparent report of the findings, accompanied by clear indications of reflexivity. This transparency allows for a thorough evaluation of the confirmability of the research. Critical self-reflection is a process that involves introspection and examination of one's own biases, preferences, and preconceptions as a researcher. It also encompasses reflecting on the research relationship, including the dynamics between the researcher and the respondents and how this relationship may influence the participant's responses to the interview questions (Lincoln & Guba, 1985). According to Smith et al. (2022), the IPA researcher makes sense of the data by engaging in a process of interpretative engagement, which involves understanding the participants' own accounts of their experiences in a double hermeneutic process. In qualitative research, reflexivity plays a crucial role in upholding transparency and ensuring the overall quality of the study (Korstjens & Moser, 2017). To ensure consistency and transparency in the interpretation of data, I have presented extracts from the participants to provide a transparent evidentiary base. This enables the reader to check the evidence supporting the claims made. One of the strategies for ensuring the trustworthiness of the findings is to recognise any personal biases that may have influenced the results. In qualitative analysis, it is crucial to demonstrate sensitivity to the data by carefully considering the meanings generated by the participants. This involves abstaining from imposing predetermined categories onto the data and instead thoroughly examining the data. The researcher subsequently derives meaning from these categories through their interpretation. By adopting this approach, the analysis can capture the nuances and complexities of the participants' experiences rather than imposing external labels or interpretations onto them (Yardley. Y, 2017). As a researcher who observes Shabbat, I recognised the potential for pre-conceived notions about the digital detox on Shabbat to limit the scope of this study. To mitigate this potential disadvantage, I collaborated with my supervisors and engaged in a consistent reflexive process throughout the research. These processes involved being mindful of my biases, reflecting on how they might affect my interpretation of the data, and taking steps to reduce research bias. By doing so, I aimed to ensure that the study captured the participants' experiences as accurately as possible. Another strategy for ensuring the trustworthiness of a study is to acknowledge any biases in sampling. In this particular study, the subject matter necessitated a biased sample, and inclusion and exclusion criteria were used to maintain homogeneity and control for confounding variables as much as possible. For diversity within the biased sample, I included individuals of both genders, and each participant's experience was subject to independent factors that make them unique, such as their personalities and environments.

Transferability aims to expand the extent to which the findings can be generalised or applied to different contexts or settings. It involves demonstrating the applicability of the research study's findings to other contexts, such as similar situations, populations, or phenomena. Strategies for enhancing transferability encompass the utilisation of thick description. This entails providing comprehensive descriptions not only of the behaviour and experiences but also of their surrounding context. By offering such rich contextual details, the behaviour and experiences can acquire meaning and become comprehensible to an outside observer.

In order to establish authenticity, researchers undertake various processes to ensure the credibility of the findings, both in terms of participant's experiences and the broader implications of the research. Authenticity, encompassed within the broader framework of establishing trustworthiness in an inquiry, goes beyond selecting a meaningful research topic and also considers the potential societal benefits of the project (James, 2008). When choosing IPA as the analytical method, my primary goal was to focus on participants' accounts and not be drawn into creating themes. During the analysis stage, I made a conscientious effort to avoid solely focusing on similarities between accounts, which could be tempting. Instead, I paid equal attention to the divergent qualities of experiences, even when the same participants appeared to contradict themselves. This allowed me to capture the richness and detail of participants' experiences while avoiding oversimplification.

5.5 Implications for Counselling and Therapy

Morris and Pickens (2017) suggest that pervasive use of technology means today's therapist will work with clients impacted by the role technology plays in their lives and relationships. Since technology plays a significant role in the daily lives of most clients, it is crucial for clinicians to investigate whether technology usage may be contributing to their presenting issues or if "unplugging" could be advantageous for specific clients based on their therapeutic objectives.

Therapists can incorporate two brief questions into their routine intake forms to assess the impact of technology on their clients' lives: "Is the utilisation of technology by family members perceived as problematic for either individuals or the family unit?" and "What effects do you believe technology usage has on you or your family members? Please mention both positive and negative consequences." Therapists may also utilise existing measures, such as the Technology Interference in Life Examples Scale (McDaniel & Radesky, 2018) to evaluate the impact of technology on their clients. If the therapist suspects that a family member is experiencing excessive technology usage, Young's (Widyanto et al., 2004) Internet Addiction Test, a validated assessment tool for Internet addiction, can help determine whether the usage is clinically problematic. The term "Internet" can be replaced with any form of technology that is reported to be problematic, such as cell phones, online gaming, or social networking sites.

Morris and Pickens (2017) further suggest that therapists should also consider educating their clients about the various outcomes associated with technology use, such as overuse, problematic or pathological use, and usage in specific social situations. This necessitates that therapists stay up-to-date with research in the field of technology. For instance, if a parent brings their child to therapy due to concerns about their technology usage, the therapist should be able to discuss recommended levels of use, assess for problematic levels of use, and be aware of potential negative outcomes. Such discussions should also include an evaluation of the parents' usage, particularly during the time spent with their children. Moreover, therapists may encounter families that feel disconnected, and while there may be multiple underlying factors, inquiring about technology usage may be advantageous since children report feeling disconnected from their parents when they use technology, and couples report similar issues in both co-parenting and spousal relationships (McDaniel & Coyne, 2014; Radesky et al., 2014). Therapists can encourage clients to discuss their perspectives on technology usage within the family. Finally, therapists should not overlook the potential positive effects of technology usage. Families may discover new ways to bond and spend meaningful time together while engaging in multiplayer online games or other forms of group entertainment.

Based on my experience as a couples counsellor, couples frequently complain about feeling ignored during shared leisure time or at the dinner table, primarily due to one partner being engrossed in their phone. This distraction caused by technology leads to a gradual sense of disconnection, with couples feeling less close to each other and perceiving a lack of prioritisation in their relationship. Similarly, children experience similar disconnection from their parents, as emotional nurturing takes a backseat to technology. Through psychoeducation, we can teach our clients to set aside time each week to focus solely on their relationship, where spending time together and feeling connected is a priority. This will require a fixed time that is dependable, can be planned for, and can be eagerly anticipated to focus on each other. By doing so, relationships and bonds can be strengthened, and couples can rely on each other to be present at an agreed-upon time, just as children can count on their parents. This can improve overall well-being for families, as they carve out dedicated time to connect with each other and prioritise those relationships.

The relationship between a counsellor and client appears to go beyond any specific intervention approach. Most counsellors subscribe to the principle that it is the relationship itself that heals (BACP, 2022; Badenoch B, 2008; Scott et al., 2009; Society, 2019), but this can sometimes be overlooked. The current cultural shift towards digitised communication and objectification of interpersonal contact raises the question of whether the next generation of counsellors will still prioritise the sense of "presence" in the therapeutic relationship that is integral to counselling. From my own perspective, a counsellor's ability to engage in meaningful interpersonal contact is more crucial than ever. Counsellors view the client-counselor relationship as the cornerstone of all therapeutic progress because it affirms human connection, validation, and participation (Webmaster, 2019). As counsellors, we possess the power to confirm our clients through the process of inclusion, offering them a relationship that can help to heal the wounds of past missed connections. To effectively encourage our clients to move from a surface-level stance to a more authentic state of participation and "being", we must relate to them as an I to a Thou (Martin & Cowan, 2019). Within our limited sphere of influence, we can work towards fostering a more compassionate and humane world. As counsellors, we must keep this objective in mind even as we aim for greater technical efficiency within a mental health "service delivery system" that may not completely align with our broader goals (Scott et al., 2009).

5.6 Implications for Society

The implications of this study for society are significant. Practising a digital detox for a day a week is accessible to anyone, and it can contribute to the well-being of individuals, families, and communities without incurring out-of-pocket costs or requiring special knowledge or equipment. For some, a more realistic starting point may be setting aside short intervals of regular time to enjoy nature, do restful activities, spend time with loved ones, or introspect without the distraction of technology. In even the busiest households, it is possible to designate one technology-free meal per week. This provides an opportunity to prepare a meal together and engage in conversation, even amidst a packed schedule.

The prevalence of technology has given rise to a novel challenge, an emerging phenomenon that has not been experienced before. The study findings revealed that the ability to observe Shabbat came with maturity and comprehension. It became evident that, for half of the participants, refraining from using their phones throughout the entirety of Shabbat was only achievable once they reached this developmental milestone. In order to maintain strong relationships with their children, parents and teachers must exhibit understanding and patience until the teenagers are ready to willingly embrace Shabbat. This understanding and support are crucial for fostering an environment where teenagers can gradually transition towards embracing Shabbat at their own pace.

Jewish communities can make further efforts to support Jewish individuals or families who want to incorporate Shabbat into their lives for those for whom Shabbat-keeping is unfamiliar. Jewish educators and parents can be more mindful of the challenges that younger generations face due to the addictive nature of technology. This realisation underscores the importance of making the general Shabbat experience a counterbalance to the thrill of technology. Families and communities should consider how Shabbat is spent, particularly with regard to the activities available for children and adolescents, to prevent boredom and breaking Shabbat. Predictability is also important so that younger Shabbat keepers can look forward to planned activities and festivities, and parents can model their own enthusiasm for Shabbat to avoid making the digital detox seem like a burden.

5.7 Strengths and Limitations of the Study

The IPA methodology used in this study has a limitation in making general claims, as it aims to explore perceptions and understandings of a particular group in their setting rather than uncovering what occurs in all settings. Nonetheless, IPA should be considered in terms of theoretical generalisability, where readers can connect the findings with existing literature and their own experiences (Smith, 2003). Although IPA is not opposed to general claims, it emphasises the gradual accumulation of similar studies to make stronger general claims. This study had a small sample size of 8 participants, which can raise questions about the transferability of findings (Charlick et al., 2016). The specific characteristics of the sample, consisting of individuals aged 18-24 years old who are single and living at home, represent a particular group. It is important to acknowledge that the findings may vary for young adults in relationships or those who no longer reside at home. These factors restrict the transferability of the findings to a broader population. However, in IPA research, prioritising depth over breadth is preferable. Analysing fewer participants in greater depth is preferable to a broader, superficial, and descriptive analysis of many individuals (Hefferon & Gil-Rodriguez, 2011).

As the sole researcher, there is a possibility that I may have missed certain perspectives or areas that another researcher might have explored while analysing the data or identifying implications. One of the strengths of this study was my personal observance of Shabbat, which helped to establish trust and rapport with the participants. This allowed the participants to feel comfortable and share their experiences freely without having to explain Hebrew or Yiddish terms to me. Conversely, this might have led to a limitation as my own established ideas about the digital detox on Shabbat might have influenced the data. These are reflected in the reflexive sections of this study.

It is noteworthy that there is currently no systematic review available on the effectiveness of digital detox on changes in mental health or relationships, and the existing literature only comprises isolated findings (Radtke et al., 2021). Due to the diverse methods of implementing digital detox, such as restricting access to certain apps or limiting usage during specific hours, it was not feasible in this study to examine each approach individually. As a result, the findings of this study may provide an incomplete picture of alternative digital detox interventions. This study specifically focuses on the particular digital detox experience undertaken in the research and is not a comparative analysis of other detox methods. Therefore, this study's findings on the experiences of a digital detox over Shabbat are significant and contribute to the limited literature on the topic.

Despite the sampling bias, the study's inclusion of a diverse sample of both men and women enriched the study with a variety of viewpoints. Initially, recruiting male participants was challenging, but efforts were made to include them, providing a broader range of perspectives (Radtke et al., 2021).

5.8 Future Research Directions

Of the nearly 15 million Jews worldwide, more than four-fifths live in the U.S. and Israel (Delle Fave et al., 2011). Depending on how the term "Jewish" is defined, there are approximately seven million Jewish individuals in the U.S. (Sheskin & Dashefsky, 2020). According to current estimates, around 37% identify as Reform, 17% as Conservative, 9% as Orthodox, 32% as nondenominational, and 4% with smaller denominations (Mitchell, 2022b). This study focuses on the experiences within the 9% of Orthodox Jews residing in the UK. Future research could benefit from exploring whether Jews from different denominations and countries have distinct experiences regarding unplugging on Shabbat.

This study has recognised Shabbat as a 25-hour weekly reprieve from technology. It is important for future research to investigate the effects of a weekly digital detox on individuals and families beyond Shabbat. Additionally, while the participants in this study reported experiencing immediate benefits from their decision to unplug, long-term outcomes were not explored, which should also be considered in future research. It may be further valuable for researchers and clinicians to investigate the efficacy of weekly "unplugging" from all technology in mitigating specific individual, relational, or familial issues. There is limited research on character strengths within the Jewish population (Schiffman et al.,

2023); therefore, future studies may explore how individuals with different personalities perceive their experiences of digital detox. Future research might also benefit from a comparison study between male and female participants who observe Shabbat.

It is important to consider the homogeneity of the group and its potential impact on their adherence to digital detox on Shabbat. Notably, within this sample of young, single adults living at home, half of the participants acknowledged breaking their digital detox. However, it is crucial to recognise that results may differ for individuals in dysfunctional or troubled families, single-parent or blended families, areas located far from Jewish communities, or those with learning or physical disabilities. Exploring these factors could yield different patterns of digital detox practices on Shabbat within these specific contexts.

5.9 Reflexivity and Conclusion

Reflexivity played a crucial role in this qualitative research study, and in addition to reflecting on my experience of the digital detox on weekdays, I also had the opportunity to experience it in real-time each week on Shabbat. This allowed me to further contemplate my own and my family's experience of the digital detox.

I make a conscious effort to focus on my home and family during Shabbat and this process begins when I switch off my phone. I experience a transitioning akin to the two worlds that was conveyed by participants. From that moment, the digital detox begins and work commitments are set aside until the following evening. At times it has been difficult when something important is remembered during the detox period that needs technology to address or when there's a desire to buy something or look something up online, but the commitment to Shabbat has always been a priority. These feelings resonated with the simultaneous relief at turning off from 'the world' whilst noticing that there were also underlying feelings of anxiety associated with digital disconnection.

During interviews, I was conscious of bracketing my own feelings about Shabbat to be open to hearing about theirs. On the other hand, my underlying innate knowledge of Shabbat was essential in allowing me to conduct the interview and hold the space from a position of shared understanding of the experiences and practices of Shabbat and the digital detox within it. An example of where I was conscious of my own experience of Shabbat whilst openly listening to my interviewee's experiences of it, was in learning how the digital detox was experienced as a unique opportunity to bond with family. Whilst I approached the interview from the perspective of a mother within the family, I aimed to understand how my participants, who were the children, were experiencing one another in a parallel experience.

During my upbringing, smartphones were non-existent, and the internet only gained popularity when I reached adulthood. Consequently, it was a new experience for me to explore what it might be like for individuals who grew up as avid internet users and would then have to completely abstain each week from this powerful tool during their formative years. I dedicated considerable time to contemplating this scenario, as it allowed me to contextualise my own positive feelings towards Shabbat, which I realised were accompanied by far fewer challenges compared to what I discovered among my participants. This process encouraged me to acknowledge both the similarities and stark differences in our experiences.

As I conducted interviews and delved deeper into the subject, my sympathy for the challenges faced by the younger generation grew significantly. Initially, I had not fully grasped the extent of these challenges when I embarked on this research endeavour. Growing up, observing Shabbat was simply a normal expectation for me. In terms of entertainment and combating boredom, there was minimal disparity between Shabbat and weekdays, as our household had limited technology and certainly no personal devices. This realisation prompted me to contemplate the generation gap and how the insights gained from this study on technology could potentially shape our approach to parenting, considering the immense challenges faced by the younger generation.

Parenting is an essential aspect of my life, and I have been practising it for over two decades. My interest in parenting, combined with my passion for an integral part of my religion, Shabbat, led me to conduct this study. It explores how children are taught to live Shabbat, which largely informs how they experience it as young adults. The impact of Shabbat is felt by all the family, not only on Shabbat itself but during the whole week, as bonds and connections are continuously strengthened and the 'real' world with 'real' people is fully experienced at regular and predictable intervals in a format and routine that is foreseen and prepared for. Shabbat is an integral part of my Jewishness because there are days that lead up to it in preparation and anticipation and days of winding down from it until it arrives again the following week.

By introducing myself as a therapist, I aimed to create an environment where participants felt comfortable and assured that I work closely with mental health issues and value hearing a wide range of experiences. This approach potentially encouraged participants to be open and candid with me, knowing that they could freely share their perspectives. Despite creating a relaxed and non-judgmental atmosphere during the interviews, there may have been a hesitancy among participants to openly discuss instances when they broke their digital detox on Shabbat. This reticence can be attributed to the significant importance of observing Shabbat for Jewish individuals, as it serves as a cornerstone of the Jewish religion. While half of the participants acknowledged breaking their digital detox during their teenage years, it remains unclear if more participants refrained from admitting such experiences. It would be noteworthy to explore the implications if more than half of the sample of Orthodox Jewish Generation Z individuals were unable to strictly observe Shabbat during their teenage years. These findings can provide valuable insights for individuals and researchers interested in this topic.

As a therapist, much of what I encounter are problems and ailments associated with being human in the present world. Stress as a result of the pace of life, overwhelming responsibilities, depression and sadness, eating disorders, loneliness, and problems in relationships, to name but a few. Of course, technology isn't the root cause of all of these problems, but it did make me think about the role technology plays in how we work, think, relate to our bodies, our image and how we apply meaning and authenticity to our lives. I have been encountering clients who have lost relationship skills and are often more influenced by messages on their mobile phones than by the people in front of them. I wanted to learn what the conditions are that allow for the possibility of human connectivity to happen, similar in some ways to how it is experienced in the therapy room. For some clients, it's the only hour in their week that they experience undivided, full attention and connection with another 'real' person not in the virtual world. This made me curious about how, as an observant Jew, I and my family, who fully engage with technology for six days a week, take a step back every Friday night and Saturday for a full 25-hour period of total digital detox where we are allowed and encouraged to just 'be' with ourselves and others.

The purpose of this thesis was to explore an aspect of my Jewish identity by collecting data that could be valuable not only to Jewish individuals interested in the digital detox aspect of their Shabbat observance but also to anyone curious about taking a weekly break from technology and the underlying factors that facilitate it. This brought me to think about the transferability of this study to other populations. I have thought a lot about whether and how the digital detox can be separated from the context of Shabbat and it seems to me that it is Shabbat that supplies the requisite conditions to make it possible. The particular conditions pertaining to Shabbat that make the digital detox possible underlie this research.

> 'The technologies of image make near what was once too distant to be seen, and they give us distance on what was too near; they allow us to speed up what was previously too slow to appear, just as they can slow down and make visible what once was too fast.' (Taylor et al., 2021, p.2).

This statement describes how technology has transformed our relationship with the world around us, technologies that have made it possible to bring distant objects and places closer to us, allowing us to see things that were once out of reach. At the same time, they have also created a sense of distance between us and what is physically close to us as we become absorbed in the digital world of images and screens. The statement also suggests that technology has the power to speed up and slow down our perception of time. It can accelerate the pace of information and communication, making things that used to take a long time to appear suddenly appear instantaneously. Conversely, it slows things down and makes visible what was once too fast for us to perceive, such as the subtle changes in facial expressions or body language that are easily missed in face-to-face interactions.

Overall, technology has fundamentally changed how we interact with the world around us, both in distance and time. While these changes have brought many benefits, they have also created challenges and complexities that we must navigate in our daily lives. Engaging with the digital world for six days a week while intentionally disconnecting for one day a week might be a way of accommodating diverse experiences of time, space, and relationships.

> *"The Sabbath is a day of rest, of mental scrutiny and of balance. Without it the workdays are insipid."*
> (Chaim Nachman Bialik, 1873-1934)

References

Adawi, M., Zerbetto, R., Re, T. S., Bisharat, B., Mahamid, M., Amital, H., Del Puente, G., & Bragazzi, N. L. (2019). <p>Psychometric properties of the Brief Symptom Inventory in nomophobic subjects: insights from preliminary confirmatory factor, exploratory factor, and clustering analyses in a sample of healthy Italian volunteers</p> *Psychology Research and Behavior Management, Volume 12,* 145–154. https://doi.org/10.2147/prbm.s173282

Aiken, M. (2016). *The cyber effect: A Pioneering Cyberpsychologist Explains How Human Behaviour Changes Online.* Hachette UK

Alabdulkareem, S. A. (2015). Exploring the use and the impacts of social media on teaching and learning science in Saudi. *Procedia – Social and Behavioral Sciences, 182,* 213–224. https://doi.org/10.1016/j.sbspro.2015.04.758

Anderson, M. W. (2003). Embodied Cognition: A field guide. *Artificial Intelligence, 149*(1), 91–130. https://doi.org/10.1016/s0004-3702(03)00054-7

Angel, M D. (1997). Exploring the Thought of Rabbi Joseph B. Soloveitchik, Hoboken, NJ, Ktav, USA. https://www.jewishideas.org/article/embracing-tradition-and-modernity-rabbi-joseph-b-soloveitchik1#_edn1, accessed 20/6/23

Arnetz, B. B., & Wiholm, C. (1997). Technological stress: Psychophysiological symptoms in modern offices. *Journal of Psychosomatic Research, 43*(1), 35–42. https://doi.org/10.1016/s0022-3999(97)00083-4

Association, A. P. (2013). *Diagnostic and Statistical Manual of Mental Disorders.* https://doi.org/10.1176/appi.books. 9780890425596

Atske, S. (2020, September 11). *Mobile Connectivity in Emerging Economies | Pew Research Center.* Pew Research Center: Internet, Science & Tech. https://www.pewresearch. org/internet/2019/03/07/mobile-connectivity-in-emerging-economies/https://www.pewresearch.org/internet/2019/ 03/07/majorities-say-mobile-phones-are-good-for-society-even-amid-concerns-about-their-impact-on-children/.

Ayyagari, R., Grover, V., & Purvis, R. L. (2011). Technostress: Technological antecedents and implications. *Management Information Systems Quarterly*, *35*(4), 831. https://doi.org/10. 2307/41409963

BACP Good practice across the counselling professions 004. (n.d.). https://www.bacp.co.uk/events-and-resources/ ethics-and-standards/good-practice-across-the-counselling-professions/gpacp004-what-works-in-counselling-and-psychotherapy-relationships/, accessed 27/8/2022

Badenoch, B. (2011). *Being a Brain-Wise Therapist: A Practical Guide to Interpersonal Neurobiology (Norton Series on Interpersonal Neurobiology).* W. W. Norton & Company.

Bakhtiari, K. (2023b, July 28). Gen-Z, The Loneliness Epidemic and the Unifying Power of Brands. *Forbes.* https:// www.forbes.com/sites/kianbakhtiari/2023/07/28/gen-z-the-loneliness-epidemic-and-the-unifying-power-of-brands/, accessed 23/8/23

Banerjee, D., & Rai, M. (2020). Social isolation in Covid-19: The impact of loneliness. *International Journal of Social Psychiatry*, *66*(6), 525–527. https://doi.org/10.1177/00207 64020922269

Bean, C. J. (2007). Book Review: Maxwell, J. A. (Ed.). (2005) Qualitative research design: An interactive approach (2nd ed.). Thousand Oaks, CA: Sage. *Organizational Research Methods, 10*(2), 393–394. https://doi.org/10.1177/1094 428106290193

Berger, R. (2015). Now I see it, now I don't: Researcher's position and reflexivity in qualitative research. *Qualitative Research, 15*(2), 219-234

Beyens, I., Frison, E., & Eggermont, S. (2016). "I don't want to miss a thing": Adolescents' fear of missing out and its relationship to adolescents' social needs, Facebook use, and Facebook related stress. *Computers in Human Behavior, 64*, 1–8. https://doi.org/10.1016/j.chb.2016.05.083

Biemann, A. (2016). *The Martin Buber Reader: Essential Writings*. Springer

Blitz, M. (2014). Understanding Heidegger on Technology, The Centre for the Study of Technology and Society, *The New Atlantis*, pp. 63–80

Bloch, A. M., Gabbay, E., Knowlton, S., & Fins, J. J. (2018). Psychiatry, cultural competency, and the care of Ultra-Orthodox Jews: achieving secular and theocentric convergence through introspection. *Journal of Religion & Health, 57*(5), 1702–1716. https://doi.org/10.1007/s10943-018-0678-z

Blum, B. (2017). 'This normal life: Texting on Shabbat? Guidelines for the observant Jew,' https://www.jpost.com/Opinion/This-normal-life-Texting-on-Shabbat-Guidelines-for-the-observantJew-481752, accessed 25/6/23

Bracken, S. (2010). Discussing the importance of ontology and epistemology awareness in practitioner research. Worcester Journal of Learning and Teaching, (4)

Buber, M. (1967). *A believing humanism: my testament, 1902-1965*

Buber, M. (1985). Pfade in utopia: Über Gemeinschaft und deren Verwirklichung

Buber, M. (2012). *I and Thou.* eBookIt.com

Braun, V., & Clarke, V. (2006). Using thematic analysis in psychology. *Qualitative Research in Psychology, 3,* 77-101.

Cao, X., & Sun, J. (2018). Exploring the effect of overload on the discontinuous intention of social media users: An S-O-R perspective. *Computers in Human Behavior, 81,* 10–18. https://doi.org/10.1016/j.chb.2017.11.035

Charlick, S. J., Pincombe, J., McKellar, L., & Fielder, A. (2016). Making Sense of participant Experiences: Interpretative Phenomenological Analysis in midwifery research. *International Journal of Doctoral Studies, 11,* 205–216. https://doi.org/10.28945/3486

Charmaz, K. (2014). Constructing grounded theory. In *Sage eBooks* (Issue 1). http://ci.nii.ac.jp/ncid/BB167 52935

Code of Ethics and Conduct | BPS. (n.d.). BPS. https://www. bps.org.uk/guideline/code-ethics-and-conduct, accessed 6/9/23

Conroy, D., Chadwick, D., Fullwood, C., & Lloyd, J. (2022). "You have to know how to live with it without getting to the addiction part": British young adult experiences of smartphone overreliance and disconnectivity. *Psychology of Popular Media.* Advance online publication. https://doi.org/10.1037/ppm000 0425

Constantino, T. E. (2008). Constructivism. In L. Given (Ed.), The Sage encyclopedia of qualitative research (pp. 116–120) [electronic resource]. Thousand Oaks, CA: Sage

Crotty, M. (2003). The Foundations of Social Research: Meaning and Perspectives in the Research Process, London: Sage Publications, 3rd edition

Dein, S, Loewenthal K M. (2013). The Mental Health Benefits and Costs of Sabbath Observance Among Orthodox Jews, Pubmed, *Journal of Religion and Health 52* (4)

Denicolo, P, Long. T, Bradley Cole, K. (2016). Constructivist Approaches and Research Methods, *A Practical Guide to Exploring Personal Meanings*, Sage, London

Dessler, E. E. (1985). *Strive for Truth*, Feldheim Publishers, Jerusalem, Israel

Diamant, A., & Cooper, H. (2009). *Living a Jewish Life, Updated and Revised Edition: Jewish Traditions, Customs and Values for Today's Families*. Harper Collins

Dictionary.com | Meanings & Definitions of English Words. (2023). In *Dictionary.com*. https://www.lexico.com/definition/digital_detox, 13 February 2023.

Digital Detox Holidays & Luxury Getaways - Carrier. (n.d.). https://www.carrier.co.uk/holiday-types/digital-detox-holidays/, accessed 6/9/23

Dimock, M. (2019). *Defining Generations: Where Millennials End and Generation Z Begins*, Pew Research Center

Donin, H. H. (2019). *To be a Jew: A Guide to Jewish Observance in Contemporary Life*

Dreyfus, H. (1995). Technology and the Politics of Knowledge, Indiana University Press, Rowman & Littlefield Publishers. Inc, New York, Oxford https://nissenbaum.tech.cornell.edu/papers/free_relation.pdf, accessed 18/6/23

Dwyer, R., Kushlev, K., Dunn, E. (2018). Smartphone use undermines enjoyment of face-to-face social interactions. *Journal of Experimental Social Psychology*, 78, 233–239

Eden, D. (2001). Job stress and respite relief: Overcoming high-tech tethers. In P. L. Perrewe & D. C. Ganster (Eds.), Exploring theoretical mechanisms and perspectives (pp. 143194). Kidlington, Oxford: Elsevier Science

Egger, I L S, Wassler, P. (2020). Digital Free Tourism – An Exploratory Study of Tourist Motivations, *Tourism Management*, Volume 79, 104098

Eisenstein, R. I. (2022). Shabbat in the modern world. *My Jewish Learning*. https://www.myjewishlearning.com/article/shabbat-in-the-modern-world/, accessed 6/9/23.

Elias, N., Lemish, D., Dalyot, S., & Floegel, D. (2020). "Where are you?" An observational exploration of parental technoference in public places in the US and Israel. *Journal of Children and Media*, *15*(3), 376–388. https://doi.org/10.1080/17482798.2020.1815228

Ellis, D A, Davidson, B I, Shaw, H, Geyer, K. (2019). Do smartphone usage scales predict behavior?, *International Journal of Human-Computer Studies*, *130*, pp. 86–92

Essel, H B, Vlachopoulos, D, Tachie-Menson, A, Nunoo, F K N, & Johnson, E E. (2022). Nomophobia among Preservice Teachers: a descriptive correlational study at Ghanaian Colleges of Education. *Education and Information Technologies*, *27*(7), 9541–9561. https://doi.org/10.1007/s10639-022-11023-6

Fairyington, S. (2018). How Apple Screen Time Helped me Stop Treating my Phone Like It's Oxygen and I'd Die Without Looking At It, Thrive Global, Well-Being, https://thriveglobal.com/stories/ways-apple-s-screen-time-feature-will-stop-you-from-staring-at-your-phone/

Fardouly, J., Diedrichs, P. C., Vartanian, L. R., & Halliwell, E. (2015). Social comparisons on social media: The impact of Facebook on young women's body image concerns and mood.

Body Image, *13*, 38–45. https://doi.org/10.1016/j.bodyim.
2014.12.002

Fave, A. D., Brdar, I., Freire, T., Vella-Brodrick, D., & Wissing, M. P. (2010). The eudaimonic and hedonic Components of Happiness: Qualitative and Quantitative Findings. *Social Indicators Research*, *100*(2), 185–207. https://doi.org/10.1007/s11205-010-9632-5

Ferrari, R. (2015). Writing narrative style literature reviews. *Medical Writing*, *24*(4), 230–235. https://doi.org/10.1179/20 47480615z.000000000329

Finlay, L. (2011). Phenomenology for Therapists, Researching the Lived World, Wiley-Blackwell, USA, UK.

Fiese, B. H., Tomcho, T. J., Douglas, M., Josephs, K., Poltrock, S., & Baker, T. (2002). A review of 50 years of research on naturally occurring family routines and rituals. *Journal of Family Psychology*, *16*, 381–390.

Fishbane, M. (1995). The inwardness of joy in Jewish spirituality. *Boston University Studies in Philosophy and Religion*, *16*, 71–88.

Forero, R., Nahidi, S., De Costa, J., Mohsin, M., FitzGerald, G., Gibson, N., McCarthy, S., & Aboagye-Sarfo, P. (2018). Application of four-dimension criteria to assess rigour of qualitative research in emergency medicine. *BMC Health Services Research*, *18*(1). https://doi.org/10.1186/s12913-018-2915-2

Frank, G., Bernardo, C. S., Tropper, S., Noguchi, F., Lipman, C., Maulhardt, B., & Weitze, L. (1997). Jewish Spirituality through Actions in Time: daily occupations of young Orthodox Jewish couples in Los Angeles. *American Journal of Occupational Therapy*, *51*(3), 199–206. https://doi.org/10.5014/ajot.51.3.199

Frankl, V. E, 1946. (2019). *Yes to Life, In Spite of Everything*, Penguin Random House, UK.

Frankl, V. E. (1963). *The Unheard Cry for Meaning: Psychotherapy and Humanism*.

Frankl, V. E., & Frankl, V. E. (1988). *The will to meaning: Foundations and Applications of Logotherapy*. Plume

Frankl, V. E. (2005). On the Theory and Therapy of Mental Disorders. In *Routledge eBooks*. https://doi.org/10.4324/97 80203005897

Frankl, V. E. (2006). *Man's search for meaning*. Beacon Press

Frankl, V. E. (2014). *The Will to Meaning: Foundations and Applications of Logotherapy*. Penguin

Friedman, M. (2008). *Buber and Dialogical Therapy: Healing Through Meeting*, Taylor & Francis, UK

Future Care Capital. (2022, December 30). *Gen Z are the loneliest generation, research finds – Future Care Capital*. https://futurecarecapital.org.uk/latest/gen-z-are-the-loneliest-generation-research-finds/, accessed 23/8/23

Garcia, A. F. (2015). Beyond Theory: Martin Buber's I and Thou and the Role of Contemplation in Integrated Relational Counseling, Routledge, Taylor and Francis Group, *Journal of Creativity in Mental Health*, 10:423-438, University of Texas, USA

Glickman, A. (2019). https://bethshalompgh.org/what-is-shomer-shabbat-originally-published-may-17-18-2019/ accessed 28/12/22

Global mobile OS market share 2023 | Statista. (2023, August 31). Statista. https://www.statista.com/statistics/272698/global-market-share-held-by-mobile-operating-systems-since-2009/, accessed 9/9/23

Gottlieb, M., & Lasser, J. (2001). Competing Values: A Respectful Critique of Narrative Research. *Ethics & Behavior*, *11*(2), 191–194. https://doi.org/10.1207/s15327019eb1102_6

Growing Up Lonely: Generation Z. (n.d.). Institute for Family Studies. https://ifstudies.org/blog/growing-up-lonely-generation-z

Guba, E. G., & Lincoln, Y. S. (1989). *Fourth generation evaluation*. SAGE

Gurock, J. S. (2006). The late Friday night orthodox service: An exercise in religious accommodation. *Jewish Social Studies: History, Culture, Society*, *12*(3), 137156.

Guba, E.G. and Lincoln, Y.S. (2005). Paradigmatic Controversies, Contradictions, and Emerging Confluences. In: Denzin, N.K. and Lincoln, Y.S., Eds., *The Sage Handbook of Qualitative Research*, 3rd Edition, Sage, Thousand Oaks, 191-215

Halpern, D. & Katz JE (2017). Texting's consequences for romantic relationships: A cross-lagged analysis highlights its risks. *Computers in Human Behavior*, 71, 386–394.

Hamburger, A. Y, Hayat, Z. (2011). The Impact of the Internet of the Social Lives of Users: A Representative Sample from 13 Countries, *Computers in Human Behaviour*, Volume 27, Issue 1

Hammarberg, K., Kirkman, M., & De Lacey, S. (2016). Qualitative research methods: when to use them and how to judge them. *Human Reproduction*, *31*(3), 498–501. https://doi.org/10.1093/humrep/dev334

Hart, C. (1998). *Doing a literature review: Releasing the Social Science Research Imagination*. SAGE.

Hefferon, K, Gil-Rodriguez, E. (2011). Interpretative phenomenological analysis, *The Psychologist*, *24*(10), 756–759

Heidegger, M. (1966). *Discourse on Thinking*

Heidegger, M. (1977). *The question concerning technology, and other essays*. Facsimiles-Garl

Heidegger, M. (2008c). *Being and time*. Harper Collins

Heidegger, M. (1969). *Discourse on Thinking, A Translation of Gelassenheit*, trans. Anderson. J M and Freund. E H, Harper & Row Publishers, New York, https://www.holybooks.com/wp-content/uploads/Discourse-on-Thinking.pdf, accessed 16/6/23

Heschel, A. J. (2005). *The Sabbath*. Farrar, Straus and Giroux.

Hiley, C. (2022), Uswitch, UK Mobile Phone Statistics, 2023, https://www.uswitch.com/mobiles/studies/mobile-statistics/#:~:text=As%20of%202021%2C%2088%25%20of,of%20adults%20had%20a%20smartphone, accessed 11/3/23

Hiniker, A, Schoenebech. S Y, Kientz. J A. (2016). Not at the Dinner Table: Parents' and Children's Perspectives on Family Technology Rules, DOI:10.1145/2818048.2819940

Hoeyer, K, Dahlager. L, Lynöe. N. (2005). Conflicting notions of research ethics: the mutually challenging traditions of social scientists and medical researchers. Soc Sci Med; 61(8):1741–9

Hoepfl, M. C. (1997). Choosing qualitative research: A primer for technology education researchers. *Journal of Technology Education*, 9(1), 47-63. Retrieved February 25, 1998, from http://scholar.lib.vt.edu/ejournals/JTE/v9n1/pdf/hoepfl.pdf

Holroyd-Leduc, J. (2002). Helewa A, Walker JM. Critical Evaluation of Research in Physical Rehabilitation: Towards Evidence-Based Practice. Philadelphia: WB Saunders Company, 2000. *Evidence-based Medicine*, 7(5), 135. https://doi.org/10.1136/ebm.7.5.135

Holloway, I., & Wheeler, S. (2010). *Qualitative research in nursing and healthcare*. John Wiley & Sons

Hoyt, D. L., Hiserodt, M., Gold, A. K., Milligan, M. C., & Otto, M. (2021). Is Ignorance Bliss? Examining the Effect of News Media Exposure on Anxiety and Depression During the COVID-19 Pandemic. *Journal of Nervous and Mental Disease*, 210(2), 91–97. https://doi.org/10.1097/nmd.0000000000001434

Huston, P. (2007). Realization. In *Fordham University Press eBooks* (pp. 106–184). https://doi.org/10.5422/fso/9780823227396.003.0005

Huttunen, R, Kakkor. L. (2021). Heidegger's critique of the technology and educational ecological imperative, Educational Philosophy and Theory, Volume 54, Issue 5, Taylor & Francis Online, accessed 15//6/23

Ibn Paquda, B. (1996). *Duties of the Heart* (D. Haberman, Trans.). Nanuet, NY: Feldheim Publishers.

James, N. (2008). Contributor for qualitative research terms. In L. M. Given (Ed.), *The SAGE Handbook of Qualitative Research Methods* (p. 118). Thousand Oaks, CA: Sage Publications.

Jarman, H. K., Marques, M. D., McLean, S. A., Slater, A., & Paxton, S. J. (2021). Social media, body satisfaction and well-being among adolescents: A mediation model of appearance-ideal internalization and comparison. *Body Image*, 36, 139–148. https://doi.org/10.1016/j.bodyim.2020.11.005

Jones, P, Bano, N. (2021). The Right to Disconnect, Alex Ferry Foundation, Autonomy Publishing, https://autonomy.work/wp-content/uploads/2021/08/the-right-to-disconnect-AutonomyFINAL.pdf, accessed 11/7/23

Kalasi, R. (2014). The impact of social networking on new age teaching and learning: An overview. *Journal of education & social policy*, *1*(1), 23-28

Kardefelt-Winther, D, Heeren. A, Schimmenti. A, Van Rooij A, Maurage. P, Carras. M, Billieux. J. (2017). How can we conceptualize behavioural addiction without pathologizing common behaviours?, *Addiction*, 112 (10), pp. 1709–1715

Konrath, S., O'Brien, E.H., & Hsing, C. (2011). Changes in dispositional empathy in American college students over time: A meta-analysis. *Personality and Social Psychology Review*, *15*, 180-98. doi:10.1177/1088868310377395.

Korstjens, I., & Moser, A. (2017). Series: Practical guidance to qualitative research. Part 4: Trustworthiness and publishing. *European Journal of General Practice*, 24(1), 120–124. https://doi.org/10.1080/13814788.2017.1375092

Krasnova E L, Abramova O, Notter I, & Baumann A (2016). *Why phubbing is toxic for your relationship: Understanding the role of smartphone jealousy among "Generation Y" users*. Twenty-Fourth European Conference on Information Systems (ECIS), Istanbul, Turkey.

Kushlev, K., Dwyer, R., & Whillans, A. V. (2019). The Social Price of Constant Connectivity: Smartphones Impose Subtle Costs on Well-Being. *Current Directions in Psychological Science*, *28*(4), 347–352. https://doiorg/10.1177/09637 21419847200

Kushlev, K., Dunn, E. W. (2019). Smartphones distract parents from cultivating feelings of connection when spending time with their children. *Journal of Social and Personal Relationships*, *36*, 1619–1639.

Kushlev, K., Proulx J., Dunn E. W. (2016). "Silence your phones": Smartphone notifications increase inattention and hyperactivity symptoms. In Proceedings of the 2016 CHI

Conference on Human Factors in Computing Systems (pp. 1011–1020). New York, NY: ACM.

Latif, M Z, Hussain, I, Saeed. R, Atif Qureshi. M, Maqsood. U. (2019). Use of Smartphones and Social Media in Medical Education: Trends, Advantages, Challenges and Barriers, *Journal of Academy of Medical Sciences of Bosnia and Herzegovina*, Acta Inform Med

Lanette, S. (2018). *The mere presence of mobile phones during Parent-Teen interactions*. https://escholarship.org/uc/item/1j709942

Lazar, A. (2015). The relation between prayer type and life satisfaction in religious Jewish men and women: The moderating effects of prayer duration and belief in prayer. *The International Journal for the Psychology of Religion*, 25(3), 211–229. https://doi.org/10.1080/10508619.2014.920603

Lemmens, P. (2011). 'This system does not produce pleasure anymore' an interview with Bernard Stiegler. Krisis. (1), 33–41.

Levin, J. (2013). Religious behavior, health, and well-being among Israeli Jews: Findings from the European Social Survey. *Psychology of Religion and Spirituality*, 5(4), 272–282. https://doi.org/10.1037/a0032601

Li, J, Pearce, P L, Low. D. (2020). Media representation of digital-free tourism: A critical discourse analysis, *Tourism Management*, 69 (2018), pp. 317–329

Li, L, Wang X. (2020). Technostress inhibitors and creators and their impacts on university teachers' work performance in higher education. *Cognition, Technology & Work*, 23(2): 315–330. doi: 10.1007/s10111-020-00625-0.

Lievrouw, L. A. (2001). New Media and the 'Pluralization of Life-World': A Role for Information in Social Differentiation',

A DAY OF DIGITAL REST

New Media & Society, volume 3, number 1. pp. 7–28: http://dx.doi.org/10.1177/1461444801003001002, accessed on 5/2/23

Lincoln, Y. S., & Guba, E. G. (1985). *Naturalistic inquiry*. sage.

Lincoln, Y. S., & Guba, E. G. (1986b). But is it rigorous? Trustworthiness and authenticity in naturalistic evaluation. *New Directions for Program Evaluation*, *1986*(30), 73–84. https://doi.org/10.1002/ev.1427

Lipman, S. (2011). Is 'Half Shabbos' a New Way of Life?, Orthodox Union, https://www.ou.org/life/parenting/is_half_shabbos_a_new_way_of_life/, 13 February 2023.

Lissak, G. (2018). Adverse physiological and psychological effects of screen time on children and adolescents: Literature review and case study. *Environmental Research*, *164*, 149–157. https://doi.org/10.1016/j.envres.2018.01.015

Loh, C. E., & Sun, B. (2022). The impact of technology use on adolescents' leisure reading preferences. *Literacy*, *56*(4), 327–339. https://doi.org/10.1111/lit.12282

Luborsky, M R, Rubinstein. R L. (1995). Sampling in qualitative research: rationale, issues and methods. *Research on Aging*, *17*: 89–113

Markee, N. (2012). Emic and Etic in Qualitative Research. *The Encyclopedia of Applied Linguistics*. https://doi.org/10.1002/9781405198431.wbeal0366

Markowitz, D. M., Laha, R., Perone, B. P., Pea, R. D., and Bailenson, J. N. (2018). Immersive virtual reality field trips facilitate learning about climate change. *Front. Psychol.* 9:2364. doi: 10.3389/fpsyg.2018.02364

Marks, L. D. (2004). Sacred practices in highly religious families: Christian, Jewish, Mormon, and Muslim perspectives. *Family Process*, *43*, 217–231

Marks, L. D., Hatch, T., & Dollahite, D. C. (2017b). Sacred practices and family processes in a Jewish context: Shabbat as the weekly family ritual par excellence. *Family Process*, *57*(2), 448–461. https://doi.org/10.1111/famp.12286

Marx, L. (1997). Technology: The Emergence of a Hazardous Concept, Social Research, Vol. 64. No 3. *Technology and the Rest of Culture* pp 965-988, https://eclass.uniwa.gr/modules/document/file.php/MSCRES102/02%20marx%20leo%20the%20emergence%20of%20a%20hazardous%20concept%20social%20researc.pdf, accessed 28/6/23

McDaniel, B. T., & Coyne, S M. (2016). "Technoference": The interference of technology in couple relationships and implications for women's personal and relational well-being. *Psychology of Popular Media Culture*, *5*(1), 85–98. https://doi.org/10.1037/ppm0000065

McDaniel, BT, Galovan, A M, Cravens I, & Drouin, M. (2018). Technoference and implications for mothers' and fathers' couple and coparenting relationship quality. *Computers in Human Behavior*, *80*, 303–313

McDaniel, B T., & Drouin, M. (2019). Daily technology interruptions and emotional and relational well-being. *Computers in Human Behavior*, *99*, 1–8. https://doi.org/10.1016/j.chb.2019.04.027

McDaniel, B. T., & Radesky, J. (2018). Technoference: Parent distraction by technology and associations with child behavior problems. *Child Development*, *89*, 100-109. doi: 10.1111/cdev.12822

Merriam, S. B. (2002). Introduction to qualitative research. *Qualitative research in practice: Examples for discussion and analysis*, *1*(1), 1-17

Mehrabian, A. (1981). Silent messages: Implicit communication of emotions and attitudes. Belmont, CA: Wadsworth Publishing.

Michaels. I. (2016). Unplugging: A Phenomenological Study of the Perceived Holistic Health Benefits from Regular Digital Detox in the Context of the Jewish Shabbat, St Catherine University, Sophia, Master of Arts in Holistic Health Studies Research Papers

Millgram, A E. (1947). Sabbath The Day of Delight, The Jewish Publication Society of America, Philadelphia, USA. Social Isolation, Wellington, Australasion Conference on Information Systems

Mintel, (2023, August 4). *UK Lifestyles of Generation Z Market Report 2023*. Mintel Store. https://store.mintel.com/ report/uk-lifestyles-of-generation-z-market-report

Misra, S., Cheng, L., Genevie, J., & Miao, Y. (2014). The iPhone effect. *Environment and Behavior*, 48(2), 275–298. https://doi.org/10.1177/0013916514539755

Mitchell, T. (2022b, October 6). *Jewish practices and customs in the U.S. | Pew Research Center*. Pew Research Center's Religion & Public Life Project. https://www.pewresearch.org/ religion/2021/05/11/jewish-practices-and-customs/accessed 7/2/23.

Morris, N., & Pickens, J. C. (2017). "I'm Not a Gadget": A Grounded Theory on Unplugging. *American Journal of Family Therapy*, 1–19.

Moya, P. (2014). Habit and embodiment in Merleau-Ponty. *Frontiers in Human Neuroscience*, 8. https://doi.org/10.3389/ fnhum.2014.00542

Muller, W. (2000). *Sabbath: Finding rest, renewal, and delight in our busy lives*. New York, NY: Bantam Books.

Murray, M. (2003). Narrative psychology and narrative analysis. In *American Psychological Association eBooks* (pp. 95–112). https://doi.org/10.1037/10595-006

Murray, S.J., Holmes, D. Interpretive Phenomenological Analysis (IPA) and the Ethics of Body and Place: Critical Methodological Reflections. *Hum Stud*, *37*, 15–30 (2014). https://doi.org/10.1007/s10746-013-9282-0

Myers, T. A., Ridolfi, D. R., Crowther, J. H., & Ciesla, J. A. (2012). The impact of appearance-focused social comparisons on body image disturbance in the naturalistic environment: The roles of thin-ideal internalization and feminist beliefs. *Body Image*, *9*(3), 342–351. https://doi.org/10.1016/j.bodyim.2012.03.005

Nakshine, V. S., Thute, P. P., Khatib, M. N., & Sarkar, B. (2022). Increased screen time as a cause of declining physical, psychological health, and sleep patterns: a literary review. *Cureus*. https://doi.org/10.7759/cureus.30051

National Trust for Scotland. (2023, February 22). *Digital detox holidays in Scotland*. https://www.nts.org.uk/stories/digital-detox-holidays-in-scotland

Navon, D., & Gopher, D. (1979). On the economy of the human-processing system. *Psychological Review*, *86*(3), 214–255. https://doi.org/10.1037/0033-295X.86.3.214

Nelson, T. A., Abeyta, A. A., and Routledge, C. (2019). What makes life meaningful for theists and atheists? Psychol. Relig. Spirituality.

Nelson, S. K., Kushlev, K., Lyubomirsky, S. (2014). The pains and pleasures of parenting: When, why, and how is parenthood associated with more or less well-being? *Psychological Bulletin*, *140*, 846–895.

Nizza, I E, Farr. J, Smith. J A. (2021). Achieving Excellence in Interpretative Phenomenological Analysis (IPA): Four Markers of High Quality, *Qualitative Research in Psychology*, Volume 18 – Issue 3, pages 369-386, Taylor & Francis Online, https://www-tandfonline-com.ezproxy.mdx.ac.

uk/doi/full/10.1080/14780887.2020.1854404, accessed 1/6/2023

Noble, H, Smith, J. (2015). *Issues of Validity and Reliability in Qualitative Research, School of Nursing and Midwifery*, Queens's University Belfast, UK; http://dx.doi.org/10.1136/eb-2015-102054, accessed 7/2/23

Nuccetelli-Hurtado/Nudler. (n.d.). *The Furniture of the World: Essays in Ontology and Metaphysics*. Notre Dame Philosophical Reviews. https://ndpr.nd.edu/reviews/he-furniture-of-the-world-essays-in-ontology-and-metaphysics/

Pascale, C. (2011). Cartographies of knowledge: Exploring qualitative epistemologies. Thousand Oaks, CA: Sage.

Pinquart, M. (2017). Associations of Parenting Dimensions and Styles with Externalizing Problems of Children and Adolescents: An Updated Meta-Analysis. Developmental Psychology, 53, 873-932. 10.1037/dev0000295

Pietkiewicz, I, Smith. J. (2014). A practical guide to using Interpretative Phenomenological Analysis in qualitative research psychology, *Psychological Journal*

Pringle, J, Drummond. J, McLafferty. E, Hendry. C. (2011). Interpretative phenomenological analysis: a discussion and critique. *Nurse Researcher*, *18*(3), 20–24

Ofcom. (2022). Making Communication Word for Everyone, Online Nation, 2022 Report, https://www.ofcom.org.uk/__data/assets/pdf_file/0023/238361/online-nation-2022-report.pdf, accessed 11/3/23

Orb, A, Eisenhauer. L, Wynaden. D. (2001). Ethics in qualitative research. J Nurs Scholar, 33(1):93–6

Ortiz-Ospina, E. (2019). *The Rise of Social Media, Our World in Data*, University of Oxford

Oxford Learners Dictionary, Digital Detox, https://www.oxfordlearnersdictionaries.com/definition/english/digital-detox#:~:text=%2F%CB%8Cd%C9%AAd%CA%92%C9%AAtl%20%CB%88di%CB%90t%C9%91%CB%90ks%2F, to%20reduce%20stress%20and%20relax, accessed 26/6/23.

Oxley, L. (2016). An examination of Interpretative Phenomenological Analysis (IPA). *Educational and Child Psychology*, *33*(3), 55–62. https://doi.org/10.53841/bpsecp.2016.33.3.55

Palandrani, P. (2022). A Decade of Change: How Tech Evolved in the 2010s and What's in Store for the 2020s, Global X ETF's, Nasdaq, https://www.nasdaq.com/articles/a-decade-of-change%3A-how-tech-evolved-in-the-2010s-and-whats-in-store-for-the-2020s, accessed 11/3/23

Patton, M. Q. (2002). *Qualitative Evaluation and Research Methods* (3rd ed.). Thousand Oaks, CA: Sage Publications, Inc

Pelcovitz, R., & Pelcovitz, D. (2014). *Life in the balance: Torah perspectives on positive psychology*. Shaar Press

Pew Research Center. (2018, February 5). *Mobile fact sheet*. Retrieved from Pew Research Center website: http://www.pewinternet.org/fact-sheet/mobile/

Phillips, R. (2019). *An Ambivalent Jewishness: Half Shabbos, the Shabbos App, and Modern Orthodoxy*, Springer

Piaget, J. (1953). *The Origins of Intelligence in Children*. New York, NY: Basic Books.

Pirutinsky, S., Rosmarin, D. H., Holt, C. L., Feldman, R. H., Caplan, L. S., Midlarsky, E., & Pargament, K. I. (2011). Does social support mediate the moderating effect of intrinsic religiosity on the relationship between physical health and depressive symptoms among Jews? *Journal of Behavioral*

Medicine, *34*(6), 489–496. https://doi.org/10.1007/s10865-011-9325-9

Ponterotto, J. G. (2005). Qualitative research in counseling psychology: A primer on research paradigms and philosophy of science. *Journal of Counseling Psychology*, *52*(2), 126–136.

Przybylski, A. K., & Weinstein, N. (2012). Can you connect with me now? How the presence of mobile communication technology influences face-to-face conversation quality. *Journal of Social and Personal Relationships*, *30*(3), 237–246. https://doi.org/10.1177/0265407512453827

Przybylski et al., 2013, A.K. Przybylski, K. Murayama, C.R. DeHaan, V. Gladwell Motivational, emotional, and behavioral correlates of fear of missing out, *Computers in Human Behavior*, *29* (4) (2013), pp. 1841–1848

Psychology Today. (2022), 3 Things Making Gen Z the Loneliest Generation, Jenkins. R, 16 August 2022, https://www.psychologytoday.com/gb/blog/the-case-connection/202208/3-things-making-gen-z-the-loneliest-generation, accessed 23/8/23

Putnam, R. D. (2000). Bowling Alone: America's declining social capital. In *Palgrave Macmillan US eBooks* (pp. 223–234). https://doi.org/10.1007/978-1-349-62397-6_12

Qi, C. (2019). A double-edged sword? Exploring the impact of students' academic usage of mobile devices on technostress and academic performance. Behav. Inform. Technol. 1–18. doi: 10.1080/0144929X.2019.1585476

Radesky, J. S., Kistin, C. J., Zuckerman, B., Nitzberg, K., Gross, J., Kaplan-Sanoff, M., Augustyn, M., & Silverstein, M. (2014). Patterns of mobile device use by caregivers and children during meals in fast food restaurants. *Pediatrics*, *33*, e843–e849.

Radtke, T., Apel, T., Schenkel, K., Keller, J., & Von Lindern, E. (2021). Digital detox: An effective solution in the smartphone era? A systematic literature review. *Mobile Media and Communication*, *10*(2), 190–215. https://doi.org/10.1177/20501579211028647

Ragu-Nathan, T. S., Tarafdar, M., Ragu-Nathan, B. S., & Tu, Q. (2008). The Consequences of technostress for end users in Organizations: Conceptual development and empirical validation. *Information Systems Research*, *19*(4), 417–433. https://doi.org/10.1287/isre.1070.0165

Ratcliffe, M. (2019). Towards a phenomenology of grief: Insights from Merleau-Ponty. *European Journal of Philosophy*, *28*(3), 657–669. https://doi.org/10.1111/ejop.12513

Raviv, Z. (2000). On truth, tradition, and respect in Jewish education. *Journal of Jewish Communal Service*, 76(4), 275-291

Reid, K., Flowers, P., & Larkin, M. (2005). Exploring lived Experience. *ResearchGate*. https://www.researchgate.net/publication/221670347_Exploring_lived_Experience

Richards, K. (2003). Qualitative Inquiry in TESOL. Basingstoke: Palgrave Macmillan

Roberts, J, Koliska, J. (2014). The Effects of Ambient Media: What Unplugging Reveals about being Plugged in, Peer Reviewed Journal, First Monday, Volume 19, Number 84, Researchgate

Roberts, P., & Priest, H. (Eds.). (2010). *Healthcare research: A handbook for students and practitioners*. John Wiley & Sons

Roberts, J A, & David, M E. (2016). My life has become a major distraction from my cell phone: Partner phubbing and relationship satisfaction among romantic partners. *Computers in Human Behavior*, *54*, 134–141.

Robinson, O C. (2013). Sampling in Interview-Based Qualitative Research: A Theoretical and Practical Guide, pp. 25–41, https://www-tandfonline-com.ezproxy.mdx.ac.uk/doi/full/10.1080/14780887.2013.801543, accessed 28/6/23

Rosenblum, J. (2012). Half Shabbos Is No Shabbos, Jewish Action, The Magazine of The Orthodox Union, Religion, https://jewishaction.com/religion/shabbat-holidays/half-shabbos-is-no-shabbos/, 13/2/2023

Sacasas, L. M. (2014, February 14). *Leo Marx – L.M. Sacasas*. L.M. Sacasas. https://thefrailestthing.com/tag/leo-marx/#:~:text=Hughes%20has%20aptly%20called%20the,to%20conceal%20every%20trace%20of, accessed 26/7/23

Sacks, J. (2014). Happiness: A Jewish perspective. *Journal of Law and Religion*, 29(1), 30–47

Sacks, J. (2019). Celebrating Life: Finding Happiness in Unexpected Places, Continuum Publishers, London, UK

Sacks, J. (2021). Morality: Restoring the Common Good in Divided Times, Hodder & Stoughton, UK

Sagioglou, C., & Greitemeyer, T. (2014). Facebook's emotional consequences: Why Facebook causes a decrease in mood and why people still use it. *Computers in Human Behavior*, 35, 359–363. https://doi.org/10.1016/j.chb.2014.03.003

Sanjari, M, Bahramnezhad. F, Khoshnava F. F, Shoghi. M, Cheraghi. M A. (2014). Ethical Challenges of Researchers in Qualitative Studies: the Necessity to Develop a Specific Guideline, https://www.ncbi.nlm.nih.gov/pmc/articles/PMC4263394/, accessed 28/6/23

Sartre, J. (2021). *Being and Nothingness*. Simon and Schuster.

Saylor Academy. (2012). *Principles of sociological inquiry; Qualitative and quantitative methods*. Washington, DC: Saylor Academy. Retrieved from https://www.saylor.org/site/

textbooks/Principles%20of%20Sociological%20Inquiry. pdfaccessed 24/8/23

Saylor Academy Open Textbooks, *Saylor Academy*. (2022, November 17). Saylor Academy. http://www.saylor.org/ books, accessed 27/8/23

Saul, J., Rodgers, R. F., & Saul, M. (2022). Adolescent Eating Disorder Risk and the Social Online World. *Child and Adolescent Psychiatric Clinics of North America, 31*(1), 167–177. https://doi.org/10.1016/j.chc.2021.09.004

Saunders, M. N. K., & Lewis, P. G. (2011b). *Doing Research in Business and Management: an essential guide to planning your project*. https://epubs.surrey.ac.uk/817620/

Schiffman, M., Cherniak, A., Schnall, E., Brooks, S., Pirutinsky, S., Shabtai, D. (2023). Positive Psychology and Judaism. In: Davis, E.B., Worthington Jr., E.L., Schnitker, S.A. (eds) Handbook of Positive Psychology, Religion, and Spirituality. Springer, Cham. https://doi.org/10.1007/978-3-031-10274-5_11

Schnall, E. (2006). Multicultural counseling and the Orthodox Jew. *Journal of Counseling and Development, 84*, 276–282. https://doi.org/10.1002/j.1556-6678.2006. tb00406.x

Scott, J., Scott, R. G., Miller, M. W. L., Stange, K. C., & Crabtree, B. F. (2009). Healing relationships and the existential philosophy of Martin Buber. *Philosophy, Ethics, and Humanities in Medicine, 4*(1), 11. https://doi.org/ 10.1186/1747-5341-4-11

Sheskin, I. M., & Dashefsky. A. (2020). United States Jewish population, 2019. In *American Jewish year book 2019* (pp. 135–231). Springer

Sinead. (2022). Right to Disconnect Legislation in Europe. *Capital GES*. https://www.capital-ges.com/right-to-disconnect-legislation-in-europe/

Singer, D., & Sokol, M. (1982). Joseph Soloveitchik: Lonely Man of Faith. *Modern Judaism*, *2*(3), 227–272. https://doi.org/10.1093/mj/2.3.227

Singh, A P, Dangmei. J. (2016). Understanding the Generation Z: The Future Workforce, Universal Multidisciplinary Research Institute Pvt Ltd

Society, C. (2019, May 22). *A relational approach to therapy*. NCS. https://nationalcounsellingsociety.org/blog/posts/a-relational-approach-to-therapy, accessed 27/8/23

Sofaer, S. (1999). Qualitative methods: what are they and why use them?, *Health Services Research*, *34*(5 Pt 2): 1101-1118

Smith, A. (2015,). *U.S. smartphone use in 2015*. Retrieved from Pew Research Center website: http://www.pewinternet.org/2015/04/01/us-smartphone-use-in-2015/, accessed 10/7/23

Smith, J., Van Langenhove, L., & Harré, R. (1995). Rethinking methods in psychology. In *SAGE Publications Ltd eBooks*. https://doi.org/10.4135/9781446221792

Smith, J. A. (Ed.). (2003). *Qualitative psychology: A practical guide to research methods*. Sage Publications, Inc.

Smith, J. A., Flowers, P., & Larkin, M. (2021). *Interpretative Phenomenological analysis: Theory, Method and Research*. SAGE

Smith, J. A. (2007). Hermeneutics, human sciences and health: linking theory and practice. *International Journal of Qualitative Studies on Health and Well-being*, *2*(1), 3–11. https://doi.org/10.1080/17482620601016120

Smith, M, Puczkó. L. (2015). *More than a Special Interest: Defining and Determining the Demand for Health Tourism, Tourism Recreation Research*, *40* (2), pp. 205–219

Speedling, B B. (2019). Celebrating Sabbath as a Holistic Health Practice: The Transformative Power of a Sanctuary in Time, *Journal of Religion and Health*, 1382-1400

Sreenivas, S. (2021). Digital Detox: What to Know, https://www.webmd.com/balance/what-is-digital-detox, accessed 20/6/23

StackPath. (2022). https://brodies.com/insights/employment-and-immigration/the-right-to-disconnect-what-is-it-and-should-employers-introduce-it/. Accessed 11/7/23

Stäheli, U., & Stoltenberg, L. (2022). Digital detox tourism: Practices of analogization. *New Media & Society*, 0(0). https://doi.org/10.1177/14614448211072808

Statista. (n.d.). *Statista – The Statistics Portal*. https://www.statista.com/aboutus/our-research-commitment/2678/federica-laricchia, accessed 12/9/23

Smartphone ownership by age 2012-2023 | Statista. (2023, August 21). Statista. https://www.statista.com/statistics/271851/smartphone-owners-in-the-united-kingdom-uk-by-age/, accessed 23/8/23

Stiegler, B. (2011). Distrust and the Pharmacology of Transformational Technologies, Information Technology, Philosophy of Technology, New Media, Digital Humanities, https://www.academia.edu/12692249/Bernard_Stiegler_Distrust_and_the_Pharmacology_of_Transformational_Technologies_2011, accessed 28/6/23

Strauss, A., & Corbin, J. (1990). *Basics of Qualitative Research: Grounded Theory Procedures and Techniques*. Newbury Park, CA: Sage Publications, Inc

Sullivan, C., & Forrester, M. A. (2019). *Doing Qualitative Research in Psychology: A Practical Guide*. SAGE Publications Limited.

Sun, Y., Yang, J., Li, M., & Liu, T. (2022). The Association Between Neuroticism and Nomophobia: Chain Mediating Effect of Attachment and Loneliness. *International Journal of Mental Health and Addiction.* https://doi.org/10.1007/s11469-022-00897-9

Smith-Gabai. H, (2011). Observing the Jewish Sabbath: A Meaningful Restorative Ritual for Modern Times. *Journal of Occupational Science, 18*(4), 347–355. https://doi.org/10.1080/14427591.2011.595891

Syversten, T, Enli, G. (2019). Digital Detox: Media Resistance and the Promise of Authenticity, Sage Journals

Syvertsen, T. (2020). *Digital Detox: The Politics of Disconnecting.* Emerald Group Publishing

Tindall, L. (2009). J.A. Smith, P. Flower and M. Larkin (2009), *Interpretative Phenomenological Analysis: Theory, Method and Research. Qualitative Research in Psychology,* 6(4), 346–347. https://doi.org/10.1080/14780880903340091

Tarafdar, M., Tu, Q., Ragu-Nathan, B. S., & Ragu-Nathan, T. S. (2007). The impact of technostress on role stress and productivity. *Journal of Management Information Systems,* 24(1), 301–328. https://doi.org/10.2753/mis0742-1222240109

Taylor, M. C., Rubenstein, M., & Carlson, T. A. (2021). *Image: Three Inquiries in Technology and Imagination.* University of Chicago Press

Telushkin, S. (2014). Shabbat is a day of rest—But does it mean I can't text my friends? Retrieved from https://www.tabletmag.com/jewish-life-and-religion/184233/shabbat-phones, accessed 25/6/23.

The Annie E. Casey Foundation. (2023, March 13). *What Are the Core Characteristics of Generation Z?* https://www.aecf.org/blog/what-are-the-core-characteristics-of-generation-z, accessed 17/6/23

Thomas, R. A. (2019). *Bernard Stiegler on a Unified vision of Humanity and Technology in education: An Analysis of Human/technical Ideology in the Writings of Today's Most Influential Educational Leaders*, accessed 28/6/23

Tomlinson, Y N, (2023). The Importance of Engaging with Ontology and Epistemology as an ECR, https://www.bps.org.uk/psychologist/importance-engaging-ontology-and-epistemology-ecr, accessed 28/6/23

Turkle, S. (2017). *Alone together: Why We Expect More from Technology and Less from Each Other*. Hachette UK

University of Maine, Social Media Statistics Details. (2021). https://umaine.edu/undiscoveredmaine/small-business/resources/marketing-for-small-business/social-media-tools/social-media-statistics-details/, accessed 23/6/23

Upadhyaya P, Acharya V. Impact of technostress on academic the productivity of university students. *Education & Information Technologies*. (2020) doi: 10.1007/s10639-020-10319-9

Urquhart, C. (2013). *Grounded theory for qualitative research: A Practical Guide*. SAGE

Vail, K., and Routledge, C. (2020). *The Science of Religion, Spirituality, and Existentialism*. Academic Press, Elsevier, New York.

Varma, H. (2018). Digital detox: the art of switching off. *INROADS – an International Journal of Jaipur National University*, 7(1and2), 8. https://doi.org/10.5958/2277-4912.2018.00023.1

Van Manen. M. (2017). But is it phenomenology? *Qualitative Health Research*, 27, 775–779

Wajcman, J. (2016). *Pressed for Time: The Acceleration of Life in Digital Capitalism*. University of Chicago Press.

Walsh, F. (2010). *Spiritual Resources in Family Therapy, second edition*. Guilford Press

Wang, X., & Li, B. (2019). Technostress Among University Teachers in Higher Education: A Study Using Multidimensional Person-Environment Misfit Theory. *Frontiers in Psychology*, *10*. https://doi.org/10.3389/fpsyg.2019.01791

Weberman, D. (2011). Sartre on the Authenticity, Required if My Choices Are to be Truly Mine. *Filozofia*, *66*(9). http://www.klemens.sav.sk/fiusav/doc/filozofia/2011/9/879-889.pdf

Webmaster, C. (2019b, May 13). *Remembering Martin Buber and the I–Thou in counseling – Counseling Today*. Counseling Today. https://ct.counseling.org/2019/05/remembering-martin-buber-and-the-i-thou-in-counseling/, accessed 19/7/23

Weiss, Z., & Levy, D. (2010). "The Eternal is with me, I shall not fear": Jewish contemplative practices and well-being. In T. G. Plane (Ed.), *Contemplative Practices in Action: Spirituality, Mediation, and Health* (pp. 103–121). Santa Barbara, CA: ABC-CLIO.

Wendland, A. J., Merwin, C., & Hadjioannou, C. (2018). *Heidegger on technology*. Routledge

Widyanto, L., & McMurran, M. (2004). The Psychometric Properties of the Internet Addiction Test. *Cyberpsychology & Behavior*, *7*(4), 443–450. https://doi.org/10.1089/cpb.2004.7.443

Williams, R. (2003b). *Television: Technology and Cultural Form*. Psychology Press.

Willig, C. (2021b). *EBOOK: Introducing Qualitative Research in Psychology 4E*. McGraw-Hill Education (UK)

Willig, C. (2008). *Introducing Qualitative Research in Psychology* (2nd edn.). Open University Press, UK

Willig, C, Billin, A. (2011). Existentialist-Informed Hermeneutic Phenomenology, In: *Qualitative Research Methods in Mental Health and Psychotherapy: A Guide for Students and Practitioners*. (pp. 117–130), City University of London Institutional Repository, Wiley-Blackwell

Willig, C. (2016). Constructivism and 'The Real World': Can they co-exist?. City Research online, City University of London, https://openaccess.city.ac.uk/id/eprint/13576/1/, accessed 12/3/23

Winner, L. (1997). *Technology and Values, Technologies as Forms of Life*, Rowman & Littlefield Publishers, Inc, Lanham, Boulder, New York, Oxford.

C. S. Wyatt, cswyatt@tameri.com. (n.d.). *Existential Primer: Theology*. (C) 2020 C. S. Wyatt. https://www.tameri.com/csw/exist/ex_theo.html, accessed 18/7/23

Yao, N., & Wang, Q. (2022). Technostress from Smartphone Use and Its Impact on University Students' Sleep Quality and Academic Performance. *Asia-pacific Education Researcher*, 32(3), 317–326. https://doi.org/10.1007/s40299-022-00654-5

Yardley, Y. (2017). Demonstrating the validity of qualitative research, The Journal of Positive Psychology, 12:3, 295-296, DOI: 10.1080/17439760.2016.1262624

Yin, R. K. (1989). *Case Study Research: Design and Methods*. SAGE Publications, Incorporated.

Zerubavel, E. (1982). The Standardization of Time: A Sociohistorical Perspective. *American Journal of Sociology*, 88(1), 1–23. https://doi.org/10.1086/227631

APPENDIX A: Recruitment Advert

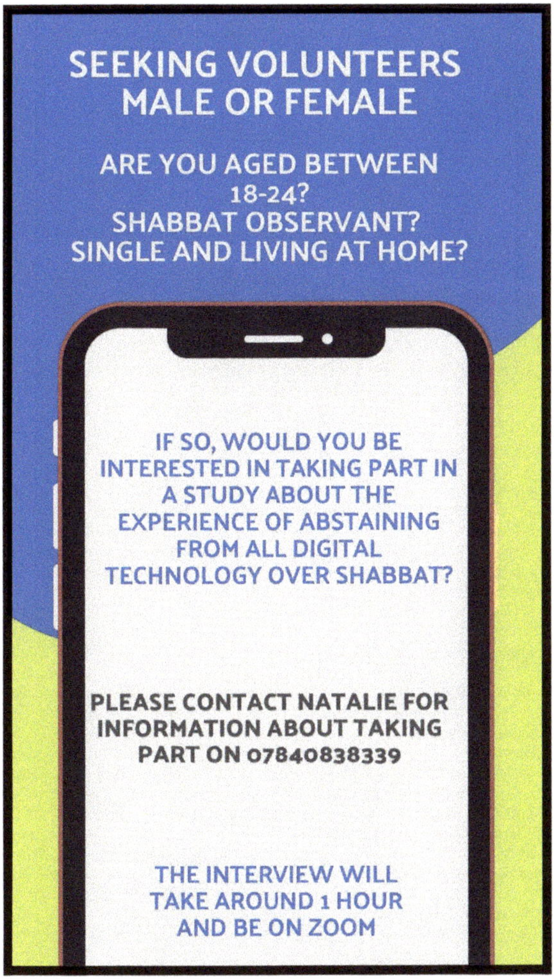

APPENDIX B: Participant Information Sheet

NSPC

*The Department of Health and Social
Sciences
Middlesex University
Hendon
London NW4 4BT*

Date: 9/2/22

<u>Title:</u>

'An Interpretative Phenomenological Analysis of Young Jewish Adults Experience of Having a Digital Detox During Shabbat'

<u>Invitation paragraph</u>

You are being invited to take part in this research study. Before you decide to participate, it is important for you to understand why the research is being done and what it will involve. Please take your time to read the following information carefully and discuss it with family, friends and any other people if you wish. Please ask if there is anything that is not clear or if you would like more information. Take your time to decide whether or not you wish to take part.

<u>What is the purpose of the research</u>?

This study is being carried out as part of my studies at NSPC Ltd and Middlesex University. Data shows that technology usage is rising year on year and that human behaviour is affected and shaped by technology (Aiken, 2016). However, there is a lack of research as to the impact of a regular digital detox on young adults. This study has been designed to learn more about your experience of abstaining from all forms of digital technology for one day per week every week of the year. I believe that data that results from interviewing participants such as yourself will be helpful to researchers and professionals who are interested in what it's like for young adults who normally interact with digital technology to completely abstain from it for 25 hours weekly over Shabbat. The impact this has on your life, your sense-of wellbeing, your relationships with family and friends may add value to the emerging field of data about the experience of digital detox for individuals and professionals who are interested in what weekly digital technology abstinence brings about.

Why have I been chosen?

You have been chosen because you responded to my advertisement seeking participants who abstain from using all digital technology during Shabbat. You are a young adult, you are single and you live at home, you therefore fit my inclusion criteria to take part in this research.

Do I have to take part?

No. You do not have to take part. Taking part is voluntary and you are free to stop taking part any time until June 2022 at which time the data from your interview will be transcribed.

What will happen to me if I take part?

If you choose to take part, you will be asked to attend one interview that will last for 45 minutes to 1 hour either via zoom or at a venue of our choosing. We will agree on a time that is convenient to you.

If we meet via zoom, you will be sent a passworded invite via email. You will be asked to read and sign a consent form and following this we will discuss your experiences, your thoughts and your feelings about what it's like to have a weekly digital detox every Shabbat.

This discussion will be confidential between us. I will ask you questions that will guide us through the topic and invite you to answer them as you see fit. There are no right or wrong answers, everything you say is important and of interest to the study as it helps me understand your experience.

Following the interview, the information you provide will be combined with the information from other participants for analysis. I will use a qualitative research method to extract the main themes of what you and other people tell me about your experience of a digital detox during Shabbat.

If you choose to be interviewed via zoom, you need to ensure that the interview will be held at a private location where you will not be interrupted. Any issues such as potential technical problems or anything else related to the zoom interview will be discussed via email prior to the interview.

What are the possible disadvantages to taking part?

Talking about your experience of observing abstinence from all forms of digital technology can in rare occasions cause distress. If so, please let me know, and if you wish, I will stop the interview. If you feel distressed during or following the interview you can talk to me about it or I can advise another therapist.

Although this is unlikely, should you tell me something that I am required by law to pass on to a third person, I will have to do so. Otherwise, whatever you tell me will be confidential. It will also require 45 minutes to one hour of your time.

What are the possible benefits of taking part?

We do not know much about the benefits or drawbacks of having a digital detox over Shabbat but it is possible that it will be helpful for people in future who are interested in the experience of abstaining from all digital devices every week over Shabbat. Being interviewed about your experience has no direct benefit although some people may find it an opportunity to reflect on their experience of digital detox over Shabbat and may find it beneficial. When the results of the research have been published I would be happy to meet again to tell you about it, if that is something you would like.

Who is organising and funding the research?

This study is being carried out as part of my studies at NSPC Ltd and Middlesex University. The research is self-funded.

What will you do with the information that I provide?

The interview will be transcribed by another person. So I will not use your full or last name in the interview and the person transcribing the interview will not know who you are. I will be recording the interview on a digital recorder, and will transfer the files to a USB stick for storage and backup. The USB stick will be encrypted when being uploaded to the computer using a secure encryption application. The interview from the recorder will be deleted once the data from the interview has been transcribed. All of the information that you provide me will be identified only with a project code and stored on the USB stick in a locked filing cabinet together with the recorder. I will be the sole holder of the key to that cabinet. The interview on the USB stick will be kept in the locked cabinet up to 6 months after I graduate and then it will be deleted and the USB stick will be destroyed. The information will always be treated as confidential. If my research is published, I will make sure that neither your name or other identifying details are used.

Data will be stored according to the Data Protection Act and the Freedom of Information Act

Who has reviewed the study?

All proposals for research using human participants are reviewed by an Ethics Committee before they can proceed. The NSPC Ethics Committee have reviewed this proposal as well as my research supervisors.

Expenses

If you choose to meet face to face I will offer to reimburse you for any travel expenses incurred.

Consent

You will be given a copy of this information sheet for your personal records and, if you agree to take part, you will be asked to sign the attached consent form before the study begins.

Participation in this study is entirely voluntary. You do not have to take part if you do not want to. If you decide to take part you may withdraw at any time without giving a reason. Whether or not you participate will not affect the relationship you have with me should we meet in future.

Concluding section

Thank you for reading this information sheet.

If you have any further questions, you can contact me at:
The Existential Academy, 61-63 Fortune Green Road, London, NW6 1DR
ns1103@live.mdx.ac.uk

If you any concerns about the conduct of the study, you may contact my supervisor:

Dr Andreas Vossler
The Open University
Andreas.vossler@open.ac.uk

Or

The Principal
NSPC Ltd. 61 – 63 Fortune Green Road
London NW6 1DR
Admin@nspc.org.uk
0044 (0) 20 7435 8067

Thank you for reading this information sheet.

Researcher:

Supervisor:

APPENDIX C: Consent Form

Middlesex University School of Science and Technology
Psychology Department
Written Informed Consent

Middlesex University London

Title of study and academic year: DcPsyche Psychotherapy and Counselling

Researcher's name: Natalie Scheiner   Date: 26/4/22

Supervisor's name and email: Dr Andreas Vossler
                                  Andreas.Vossler@open.ac.uk

- I have understood the details of the research as explained to me by the researcher, and confirm that I have consented to act as a participant.

- I have been given contact details for the researcher in the information sheet.

- I understand that my participation is entirely voluntary, the data collected during the research will not be identifiable, and I have the right to withdraw from participating in the project at any time without any obligation to explain my reasons for doing so.

- I understand that I can ask for my data to be withdrawn from the project until the study is published.

- I further understand that the data I provide may be used for analysis and subsequent publication for my doctoral thesis, and I provide my consent that this may occur.

- I understand that my raw data will be stored securely and anonymously by The New School of Psychotherapy and Counselling for up to 10 years after the work is submitted

_____   _____
Print name   Sign Name

date: _____

To the participant: Data may be inspected by the Chair of the Psychology Ethics panel and the Chair of the School of Science and Technology Ethics committee of Middlesex University, if required by institutional audits about the correctness of procedures. Although this would happen in strict confidentiality, please tick here if you do not wish your data to be included in audits: _____

APPENDIX D: Interview Schedule

Sub-questions:
- How does the digital detox affect your sense of well-being?
- How does the digital detox impact how you relate to your family
- How does the digital detox impact how you relate to your friends
- What was it like to digitally detox when you were younger?

1. **What is it like to switch your phone off before Shabbat?**
- What is it like during the time that you refrain from using your digital technology?
- What do you feel when you switch it back on again?
- Are there advantages to having a digital detox?
- Could you digitally detox on any day of the week?
- Have you ever considered stopping your digital detox?

2. **What kinds of things have an impact on the detox experience? Makes it easier to digitally detox?**
- Are there things that make it more difficult to digitally detox?
- What makes it more difficult?
- What makes it easier?

3. **Do you remember what it was like to digitally detox when you were younger?**
- Was it easier or more difficult to digitally detox when you were younger?

4. **How does a digital detox affect your relationships, if at all?**
- How do you experience the impact on family relationships
- How do you experience the impact on the relationship with friends?

5. **How does a digital detox affect your sense of well-being, if at all?**

6. **Is a digital detox something you would recommend?**
- For which groups of people might it be useful/not useful
- In what kind of situations will it be useful/not useful

APPENDIX E: Section of One Transcript with Notes

Experiential Statements	Person	Verbatim	Exploratory Notes
He experiences technology as being highly stimulating, and as a result, it can be a struggle to be alone. P7. Mendel	M.24	For sure, yeah and anyway, in my experience. It all comes back to a teenager who needs to be stimulated all the time ehm, and I think teenagers, from my personal experience and from friends that I have, who struggle being alone and just being able to chill with themselves or whatever and ehm, and that's where the phone is so good at being the constant stimulation thing.	Phones provide stimulation, which is addictive for teenagers. Phones replace being alone. Being alone is hard.
	N.25	And you mentioned that now you enjoy being on your own on Friday nights without your phone.	
He feels that a digital detox is more valuable as responsibilities and stresses increase. P8. Mendel	M.25	I think that it's a process of maturity as well ehm, so again, I think you can't expect a 16 or 17-year-old or even 20 whatever year-old to, you know, be so put together with themselves that they're very happy to just sit there and you know ehm but I think that as life gets more stressful and there are more responsibilities and there is more happening ehm personally for me it's just really good to have that sort of a couple of hours of just nothingness ehm and I really look forward to it actually these days ehm yeah.	As he got older and life became more stressful, he appreciated the break from technology more. It's okay to be alone, he can cope with it now that he's older.
	N.26	So you're describing it positively, having a digital detox time.	
	M.26	Yeah, at this stage of my life.	
	N.27	At this stage of your life. And can you explain what the benefits are?	
	M.27	Ehm, I'm trying to avoid using just like general words. yeah, it's great for my mental health …	
	N.28	Can you be more specific?	
He has time to reflect on his week over Shabbat, it's a way to punctuate the week and to reconcile before beginning another week. It's also a recharge. P8. Mendel	M.28	I'm trying to think of a specific thing. Ehm, I think it allows me to reflect on my previous week, ehm, like during the week, you know, it's Monday, and before you know it, it's Friday, and it's, sometimes I have, you know it's a shame cause you know you can't write on Shabbat and you have these sort of oh moments, and maybe I should do this slightly differently or, and which you don't get during the week and so I think that's probably first of all allowing the space and the time to reflect on different things. I think that especially nowadays when I know everyone says this that life moves so fast, ehm, and I think having a few hours to catch up and like sort of take it all in, ehm, I don't know if that makes sense like for example I don't know like you're building something very quickly and you always need like a couple of weeks to like touch on everything afterwards and it's like to level out the ground and like breathe a breath of fresh air and you know start again, ehm, I don't so yeah reflection, ehm, letting everything sink in, and for me personally, recharge as well cause I don't see how you could keep going, like my energy levels just drop and it comes to the routine thing like I have a lot of non-Jewish friends in the x for example who are very happy to come in on Shabbat and work and you know do 7 day weeks ehm but then on a random Tuesday like, at like for about 3 or 4 days they'll just be gone, ehm, because they're just catching up on sleep or whatever it is and I'm sure every work environment is different you know like mine is not particularly structured,|ehm so I guess it also kind of puts a structure to your week, yeah.	It's a time for reflection on the week; there is space and time for reflection on Shabbat, and time is there to catch up. It's like drawing in breath so you can start again. A recharge is necessary. It puts structure to the week.

APPENDIX F: Preliminary Superordinate Themes and Sub-Themes from the Pilot Interview

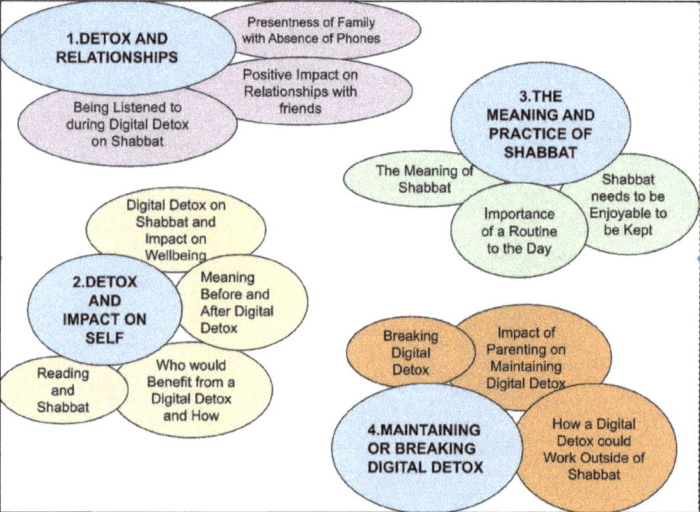

- **1. DETOX AND RELATIONSHIPS**
  - Presentness of Family with Absence of Phones
  - Positive Impact on Relationships with friends
  - Being Listened to during Digital Detox on Shabbat
- **2. DETOX AND IMPACT ON SELF**
  - Digital Detox on Shabbat and Impact on Wellbeing
  - Meaning Before and After Digital Detox
  - Reading and Shabbat
  - Who would Benefit from a Digital Detox and How
- **3. THE MEANING AND PRACTICE OF SHABBAT**
  - The Meaning of Shabbat
  - Shabbat needs to be Enjoyable to be Kept
  - Importance of a Routine to the Day
- **4. MAINTAINING OR BREAKING DIGITAL DETOX**
  - Breaking Digital Detox
  - Impact of Parenting on Maintaining Digital Detox
  - How a Digital Detox could Work Outside of Shabbat

APPENDIX G: Debriefing Sheet

New School of Psychotherapy and Counselling

254-256 Belsize Road
London
NW6 4BT

Debriefing Information Sheet for Participants

Title of Study:
An Interpretative Phenomenological Analysis of Young Jewish Adults Experience
of Having a Digital Detox During Shabbat

Academic Year: 2022

Researcher:
Natalie Scheiner
Email: ns1103@live.mdx.ac.uk

Research Supervisor:
Dr Andreas Vossler
Email: andreas.vossler@open.ac.uk

Institution Information:
NSPC
Alfred Court
61-63 Fortune Green Rd
London
NW6 1DR
020 3515 0223

Study Title:
DcSyche Psycotherapy and Counselling

Date: 10/2/22

I would like to thank you for participating in this research and check that you are still willing for your contribution to be used.

The nature of this study was to learn about the experiences of single young adults living at home, aged between 18 and 24 years old who digitally detox every Shabbat. There are many people who digitally detox from their devices, however this study was interested in the experiences of people who have a complete weekly digital detox for 25 hours from all technological devices during Shabbat.

The findings, which come from your participation may help others, either individuals, community leaders or professionals, who are interested in the experience of complete abstinence from all forms of digital devices for a full day each week.

If you have any further questions you wish to discuss, please get in touch with me on my email address above. This email address will be live until 2024.

If you have found any of the material that was discussed upsetting in any way, or if it has brought up experiences that you would like to follow up on, the list of resources below may be helpful.

The United Kingdom Counselling Psychology (UKCP) website has a list of therapies who offer psychotherapy. You can find this at:
https://www.psychotherapy.org.uk/find-a-therapist/?Distance=10

Mind Mental health charity offers free therapy and counselling. They can be found at:
https://www.mind.org.uk/information-support/drugs-and-treatments/talking-therapy-and-counselling/about-talking-therapies/

Ease Wellbeing is a short term counselling service that offers low cost counselling. They can be found at:
https://easewellbeing.co.uk/

Raphael is a local Jewish counselling service offering counselling to all sectors of the Jewish and wider communities. They can be found at:
https://www.raphaeljewishcounselling.org/

www.ingramcontent.com/pod-product-compliance
Lightning Source LLC
Chambersburg PA
CBHW040142270326
41928CB00023B/3302